The Complete Guide to
NATURAL SOAPMAKING

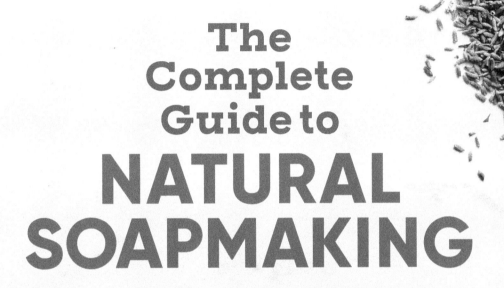

The Complete Guide to
NATURAL SOAPMAKING

Create 65 All-Natural Cold-Process, Hot-Process,
Liquid, Melt-and-Pour, and Hand-Milled Soaps

Amanda Gail Aaron

ALTHEA
PRESS

For general information on our other products and services or to obtain technical support, please contact our Customer Care Department within the United States at (866) 744-2665, or outside the United States at (510) 253-0500.

Althea Press publishes its books in a variety of electronic and print formats. Some content that appears in print may not be available in electronic books, and vice versa.

Photography © 2018 Marija Vidal; cover, pp.ii-iii, iv-v, vi-vii, ix, x-1, 8-9, 24-27, 123, 132-133, 167, 180-181, 195, 204-205, 221, 232-233, 247, 254-255 & 266. Photography © 2018 Amanda Gail Aaron; pp.30-35, 39, 41-43, 45-46, 48, 50-51, 53- 55,137-139, 143, 145, 147, 184-187, 208-209, 213-218, 237-238 & 241-244.

Cover Designer: Katy Brown   Editor: Katharine Moore
Interior Designer: Lauren Smith   Production Editor: Erum Khan
Photo Art Director: Karen Beard

ISBN: Print 978-1-64152-154-3 | eBook 978-1-64152-155-0

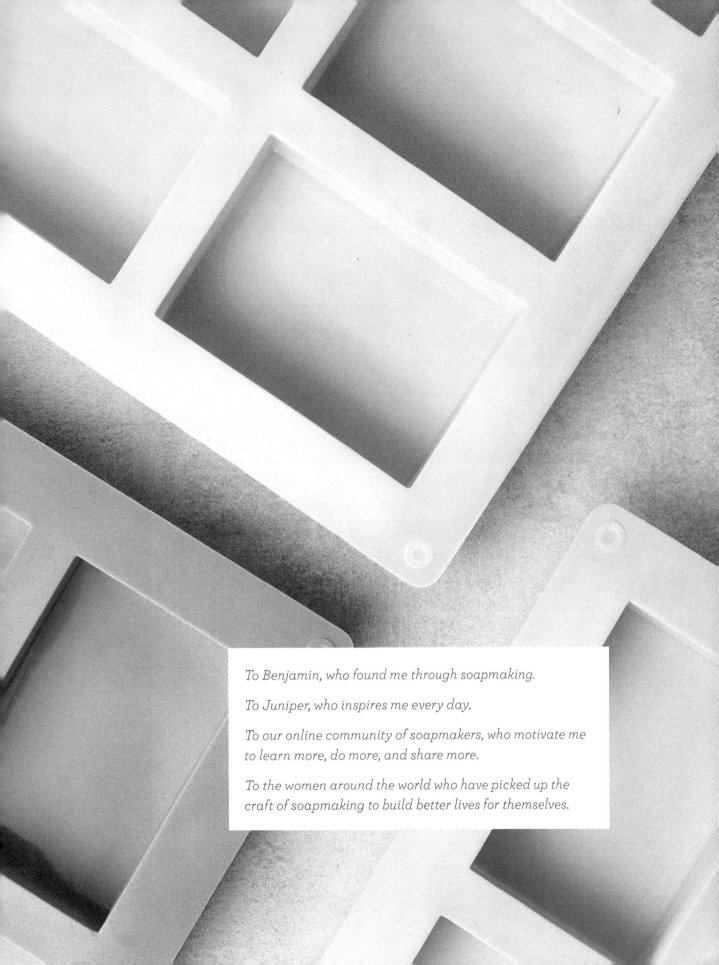

To Benjamin, who found me through soapmaking.

To Juniper, who inspires me every day.

To our online community of soapmakers, who motivate me to learn more, do more, and share more.

To the women around the world who have picked up the craft of soapmaking to build better lives for themselves.

Contents

Introduction   viii

01 All About Soapmaking   1

02 Essential Equipment and Ingredients   9

03 Cold-Process Soapmaking   25

04 Hot-Process Soapmaking   133

05 Liquid Soapmaking   181

06 Melt-and-Pour Soapmaking   205

07 Hand-Milling Soap   233

08 Finishing Touches   255

Measurement Conversions   267
Glossary   268
Resources   269
Recipe Label Index   273
Index   278

Introduction

I've been making soap since 2008. I was wandering the aisles of the local craft store and ended up in front of the candle and soap supplies. Out of curiosity, I decided to try a melt-and-pour soapmaking kit. I went home, made the soap, and was just amazed! I loved working with the colors and scents and making something useful with my own two hands. I quickly started researching soapmaking and discovered cold-process soap.

My first batch of cold-process soap was a 100 percent olive oil soap that went horribly wrong. I added too much water, and it took forever to blend. I poured it before it ever really emulsified, and I woke up to a mess in my mold the next morning. But, undaunted, I carried on.

After a few successful creations, I fell in love with soapmaking, and my house filled with supplies and racks of curing soap. I sold soap for a bit, but I soon discovered my passion: teaching soapmaking to others. I started the Lovin' Soap blog, where I could share tutorials and articles on soapmaking, and I began teaching classes wherever I could find a space and some students. I then started a nonprofit with my husband, through which we travel the world and teach women's groups in developing countries how to make soap and start a business. We realized that our small soapmaking nonprofit could have an impact in communities by creating economic opportunities for women and promoting handwashing. The people who attended our classes went on to create their own small businesses selling their soap creations.

When explaining what I do for a living, I like to tell people that three of the oldest professions in the world are prostitution, beer brewing, and soapmaking. People always get a chuckle out of that grouping of ancient ventures. Recipes and descriptions of the soapmaking process have been found dating back to as early as 2200 BCE. A Mesopotamian clay tablet was discovered that contained basic directions for making soap using cassia oil and potash, a homemade lye made from leaching water through ashes. Wealthy Babylonians would have servants rub their bodies with what are still today the basic components of soap—animal fats, water, and lye.

In the 1800s and 1900s, soapmaking was a utilitarian household chore. Families made soap to use around the house and to bathe with. Back then, soapmakers butchered pigs and cows, saving the fat and rendering it down for the process. They then ran water through ashes, much like the Babylonians who came thousands of years before them, to make the potash. Water was mixed with the potash and then added to the rendered animal fats, producing a soft, rudimentary soap. This soap could be hardened with salt to produce a solid, longer-lasting bar for the bath. This basic soap would sometimes end up being harsh or biting on the skin, as calculations for exact measurements of ingredients were not available at the time.

Today we know exactly how much lye is needed to saponify (page 268) a specific amount of fatty acids, which allows us to create soap that is mild and generally pleasing to the skin. We can use the cold-process method to swirl colors and create beautiful, artistic soaps. Hot-process soapmaking creates a more utilitarian soap, with a focus on preserving the additives. We can also make rich amber liquid soaps.

There is a broad variety of soapmaking techniques, and countless ingredients can be combined for different applications, textures, and even colors. This book is a great resource for all types of soapmaking and will show you, step-by-step, how to create dozens of different products with unique characteristics and applications.

"Majik, majik!" ("magic," in Haitian Creole) exclaimed a group of women in Haiti after we taught them to make their first batch of soap. The women, who lived in a tent camp in the capital, Port-au-Prince, were as moved as I was the first time I experienced the alchemistic process of combining oils with lye to create a totally new substance. My hope is that when you're done reading, you, too, will have the confidence and the inspiration to start your own soapmaking journey and experience this magic for yourself.

01

All About Soapmaking

With so many options, you may be wondering where to get started. We'll explore the different types of soapmaking processes so you can choose the one that's best for you. We'll also go over some basic terminology and, most important, lye safety. But don't be intimidated: I've taught all over the world in places with varying levels of resources—this craft doesn't require cutting-edge or expensive equipment, just care and creativity.

The Pleasure of Natural Soapmaking

Soapmaking is equal parts science and art. By making your own soap, you get to control exactly what goes into it. For me, soapmaking is like using a paintbrush and a palette of beautiful colors. You can create soap with swirls, mirroring paper-marbling techniques that are centuries old. Many soapmakers match colors to scents; for example, lavender soap is colored purple, mint is colored green, and citrus is colored orange. A batch of natural soap is a blank canvas for you to decorate using colors, additives, and design techniques.

Here's the science part: Soap is the result of combining fatty acids (oils, butters, and fats) with lye (sodium hydroxide or potassium hydroxide). When you combine fatty acids with lye, the mixture goes through a chemical reaction called *saponification*. Here, the molecules of the fatty acids break apart, combining with the lye molecules. This process creates a substance made from the salts of fatty acids, natural glycerin (which is a by-product of the process), and if you superfatted your recipe by using extra base oils, you will wind up with extra natural emollient oils that aren't turned into soap. Chemically speaking, soap is a salt.

Soap works by emulsifying the oils and dirt on the skin with water and holding this mixture in suspension, allowing it to be washed down the drain.

The term *natural* doesn't have an official definition when it comes to soapmaking, and soapmakers' opinions vary on the topic. One soapmaker might believe that oxides and ultramarines, colorants in some soaps, are natural because even though they are made in a lab by humans, their chemical makeup is nature-identical, meaning they end up with the same chemical makeup as those found naturally. Other soapmakers will define them as synthetic and not natural because they are made in a lab. Lye, which is used in all soaps, isn't a natural ingredient. It is produced synthetically.

When it comes to soapmaking and the term *natural*, most soapmakers agree that a more natural soap can be made by using natural colorants, essential oils, and additives.

In this book, here is what I mean when I use the term *natural soapmaking*. The recipes in this book will include:

Natural colorants: You won't find colorants such as micas, cosmetic pigments, ultramarines, iron oxides, dyes, or lakes. Instead, we'll color soap using spices, herbs, clays, purées, and juices. We do use zinc oxide for its skin benefits and to color soap white. You can choose to use it or not.

Natural scents: Instead of using synthetic fragrance oils, we'll use essential oils, which are scents extracted from plant material.

Natural additives: If you want to make a naturally exfoliating soap, you can use things like seeds and clay instead of synthetic exfoliates like plastic beads, which are bad for the environment. Other natural additives include milk powders and vegetable or fruit powders.

I do include some melt-and-pour soap recipes in this book. Although melt-and-pour soap is not as natural as cold-process soap, you can find organic bases that create a more natural soap than some bases you might find in craft stores.

I avoid palm oil in the recipes as well because of the industry's link to deforestation, animal cruelty, climate change, and human rights issues. Consumers are starting to take notice and demand palm-free products.

I find great satisfaction in making something with my own two hands that I use every day. The soap that you'll make here is good for your skin and the environment. I hope you enjoy this journey into natural soapmaking and that it provides you with as much pleasure and satisfaction as it has for me.

Classic Soapmaking Techniques

Cold-process soapmaking is what most people think of when they hear the term *soapmaking*, but there are other techniques that are great fun and yield a wide variety of soaps.

COLD-PROCESS SOAP

Cold-process soap is the most common soapmaking, or soaping, technique. Here you combine a sodium hydroxide solution (lye) with fatty acids (oils, butters, or fats), emulsify them together, and pour into a mold. You can add scents, color, and additives during this process. It can also be swirled, layered, stamped, and piped. The soap is then left to work its magic through the saponification process. During this time, cold-process soap goes through an exothermic reaction, which means it generates its own heat. It is called cold-process soap because no heat is added by the soapmaker. The chemical reaction of saponification occurs usually within 24 hours, and you are left with soap. Cold-process soap needs to cure for four to six weeks. This will ensure that the majority of the water has fully evaporated so the soap won't dissolve quickly.

HOT-PROCESS SOAP

Hot-process soap is like cold-process soap, except you heat the soap to force it through the saponification process. You can cook the soap in a slow cooker, double boiler, or oven. Once the soap is cooked, you add essential oils, colorants, and additives. The soap is then spooned into a mold and left to harden. Once hard, your soap can be unmolded and cut. It is technically ready to use right away; however, hot-process soap still needs at least a two-week cure to allow some water to evaporate. One benefit to making hot-process soap is that the lye is no longer active by the time you add your essential oils. This means that you can usually use less essential oil than you would in cold-process soap, and the scents tend to come through stronger and more stable.

LIQUID SOAP

Liquid soap is made a lot like hot-process soap, except that potassium hydroxide is used to saponify the oils. You bring your base oils and lye solution to "trace" (see Recognizing Trace, page 34) and then cook the mixture until it is neutral. The cloudy mixture turns translucent with an amber color, resulting in a liquid soap paste. You then dilute the paste and add essential oils for scent. Liquid soap is great for guest bathrooms and can be dispensed in a pump.

MELT-AND-POUR SOAP

Melt-and-pour soap is the best option for those who don't want to use lye. The melt-and-pour soap base is made with lye, but it contains no active lye that you would have to handle. To make melt-and-pour soap, you purchase a melt-and-pour base, chop it up, gently melt it, and then add color, scent, and additives. You pour it into a mold, and as soon as it hardens, you can unmold it. Melt-and-pour soap is ready to use right away; no cure time is needed. It's a fun activity to do with children.

HAND-MILLING SOAP

Hand-milling is another great process for those who don't want to use lye. To make hand-milled soap, you either purchase or make an unscented cold-process or hot-process soap. Then you shred it and heat it to soften. Once it turns into a soap gel, you can add scent, additives, and color, and then scoop it into a mold. Once it hardens, it can be unmolded and cut. Like hot-process soap, it is safe to use right away, but it does benefit from a bit of a cure to allow the water to evaporate. Hand-milled soap isn't as smooth looking as cold-process soap—it has a rustic look. Because the soap is so thick, it can be harder to create a design, but it can be layered and swirled to add interest. Hand-milling is also a great technique to re-batch (make again) a soap that didn't come out quite right.

Safety First

Although soapmaking can be safe and fun, some safety precautions are necessary when working with caustic materials.

* Sodium hydroxide and potassium hydroxide can burn your skin, especially when combined with water to create a lye solution. To protect yourself from splashes, always wear gloves to protect your hands and goggles to protect your eyes (see Safety Gear, page 12).

* If you do get a splash of lye solution on your skin, rinse with water for five to seven minutes. You can typically get it rinsed off before it burns your skin. If you do get a burn, seek medical attention.

* If you get lye in your eye, flush with water for 15 minutes and seek medical attention.

* Soap batter is caustic until it goes through the saponification process, which usually takes about 24 hours. Traced soap can still burn your skin, so rinse with water if you get any on you during this time.

* Regular white vinegar neutralizes lye, but it does so by flashing it out, or heating quickly to a really high temperature. Vinegar should never be used on skin or in eyes to neutralize lye because it could cause serious burns. Instead, use vinegar on countertops or floors to neutralize lye that might have spilled.

* If you spill lye solution on the counter or floor, soak it up using towels and launder them as usual; use vinegar in your rinse cycle to neutralize any lye that might be left in your machine. Spray your counter or floor with a vinegar solution to neutralize any lye left on surfaces, then wipe them down, wearing gloves.

* Be sure to store your sodium hydroxide and potassium hydroxide in airtight containers that are clearly marked. Sodium hydroxide beads look like regular table sugar. Make sure everyone in your household who is old enough to understand knows that it is a dangerous chemical and should be left alone. If you have children in the house, store it away from curiosity and reach.

* Always add your sodium hydroxide or potassium hydroxide to the water when making a solution—never the other way around. If you were to pour the water into your caustic, it could create a crust, trapping vapors underneath. The solution can then literally explode out of your container.

* The caustics we use for soapmaking are also used as drain cleaners, so a lye solution is safe to pour down the sink. Follow by rinsing the sink with plenty of water.

These precautions might make lye sound scary and intimidating, but I simply want to prepare you so you can avoid any issues. I compare working with lye to working with harsh everyday household chemicals such as bleach, Ajax, drain cleaner, pool chemicals, etc. These all must be safely used and stored. Accidents are rare in soapmaking, especially if you wear safety gear and respect the lye.

How to Use This Book

Now that we've discussed some of the basics, the next chapter will go over the equipment and ingredients that you'll need to make natural soap. The main processes—cold-process, hot-process, liquid, melt-and-pour, and hand-milling—are divided into five chapters. Each chapter includes the basic soapmaking steps for that process, followed by some more advanced design techniques and recipes. In the final chapter, I'll share some tips for how to package and sell soap, for those of you who may be interested in moving from hobby to small business.

If you are new to soapmaking, I recommend reading this book from start to finish so you'll have a broad understanding of the equipment, ingredients, safety, and different soapmaking processes. I encourage you to start with cold-process soap by selecting one of the basic recipes. Once you get a handle on making a basic batch of soap, you can branch out into design techniques and different processes such as hot-process and liquid soap.

Melt-and-pour and hand-milling are also great for beginners. If you're looking for soap to make with children, you'll want to choose one of these, since neither process involves working with lye.

Once you're ready to formulate your own recipes or modify base oils in a recipe, you can read through Creating Your Own Cold-Process Soap Recipe (page 256). Before you substitute base oils in a recipe, make sure you run the new recipe through a lye calculator (see page 271).

If you already have experience making soap, I hope this book will further explain soapmaking topics that might be a bit fuzzy to you, or teach you a fun new technique, design, or blend.

Soapmaking is a lot like baking. Everyone has their own way to make a basic chocolate cake. Take my processes and make them your own. You'll soon find your own personal soapmaking stride!

02

Essential Equipment and Ingredients

Now that you have an overview of the soapmaking processes and safety procedures, let's explore the equipment and ingredients you'll need to gather so you can make natural soap in your own home.

Soapmaking Gear

You don't need much specialty equipment when making soap. You might even have many of these items at home.

EQUIPMENT

Following is a list of equipment that you'll need to make soap. Some of these items can be found at kitchen stores, or you can order them online from soap suppliers or online marketplaces. Pay careful attention to what your containers are made from, as lye can react to certain materials.

Digital scale: Most ingredients, including liquids like base oils, lye, water, and essential oils, will be added to your batch by metric weight, not volume. Manual scales are not as accurate as digital ones. An inexpensive digital scale can be found in most kitchen stores or ordered online.

Stick blender: Once you combine your oils and lye solution, you'll need to mix to emulsify. This was traditionally done by hand, but it can take up to an hour this way. Modern soapmakers use stick blenders (also known as immersion blenders) to mix their soap to trace. It cuts the time down to minutes.

Molds: Your soap will be fluid when poured, so you'll need a mold to contain it as it saponifies and hardens. My favorite molds are silicone, because you don't have to line them. You can also use cardboard boxes or wooden boxes, but you'll need to line them with freezer paper.

Cutter: You may need to cut your soap after you unmold it, depending on the mold shape you use. You can use a stainless-steel knife, dough scraper, wavy vegetable crinkle cutter, or any number of soap cutters sold by suppliers.

Mixing utensils: You'll need some silicone spatulas to scrape out your soap. Stainless-steel spoons are nice for scooping out solid oils and butters. Avoid any metal except for stainless steel, and avoid wooden utensils, as they can splinter over time.

Milk frother: This handy little mixer is used to mix colorants into divided soap. It doesn't thicken soap like a stick blender, keeping your soap fluid for advanced designs.

Measuring spoons: Have a set of either stainless-steel or plastic measuring spoons on hand for measuring additives.

Dry lye container: A dry lye container can be used to weigh your dry sodium hydroxide or potassium hydroxide before adding it to your water. This container can be stainless steel, glass, or plastic. I sometimes even use disposable plastic cups.

Lye solution container: This is the container that you'll typically use to weigh your water and then add your caustic to make a solution. Never use a glass container, even one known to hold up against drastic heat fluctuations. Lye can etch glass containers, eventually causing them to shatter. Use chemical- and heat-resistant plastics such as food storage containers, plastic pitchers, or paint-mixing containers from the hardware store that have the plastic code #5 on the bottom. You can also use stainless-steel bowls or pots.

Batch container: A batch container will hold your oils and lye solution for you to mix to trace. You can use stainless-steel pots or bowls, large glass mixing bowls, and plastic containers with the plastic code #5 on the bottom, including paint-mixing containers, plastic pitchers, and plastic buckets.

Mixing containers: These are the containers that you'll divide your soap into to color and swirl. I like to use small plastic paint-mixing containers or food storage containers. You can also use disposable plastic cups.

Slow cooker: A slow cooker is used to make hot-process, liquid, and hand-milled soaps. You can also use a double boiler or a stainless-steel pot in the oven, but a slow cooker is my favorite vessel for cooking soap.

Small glass container for measuring essential oils: Essential oils can eat through plastic and Styrofoam, so use glass to weigh your essential oils. I like to use small canning jars, shot glasses, or small glass measuring cups.

Small containers for premixing colorants: You can premix your colorants in small shot glasses, small disposable bathroom cups, or small kitchen prep bowls. Since these containers won't touch the active lye, they can be made of any material.

If you're just getting started, you may also want to pick up an infrared thermometer to test the temperature of your melted oils and lye solution. Over time, you'll be able to judge the temperature just by touching the container.

Scour your local thrift stores for inexpensive items. I've had luck finding slow cookers, stick blenders, stainless-steel bowls and pots, utensils, and measuring spoons. Anything you use for soapmaking should never again be used for cooking food. Have a dedicated set of equipment for soapmaking; I recommend labeling these items as "soap only."

SAFETY GEAR

Potassium hydroxide and sodium hydroxide are both caustic chemicals and can burn your skin. Wear chemical-resistant (latex, nitrile, PVC, or neoprene) gloves to protect your hands and goggles to protect your eyes. Even if you wear glasses, you'll want safety goggles that fit over them to protect you from splashes.

SETTING UP

Soapmaking can be done safely right from your kitchen, garage, basement, or any other room where you have some work space, using either countertops or a table. You'll need easy access to a sink for cleanup and for safety in case you need to rinse lye solution or soap off your skin.

You'll need to mix your lye solution in a well-ventilated space—in either your work space or another location such as a backyard, garage, or patio. Be sure the area is protected and that no one will come upon it unexpectedly.

CLEANING UP

Here are some tips for cleaning up after you make soap.

* **Lye solution:** This can be poured down the drain, as it is used as a drain cleaner. Never put raw soap down the drain, though, as it can cause clogs very easily.

* **Dry lye container and lye solution container:** Rinse with water and wash with soap.

* **Batch and mixing containers:** Before washing, always use paper towels to wipe the raw soap out of containers and discard the paper towels. Then rinse and wash your containers as usual. Some soapmakers recommend wiping with cloth towels, allowing the towels to sit overnight to saponify, and then laundering. But the superfat (excess oil) in soap can clog your washing machine and leave a gunky residue, so I don't recommend this.

* **Stick blender and utensils:** Wipe down with paper towels and then wash with soap and water.

* **Molds:** If you're using silicone molds, rinse the soap off. No need to wash. If you're using wooden molds and some soap escaped your liner, just use a knife or scraper to scrape off the hardened soap; no need to wash.

* **Dishes:** Some soapmakers leave all their soapmaking dishes until the next day, when everything has turned to soap and can be rinsed and put away.

* **Work space:** A vinegar solution can be used to spray down your work space to neutralize any lye that might have gotten onto surfaces. I also keep a spray bottle of isopropyl alcohol to clean up oily residue from my scale, stick blender base, and bottles of oils that might dribble as I pour.

* **Gloves:** Wear gloves as you're wiping down containers and your stick blender, as traced soap is still caustic and can burn.

Lye

Sodium hydroxide (NaOH) and potassium hydroxide (KOH), also known as lye, are the caustic chemicals used to turn oils and fats into soap. Sodium hydroxide creates a solid soap that is cut into bars. Potassium hydroxide creates a soft soap paste that is diluted to create liquid soap. These caustic chemicals can burn your skin, so always be sure to wear gloves and goggles when handling the dry chemical, solution, and raw soap.

Store your lye in a cool, dry place. As soon as you weigh out the lye for your batch, close the container tightly. Lye likes to draw moisture from the air, and if left open, it can be ruined by absorbing water and clumping up.

If your measurements were correct, all the lye solution should be gone once it has been combined with the oils and fats and the mixture has saponified. The soap is safe to use.

Although you might hear the term *lye-free soap*, there is no such thing. All soap is made with lye at some point in the process. Melt-and-pour base is typically called lye-free soap, but it is made of oils and butters that were saponified using sodium hydroxide. There is none left in the saponified base that you buy.

Carrier Oils

You'll find a variety of common soapmaking oils out there, and each has particular properties once saponified in soap. Every soapmaking oil requires a slightly different amount of lye to saponify into soap.

SAFETY FIRST: If you make recipe substitutions or even just *modify* the amounts of an oil in your recipe, be sure to run your new recipe through an online lye calculator to get the required amount of lye (see Lye & Essential Oil Calculators, page 271). If you don't recalculate your recipe, you run the risk of creating a lye–heavy soap that can burn your skin.

COCONUT OIL

Coconut oil gives soap big, fluffy lather. It creates a hard white bar of soap. It is a high-cleansing oil and easily strips the skin of natural oils, leaving a tight and dry feeling. Because of this, it's usually combined with olive oil and other oils and butters. Use either 76-degree or 92-degree coconut oil. Do not use fractionated (liquid) coconut oil or your soap won't harden.

Substitutions: Palm kernel oil and babassu oil. Recalculate the lye amount using a lye calculator.

LARD AND TALLOW

Lard and tallow are animal fats that create a medium-cleansing hard white bar of soap with medium lather. Soapmakers like to combine them with coconut oil and olive oil to make a more balanced soap.

Substitutions: Lard and tallow can be used interchangeably without recalculating the lye amount.

OLIVE OIL

Unlike coconut oil, olive oil creates a low-cleansing bar of soap, which means that it doesn't strip the skin of natural oils. It has a low lather, meaning it doesn't produce many bubbles. Combining it with coconut oil boosts the soap's lathering abilities. A soap high in olive oil is great to use for babies or for those with sensitive skin who require a gentler cleansing. Olive oil is slow to trace and slow to harden. I like to use a high percentage of olive oil in recipes that include swirling, to give me plenty of time to divide and color my soap. I prefer to use regular olive oil, although pomace olive oil is cheaper. Pomace olive oil can cause your soap to trace quickly. It is simply a matter of preference.

Substitutions: Rice bran oil is the best substitute for some or all of the olive oil in your recipe, but you can also substitute high oleic sunflower oil, high oleic safflower oil, canola oil, sweet almond oil, apricot kernel oil, or avocado oil. Recalculate the lye using a lye calculator.

HIGH OLEIC LIQUID OILS

High oleic sunflower oil, high oleic safflower oil, rice bran oil, sweet almond oil, neem oil, canola oil, apricot kernel oil, and avocado oil are high in oleic acid and create a low- to medium-cleansing soap with a longer shelf life. The resulting soap ranges from soft to medium in hardness. Those oils with palmitic acid, such as avocado and rice bran oil, create firmer bars than other oils in this category. These oils are typically combined with coconut oil and olive oil to add conditioning lather to a bar of soap, as well as label appeal.

Substitutions: These oils can be used interchangeably in a recipe. Recalculate the lye using a lye calculator.

HIGH LINOLEIC AND LINOLENIC LIQUID OILS

Sunflower oil, safflower oil, soybean oil, grapeseed oil, cottonseed oil, and hemp seed oil are high in linoleic and linolenic acids and create a low- to medium-cleansing soap with a short shelf life. The resulting soaps are soft, sticky, and hard to unmold. Because these oils can be prone to rancidity, use them in small amounts in your recipe. Both sunflower and safflower oils can be purchased in high oleic versions that have a much longer shelf life.

Substitutions: These oils can be used interchangeably in a recipe, or you can substitute a high oleic liquid oil to make a more stable formula. Recalculate the lye using a lye calculator.

JOJOBA OIL

Jojoba oil is a liquid wax that mirrors the properties of sebum in our own skin. It doesn't lather much in soap and can create a sticky bar, so use in small quantities.

Substitutions: There is no oil quite like jojoba oil. If you don't have it, substitute in a high oleic liquid oil from the the previous list. Recalculate the lye using a lye calculator.

CASTOR OIL

Castor oil is a solvent. It boosts the lathering ability of soap by making the soap more soluble in water. It is great in any formula where you want a bit more lather. If you use too much, it can create a sticky soap with a draggy feel on your skin.

Substitutions: There are no other oils like castor oil. If you don't have it, you can use any of the high oleic oils in your formula. It will change the feel of the bar slightly. Recalculate the lye using a lye calculator. You can also add solubility to your soap by adding sugar (see page 20).

COSMETIC BUTTERS

Butters such as shea butter, cocoa butter, mango (kernel) butter, sal butter, kokum butter, and illipe butter contribute hardness and body to soap. They help stabilize lather and create a soap that lasts longer in the shower. They are low-medium cleansing and have a low-medium lather. You can use either raw or refined butters in your soap.

Why No Palm Oil?

Many soapmakers wish to make soap palm-free. The palm oil industry has some negative impacts on the environment, most notably deforestation and the loss of natural habitats to palm oil plantations. This deforestation displaces animals and even indigenous people who aren't given fair compensation or even consultation before their lands are taken. The clearing of these rain forests plays a big role in global warming, releasing carbon dioxide into the atmosphere.

There are movements toward creating sustainable sources of palm oil, but, so far, those efforts are fraught with controversy, corruption, and fraudulent certifications and labeling.

This used to be an issue that the regular person outside of the food and cosmetic industry just didn't hear about. But things are changing and consumers are increasingly demanding palm-free products. A few large cosmetic companies in the US have omitted palm oil from their products, and many smaller cosmetic companies and soapmakers are following their lead.

Substitutions: These butters can be used interchangeably in a recipe. Recalculate the lye using a lye calculator.

Natural Colorants

There is a rainbow of natural colorants out there that we can use to color soap. Here are some of my favorites.

Spice and herb powders: You might have cinnamon, turmeric, paprika, annatto seed, parsley, and sage in your kitchen cabinet right now. These all make great natural colorants for soap. Other spices and herb powders include indigo, madder root, alkanet root, black walnut hulls, peppermint, spirulina, beet root, yellow dock root, and nettle leaf. Spice and herb powders can be added to soap in three ways:

* **Oil infusions:** Some spices and herbs release their colors into oil easily. You can then use this oil in your recipe to color your soap a natural color.

* **Added to the lye solution:** Few spices and herbs do well when added to the lye solution, but indigo creates a nice color this way.
* **Added to oils or trace:** Most herbs and spices can be added to your base oils before combining with the lye solution. If you're swirling your soap, you can add the powders to your traced and divided soap. Adding powder to traced soap can result in speckled soap.

Clay: Clays come in many colors and make great natural colorants in soap. They also have drawing and purifying properties on the skin. Be sure to get cosmetic clays for your soap. Add clay to the lye solution for a solid soap to help draw out the color, or add it to traced and divided soap to swirl.

Cosmetic charcoal: Cosmetic charcoal is my favorite natural black colorant. Charcoal is great for treating acne and drawing oil and toxins from the skin.

Zinc oxide: Zinc oxide is what most natural soapmakers use to color their soap white. It also soothes irritated and troublesome skin.

How much to use: Usage rates, or the amounts of colorant you should use, vary based on the depth of color you wish to achieve. I use 1 teaspoon to 1 tablespoon per 450 grams of base oils. Start by adding a little, and add more if you want a darker color. If you add the amount listed in a recipe but want a darker color, add more. You don't have to follow a recipe exactly when it comes to color.

Force your cold-process soap through gel phase (see page 35) to get deeper and brighter colors.

Natural Additives

Natural additives give soap character, label appeal, and usefulness. Here are some of my favorite additives for natural soap. I include a recommended usage rate under each additive, but feel free to use less or more.

Seeds: You can use blueberry, cranberry, raspberry, strawberry, poppy, chia, cardamom, or cumin seeds to create an exfoliating soap. Add up to 1 teaspoon per 900 grams of base oils in your recipe. Add to your base oils before combining with the lye solution.

Creating an Oil Infusion

Using an infused oil in your soap is a great way to naturally color it without getting the speckles you might get from adding herbs or spice powder directly to your soap. Try infusing annatto, paprika, alkanet root, or turmeric to start, as these infuse easily. Here's what I do:

Step 1: Add 40 to 60 grams of a spice or herb powder to a clean, dry canning jar. You can even put the powder into a heat-sealable tea bag. That way, you don't have to strain it before using your oil; you just remove the tea bag.

Step 2: Add 240 grams of olive oil to the jar. You can use any liquid oil, but olive oil is a stable oil used in most recipes.

Step 3: Close your jar and allow the color to infuse. For cold infusion, store your infusion in a cool, dry cupboard for up to 4 weeks. You can shake it every now and then to mix up the colorant and oil. For a warm infusion, adding heat helps the colorant release its color easily. Fill a slow cooker or pot with water. Place the jar into a slow cooker turned to medium or a pot over low heat, and allow your infusion to heat for 10 to 20 minutes. The heat will quickly draw out the color. Give the jar a shake every 5 minutes or so.

Step 4: When you're ready to use your infusion, substitute it for some of the olive oil that your recipe calls for. Use a little for a light color or a lot for a darker color. For example, if your recipe calls for 360 grams of olive oil, you can use 360 grams of your infused oil for a darker color, or 100 grams of infused oil and 260 grams of regular oil for a lighter color—or any combination you wish.

Oatmeal: Oatmeal is soothing to the skin, and any type works in soap. Whole oats are quite scratchy, so I like to grind them down to a powder. Add up to 1 tablespoon per 450 grams of base oils in your recipe. Add to your base oils before combining with the lye solution.

Coffee: Coffee is a fun exfoliant. Add up to 1 tablespoon per 450 grams of base oils. You can add the ground coffee to your lye solution to draw out the color, or add to your base oils before combining with the lye solution.

Dried herbs: Dried and crushed herbs such as peppermint, rosemary, sage, basil, and spearmint can be added to soap as an exfoliant. Add up to 1 teaspoon per 450 grams of base oils in your recipe. Add to your base oils before combining with the lye solution.

Milk powders: Milk powders can give soap a lotion-like and creamy lather. You can use goat milk, buttermilk, or coconut milk powders. Add up to 1 tablespoon per 900 grams of base oils in your recipe. Add to your base oils before combining with the lye solution. Use a stick blender to break up any clumps.

Dried flowers: Most dried flowers will turn brown or black inside of your soap. Lavender added to soap turns black and looks exactly like mouse poop. Calendula, however, stays nice and yellow. I recommend adding dried flowers to the top of your soap as a decoration so they have a better chance of keeping their color. Some of my favorite dried flowers include calendula, chamomile, rose petals or buds, and cornflowers.

Sugar: Sugar can include white sugar, brown sugar, honey, agave, and maple syrup. Sugars boost the lather of a soap by creating a more soluble soap. Anything granular needs to be dissolved before adding it to your soap. You can dissolve it into your warm lye solution. Honey, agave, and maple syrup can be melted into solid oils and butters right after you melt them. Sugar can heat soap, so use cool temperatures and do not insulate your soap (see Gel Phase, page 35).

Salt: Salt can help harden your soap, making it easier to release from silicone molds. Add up to 1 teaspoon of sea salt or table salt per 900 grams of base oils to your hot lye solution to dissolve.

Essential Oils

When we taught soapmaking in Haiti, one woman exclaimed that smelling the soap took her back in time to when she lived with her grandmother as a child. Scent is very powerful. It really can transport you to different places and times in your life. Essential oils are used to naturally scent soap, and they have aromatherapeutic properties. These oils are extracted from part or the whole of a plant.

Essential oils are categorized into different notes, including top notes, which are bright, sharp, moving, dancing, and sometimes fleeting oils (meaning they can dissipate from the soap slightly); base notes, which are strong, pungent, bottom, heavy, grounding, and anchoring oils; and middle notes, which round out and help add complexity to a blend. When blending them, try to include at least two of the note groups, if not all three.

Here are some common essential oils and their characteristics:

Top Note	**Peppermint, corn mint, and spearmint:** Refreshing, stimulating, and cooling to the skin. Give soap a fresh and clean smell.
	Orange, lemon, and grapefruit: Happy and uplifting. Can improve any mood. Choose "folded" (fractionated) citrus oils for better staying power in soap.
Top-Middle Note	**Litsea:** Bright and uplifting, with a lemony fragrance. Helps anchor more fleeting citrus essential oils in a blend.
	Lavender: Calming, relaxing, and balancing, with antiseptic and antibacterial properties. One of the most common essential oils used in soap.
	Lime and bergamot: Bright like other citrus oils, but also musky. Add depth and complexity to a blend.
	Clary sage: Sweet and herbaceous, mood enhancing, and balancing.
Middle-Base Note	**Clove bud, cinnamon leaf, cassia, and nutmeg:** Warm, spicy, and musky. Invigorating and warming. Spice essential oils can deepen any blend and are great for holiday blends. They can cause a soap to trace quickly, so hand-stir if your blend contains a spice.
Base Note	**Patchouli:** Spicy, musky, and sweet. Grounding and balancing. A wonderful base note to add depth to a blend.
	Cedarwood: Woody and clean smelling. Calming and soothing.

Following, you'll find five of my favorite soapmaking essential oil blends for beginners. You can substitute them in any of the cold-process soap recipes, or in your favorite 900-gram oil cold-process soap recipe.

* Lavender (35 grams) and peppermint (10 grams)
* Orange (35 grams) and patchouli (10 grams)
* Cedarwood (15 grams), lavender (25 grams), and patchouli (5 grams)
* Lemon (30 grams) and lavender (15 grams)
* Orange (20 grams), lemon (15 grams), and litsea (10 grams)

Usage rates in soap: Soapmakers follow different usage rates; but here is what I recommend. Some essential oils, such as spices, should only be used in small quantities in a blend. Be sure to use an essential oil calculator (see page 271) to determine safe amounts to use.

* Cold-process soap: 15 to 30 grams per 450 grams of base oils
* Hot-process soap: 15 to 20 grams per 450 grams of base oils
* Melt-and-pour soap: 1 to 2 percent of soap base
* Hand-mill soap: 2 to 3 percent of grated soap base
* Liquid soap: 1 percent of diluted liquid soap

Essential Oil Safety

Every essential oil has a safe usage rate in soap. Some oils can be skin sensitizers, especially spices such as clove, cinnamon, cassia, and nutmeg. You'll want to use spices in very small percentages of your blend. To find out how much of an essential oil or blend is safe to use in soap, use an online essential oil calculator (see page 271). All the blends in this book use safe usage rates.

If you are pregnant, experts recommend avoiding essential oils altogether during your first trimester. During your second and third trimesters, it is generally safe to use bergamot, grapefruit, lavender, lemon, lemongrass, lime, litsea, orange, patchouli, peppermint, tea tree, and ylang-ylang. Avoid basil, cassia, cedarwood, cinnamon, clary sage, clove, juniper berry, nutmeg, rosemary, and thyme during pregnancy. Check with your health care provider before using any essential oils.

Essential oils should be treated like medicine in many cases. If you have certain medical conditions or are taking medication, you should avoid working with certain essential oils. For example, people with epilepsy should avoid stimulating essential oils such as eucalyptus, rosemary, sage, and sweet fennel. Those with low blood pressure should avoid sedating oils such as lavender, sage, and ylang-ylang. Refer to the essential oil safety resources (page 272) to research which essential oils should not be used in your circumstances.

Little ones should not have access to essential oils, as children are much more sensitive to the effects of the oils and more easily absorb them into their system. If your child is making soap, I recommend that you add the essential oil to their soap; if they are older, at least make sure they are wearing gloves and that the undiluted oil does not get on their skin. Avoid using spice, mint, and camphor essential oils as well as lemongrass and juniper with children.

Always wear gloves when working with essential oils, as you don't want your skin to absorb undiluted oils, especially if you're pregnant. If you do get essential oils on your skin, wash with soap and warm water immediately. Allowing undiluted essential oils on your skin time after time can cause you to become allergic to them, even to seemingly safe oils such as lavender and tea tree.

Store essential oils in a cool space out of direct sunlight. Refer to pages 20 to 22 for additional information.

Sea Clay & Avocado Soap, page 115

Basic Beginner Soap—Vegan, page 58

Coffee Scrub Soap, page 98

Kombucha Soap, page 106

Basil, Lavender & Mint Soap, page 121

Oatmeal Soap, page 70

Charcoal Soap, page 72

Lemon Turmeric Soap, page 104

03

Cold-Process Soapmaking

Cold-process is my favorite soapmaking method. The fluidity of the soap allows for endless swirling and design. The soap comes out smooth and refined looking. Unlike hot-process soap, you pour it and let it saponify in the mold for 24 hours. It's always fun to wake up the next day and cut your soap.

Garden Herb Soap, page 118

Rose Clay Soap, page 74

Tomato & Herb Soap, page 112

100% Coconut Oil Soap—Laundry Soap, page 68

Lavender & Geranium Soap, page 96

Apple Cider Vinegar Soap, page 100

Carrot & Honey Soap, page 128

Juniper's Soap, page 80

Recipes

* Basic Beginner Soap—
  Lard or Tallow   56

* Basic Beginner Soap—Vegan   58

* Castile Soap   60

* Bastile Soap with Coconut Oil   62

* Bastile Soap with Shea Butter   64

* 100% Coconut Oil Soap—
  20% Superfat   66

* 100% Coconut Oil Soap—
  Laundry Soap   68

* Oatmeal Soap   70

* Charcoal Soap   72

* Rose Clay Soap   74

* Lavender Mint Soap   76

* Neem Soap   78

* Juniper's Soap   80

* Almond Orange Soap   82

* Bay Rum Soap   84

* Chamomile Tea Soap   86

* Coconut Milk & Cedarwood Soap   88

* Cocoa & Honey Soap   90

* Dandelion, Nettle & Aloe Soap   92

* Sea Clay & Eucalyptus Soap   94

* Lavender & Geranium Soap   96

* Coffee Scrub Soap   98

* Apple Cider Vinegar Soap   100

* Cypress, Lavender & Sage Soap   102

* Lemon Turmeric Soap   104

* Kombucha Soap   106

* Egg & Turmeric Soap   109

* Tomato & Herb Soap   112

* Sea Clay & Avocado Soap   115

* Garden Herb Soap   118

* Basil, Lavender & Mint Soap   121

* Patchouli Orange Soap   124

* Plantain-Infused Lavender Soap   126

* Carrot & Honey Soap   128

* Ocean Breeze Soap   130

Cold-Process Soapmaking
Step-by-Step

Before we get started, I'd like to share a few different process variations when it comes to melting your oils and adding colorants and additives.

Melt Your Oils

To make cold-process soap, all your solid oils and butters need to be melted. There are two options:

Microwave: This is the most common method for melting solid oils and butters. Weigh your solid oils and butters into a microwave-safe container. Heat just until melted—don't overheat. This is the process used throughout this section.

Double boiler: You can also melt your solid oils and butters using a double boiler.

Color Your Soap

For cold-process soap, you can add color and additives in two different ways:

Add to base oils: If you are making a single-colored soap, add your colors and additives directly to the oils before adding your lye solution. This ensures that everything is mixed well.

Add to emulsified soap: If you want to divide your soap to swirl, you can divide your emulsified soap and then add colors and additives.

Make Your Soap

Let's make cold-process soap!

~~~~~~

SAFETY FIRST:

* Remember to wear goggles and gloves for safety.
* Mix the lye solution in a well-ventilated area with access to a sink for flushing with water in case of accidents.
* Keep your work space free from distractions, especially small children and pets who can land underfoot.
* Always pour the lye into the water, not the other way around.

~~~~~~

Prep ahead: Weigh your essential oils into a small glass container.

Step 1: Place a lye solution container on the scale and press the tare button to zero the scale. (The tare button on your scale will zero out the weight of the measuring container and leave the scale at zero, so you can weigh just what you put into the container and not the container itself.) Weigh the water in the container and set aside. Remember, don't use glass for this container.

Step 2: Place a dry lye container on the scale and press the tare button to zero the scale. Weigh the sodium hydroxide.

Step 3: Following safety precautions, pour the sodium hydroxide into the water (not the other way around) while stirring. Remember never to pour the

Prep Ahead

Step 1

Step 2

Step 3

Step 3, continued

Step 4

Step 5

Step 6

Step 7

water into the sodium hydroxide or a violent reaction can occur. Turn your head and lean away from the lye solution so you aren't breathing in fumes. Stir until all the granules have dissolved. The lye will dissolve quickly, usually in less than one minute. Set aside to cool.

Step 4: Place a microwave-safe bowl on the scale and press the tare button to zero the scale. Weigh each solid oil and butter from your recipe in the bowl, pressing the tare button in between oils to zero the scale.

Step 5: Heat the bowl in the microwave until the solid oils and butters are just melted.

→

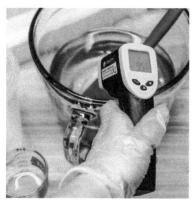

Step 9

Step 10

Step 10, continued

Step 6: Place the bowl of melted oils and butters on the scale and hit tare. One by one, weigh each liquid oil from your recipe in the bowl, pressing the tare button in between. Adding the room-temperature liquid oils to the melted oils and butters helps drop the temperature of the complete base oil mixture. You should now have all your base oils and butters weighed out in one bowl, all in a liquid state.

Step 7: Add your essential oils to the prepared base oils.

Step 8: If you are creating a single-colored soap, add your colors and additives to the oils now. If you are dividing your soap to swirl, wait until the soap has traced. This is further explained in the Decorative Techniques section (page 39).

Step 9: Check the temperature of your base oil mixture and lye solution using an infrared thermometer. Be sure to blend each mixture before you take the temperature, as the thermometer takes the surface temperature. For cold-process soap, a good range for both mixtures is between 80°F and 110°F.

Step 10: Pour the lye solution into your melted oils and mix to trace (see sidebar, page 34). Be sure to "burp" your stick blender first by tilting it to the side once you put it into the mixture. This helps prevent air bubbles in your soap. When your stick blender is turned on, keep it submerged in the soap or it will splatter soap everywhere.

Step 11

Step 11, continued

Step 14

Step 11: Pour your soap into a mold and allow to saponify for 24 hours. You do not need to insulate it unless you want to force gel phase.

Step 12: After 24 hours, you can unmold the soap. If you're using a silicone loaf mold or a silicone individual cavity mold, pull the sides of the mold away from the soap; if it pulls away easily, it's ready to come out. Turn the mold over and push down with your thumbs. The soap should start moving out. If the sides are sticking, wait another 24 hours and try again. If you're using a lined mold, it should be easy to pull the soap out.

Step 13: Cut your soap using a stainless-steel knife, dough scraper, or a specialized soap cutter. I like to slice my loaves into one-inch bars, but it is

a matter of preference. Try a couple of different widths and see what feels good in your hands.

Step 14: Allow the soap to cure in a cool, dry space for at least 4 weeks. Place your bars standing up on a shelf or table, spaced apart to allow air to flow around them. During the cure, the last bit of saponification takes place and water evaporates, creating a hard bar of soap that is gentle and lasts a long time in the bath.

Step 15: If you'd like to package your soap, wait until after the curing period to do so. Once your soap has cured, you can store it in cardboard boxes or plastic shoeboxes with holes punched in them. They will continue to need airflow to breathe.

Recognizing Trace

It's true that oil and water don't mix. And if you were to simply pour your lye solution into your prepared oils and then pour it all into the mold, it would separate and you'd be left with a caustic, oily mess. Before you pour your soap into the mold, you must mix it to create a stable emulsion. Soapmakers call this process *trace*. To test for trace, pull your turned-off stick blender out of your mixed soap and drizzle some soap back onto the surface. If it sits a bit on the surface and you can see it, then you have reached trace. Your soap is emulsified and you can now pour it into your mold.

To create swirls, you can mix your soap until it is fully emulsified but not showing trace. This will give you plenty of time to divide your soap to color. Here I'll show you the difference and what to look for.

The lye solution has been added to the oils, and you can clearly see the separation between the two.

As you mix, things start to come together, but you can still see oil streaks.

Now the soap is emulsified, solid in color, and there are no oil streaks. This will make soap. Emulsified soap is perfect for dividing into containers to color for swirling.

Here the soap has clearly traced. You can see the drizzle of soap sitting on the surface.

Gel Phase

Gel phase is the heating phase of saponification. It can be quite shocking to see soap starting to go through gel phase. Your soap will heat up and start to turn dark and translucent in the center. As it continues to heat up, the soap going through gel phase will spread to the sides. As it cools, your soap will lighten up a bit and become opaque.

Soap doesn't have to go through gel phase. If you make soap using cool temperatures, your soap might not gel and that's okay.

If your soap does go through gel phase, it will probably be easier to unmold because it will be harder and less sticky. Gel phase does make natural colorants brighter. If you want to force gel phase to get the brightest natural colors in your soap, you can try a few things:

- Insulate your soap by covering it with a piece of wood or placing a cardboard box over your mold. You can even cover it with some blankets. Check it every now and then to make sure it isn't overheating. A crack will form if it is overheating.

- You can oven-process your soap to force it though gel phase. Preheat the oven to warm, or about 170°F. As soon as your soap is in the mold, turn the oven off, place the soap in the oven, and let it sit overnight. The warm oven will force it to gel. Make sure that your mold can withstand the higher heat in the oven. Most silicone molds work well.

- You can also place your soap on a heating pad. This will usually force gel phase to occur.

Cold-Process Soap Pro Tips

- Take your time when making soap. As you go through the process, check off each step, since it's easy to forget a base oil or scent. I like to place all of my ingredients to the left of my scale, and as I add them to my batch, I move them to the right of my scale. That way I know I didn't miss anything.

- Temperatures matter when it comes to cold-process soapmaking. I recommend keeping the temperatures of your lye solution and oil mixture between 80°F and 120°F. They do not need to be the same temperature; for example, your lye solution can be 93°F and your oil mixture can be 110°F. The warmer your ingredients, the faster your soap will move to trace. If you want to swirl your soap, try a temperature between 80°F and 90°F to give yourself plenty of time to divide and color your soap. I recommend using an infrared thermometer to check your temperatures. Once you get more experience, you'll be able to touch the sides of your container and feel that they are at the ideal temperature.

- Always follow a recipe exactly. Every oil requires a specific amount of sodium hydroxide to saponify. If you substitute oils or change oil amounts, be sure to run your new recipe through a lye calculator (see page 271) to get the new lye amount.

- Water or liquid amounts can fluctuate in soap. Using more liquid creates a soap that is slower to move to trace. A soap made with more water might require more time in the mold to harden. Using less water can create a soap that hardens more quickly and allows you to unmold and cut sooner.

- When you are trying a new recipe, use your stick blender sparingly. The soap might move quickly to trace because of its ingredients. Rotate between pulsing with your stick blender and mixing with it turned off. If a recipe contains spice essential oils or any ingredients with sugar, such as milk, sugar, honey, agave, purées, beer, wine, etc., your soap might move quickly to trace.

Cold-Process Soap Troubleshooting

**Issue:
Soap cracks
or volcanoes
out of the mold.**

CAUSE/WAYS TO PREVENT: This is usually a sign that your soap has overheated. Make your next soap using cooler temperatures and don't insulate your mold.

FIX: If your soap is cracking, put it in front of a fan or in the freezer. If your soap has volcanoed out of the mold, you can usually just scoop it up and put it back into the mold.

**Issue: Soap has
a layer of oil on
top of it.**

CAUSE/WAYS TO PREVENT: This can happen because of two things: overheating or not mixing enough. Use cooler temperatures, and make sure that you are at trace before you pour your soap into the mold.

FIX: If it is just a little oil, wait 24 to 48 hours to see if it will reabsorb. If it is a lot of oil that won't reabsorb, dump the whole mixture into a slow cooker. Use your stick blender to mix back to trace and hot-process your soap following the hot-process instructions (page 135).

**Issue: Soap is
brittle or chalky.**

CAUSE/WAYS TO PREVENT: This can happen if you have excess lye in your soap. Check your scale to make sure it is weighing your ingredients correctly and double-check your recipe to make sure it has the correct amount of lye for the amount of oils used. You can run it through a lye calculator.

FIX: I don't usually recommend re-batching lye-heavy soap because you don't know exactly how much oil you need. Just toss it out.

**Issue: Soap is
sticking to a
silicone mold.**

CAUSE/WAYS TO PREVENT: To prevent this, use a recipe high in hard oils and butters. You can also use a water discount (reduce the amount of water you use). Soaping at a higher temperature and forcing gel phase can also help firm up your soap enough to unmold it.

FIX: If you know that you followed the recipe correctly, wait a day or two to unmold. Your soap will dry out and firm up enough to unmold.

Issue: Your soap "rices" after adding a fragrance or essential oil—it looks like there are hard lumps of rice in your mixture.

CAUSE/WAYS TO PREVENT: Ricing happens when you add a finicky fragrance or essential oil. It usually occurs with fragrance oils, so check with the manufacturer to make sure your fragrance is stable in cold-process soap.

FIX: Try mixing your soap by hand to see if it will smooth out. If it won't, place it into a slow cooker and use the hot-process method to finish it.

Issue: Your soap seizes (hardens) while you're mixing it.

CAUSE/WAYS TO PREVENT: Seizing usually happens because your soap is too hot or because a fragrance or essential oil causes the reaction. Work at a lower temperature and use fragrance oils that work with cold-process soap. Spice essential oils are notorious for seizing soap, so use in small amounts or avoid altogether.

FIX: If your soap seizes, transfer it into a slow cooker and finish it using the hot-process method.

Issue: Your soap has pockets of oils or lye.

CAUSE/WAYS TO PREVENT: This usually happens when you don't mix enough or your soap gets thick unexpectedly without emulsifying fully.

FIX: Shred your soap and use the hand-milled method to finish it.

Embossing or Stamping Your Soap

One of the easiest ways to decorate a bar of soap is to use a soap stamp to emboss it. There are countless soap stamp designs available, ranging from natural elements such as trees and flowers to text such as *goat milk* or *natural.* You can even find companies that will create a soap stamp from your logo or design. Stay away from rubber paper–crafting stamps, as they don't work in soap. This technique can be used with any of the recipes in the cold-process section.

Step 1: Make your soap and let it saponify for 24 hours.

Step 2: Unmold and cut your soap into bars.

Step 3: Lay your bar of soap flat on a hard surface. Press your soap stamp straight down into the soap. If your soap seems hard and the stamp doesn't press down, you can use a small mallet to bang it into the soap. If your stamp enters the soap too easily and the design is mushing together or soap is sticking to the stamp, then your soap might be too soft. Wait a couple of days and try again. If it is still too soft, try after a week.

Step 4: After stamping your soap, you can leave it as is, or you can dust the design with a natural colorant, such

as a clay. This makes the design pop and gives it some interest. I spray a bit of alcohol onto the surface of the stamped soap; this helps the natural colorant stick. Use a fine-mist sprayer and spray only once. Then dust a little natural colorant over the stamp and wipe off the excess using a paper towel. This helps smooth out the colorant and fill in the stamp impression.

Step 5: Let the soap cure as usual.

In-the-Pot Swirl

This design uses a loaf mold to create a beautiful swirl that you'll see once you cut your soap. This is a very simple technique to try, especially if you haven't tried swirling before. It is called an in-the-pot swirl because you divide some of your soap into containers to color, and then you pour them back into your base, swirl gently, and pour into your mold. As you do this, the soap continues to swirl together. You can use two colors to create a simple swirl, or as many colors as you're brave enough to try!

Prep ahead: Weigh your essential oils into a small glass container.

Step 1: Weigh the water into your lye solution container.

Step 2: Weigh the sodium hydroxide into your dry lye container.

Step 3: Following safety precautions, pour the sodium hydroxide into the water while stirring. Turn your head and lean away from the lye solution. Stir until all the granules have dissolved. Set aside.

Step 4: Weigh and melt the solid oils and butters.

Step 5: Weigh the liquid oils into the melted oils and butters.

Step 6: Add your essential oils to the prepared base oils.

Step 7: Check the temperature of your base oil mixture and lye solution. For swirling soap, a good range for both mixtures is between 80°F and 90°F.

Step 8: Pour the lye solution into your melted oils and mix to emulsion (for more details, refer to Recognizing Trace on page 34).

Step 9: Divide your soap into separate containers for each color that you want in your swirl. For this swirl, I like to keep at least half of my soap uncolored as a base, or colored white using zinc oxide powder, and then divide the rest in individual cups to color. Leave your base soap in the original mixing container. How much soap you color for your swirl is up to you.

Step 8

Step 9

Step 11

Step 11, continued

Step 11, continued

Step 12

Step 10: Add colorant to each container, and mix using a spoon or a milk frother. Avoid using a stick blender, as it will thicken the soap further. At this point, your soap should be at light to medium trace.

Step 11: Pour your colored soap(s) back into the base. I like to rotate through each color about three times and pour them in three different spots, pouring each color right on top of the last. Hold your colored soap up high when pouring so it will penetrate down into your base soap.

Step 12: Using a small silicone spatula, give the soap one swirl. Don't over-swirl in the container or it will muddy the soap.

Step 13

Step 13, continued

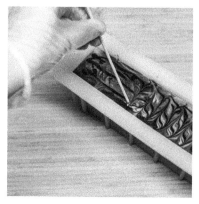

Step 14

Step 15

Step 16

Step 13: Pour the soap into your loaf mold. As you pour, it will swirl even more.

Step 14: Swirl the top of the soap with a skewer if you'd like.

Step 15: Allow the soap to saponify for 24 hours.

Step 16: Unmold your soap, cut into bars, and allow to cure in a cool, dry space for at least 4 weeks.

Avoiding Ash

Ash is a pesky little problem that's common in cold-process soap. Occasionally you'll make a soap and wake up the next morning to find it covered in a fine dusting of white powder. This powder is sodium carbonate, which forms where active sodium hydroxide meets air. It's harmless and simply an aesthetic issue. To prevent ash, you just need to create a barrier between the soap and the air. Some soapmakers cover their soap with plastic wrap, but if you swirl your soap, plastic wrap can ruin your design. Alcohol can be used to create a barrier as well. Spray your soap in the mold with isopropyl alcohol (91 percent or the highest you can find). Don't spray it right after you pour if your soap is still really fluid, as it can pick up the colors and move them. Wait until after your soap has set up a bit and has become dull, usually 10 to 20 minutes. Saturate it to the point that it is fully wet, but stop before the alcohol starts pooling on the soap. Let it sit and then spray again after an hour or two. This will keep that pesky ash away.

If your soap has ash, there are some ways to remove it:

- Run the soap under warm water and use a paper towel to scrub off the ash.

- Use a handheld steamer to steam it away. Hold the steamer a couple of inches above your soap and steam for 20 seconds. Once your soap dries, the ash will be gone.

- Use a vegetable peeler to scrape the ash off the top of cut bars.

Simple Slab Swirl

There are two main styles of high-volume molds that you can use when making a batch of soap: slab molds and loaf molds. A slab mold creates a design on the surface of the soap. What you see when you pour your soap is what you'll end up with on the surface of each bar.

This design uses a slab mold to create a beautiful swirl on the surface of your soap.

SAFETY FIRST: Remember to wear goggles and gloves. Mix the lye solution in a well-ventilated area with access to a sink for flushing with water if necessary. Keep your work space free from distractions, small children, and pets.

Prep ahead: Weigh your essential oils into a small glass container.

Step 1: Weigh the water into your lye solution container.

Step 2: Weigh the sodium hydroxide into your dry lye container.

Step 3: Following safety precautions, pour the sodium hydroxide into the water while stirring. Turn your head and lean away from the lye solution. Stir until all the granules have dissolved. Set aside.

Step 4: Weigh and melt the solid oils and butters.

Step 5: Weigh the liquid oils into the melted oils and butters.

Step 6: Add your essential oils to the prepared base oils.

Step 7: Check the temperature of your base oil mixture and lye solution. For swirling soap, a good range for both mixtures is between 80°F and 90°F.

Step 8: Pour the lye solution into your melted oils and mix to emulsion (for more details, refer to Recognizing Trace on page 34).

Step 8

Step 9

Step 11

Step 9: Divide your soap into separate containers for each color that you want in your swirl. I like to keep at least half of my soap uncolored as a base, or colored white using zinc oxide powder, and then divide the rest into individual cups to color. How much soap you color is a matter of preference.

Step 10: Add colorant to each container, and mix using a spoon or a milk frother. Avoid using a stick blender, as it will thicken the soap further. At this point, your soap should be at light to medium trace.

Step 11: Once everything is mixed, pour your base soap into your mold.

Step 12: Pour in your colored soap. I like to rotate through each color about four times and pour them in straight lines all going in the same direction. This will create a crisp swirl. Hold your pouring container up high for the colored soap to penetrate down into the base soap. When you get to the last pour for each color, hold the soap close to the mold so it will fall on the surface of the base soap. You want each color on the surface of the soap, as this is what you'll be swirling.

→

Step 12

Step 12, continued

Step 13

Step 15

Step 13: Use a small silicone spatula to swirl your soap. Push it all the way down to the bottom of your mold so it will swirl the soap throughout the bars. I move the spatula through the lines, breaking them into a swirl as the spatula drags the soap.

Step 14: Allow the soap to saponify for 24 hours.

Step 15: Unmold your soap, cut into bars, and allow to cure in a cool, dry space for at least 4 weeks.

Tiger Stripe Swirl

This design uses a loaf mold to create a beautiful swirl that you'll see once you cut your soap. It is called a tiger stripe swirl because when you cut it, it looks like tiger or zebra stripes. This is a simple swirl for beginners because it is beautiful whether your soap is nice and fluid or it thickens up a bit.

SAFETY FIRST: Remember to wear goggles and gloves. Mix the lye solution in a well-ventilated area with access to a sink for flushing with water if necessary. Keep your work space free from distractions, small children, and pets.

Prep ahead: Weigh your essential oils into a small glass container.

Step 1: Weigh the water into your lye solution container.

Step 2: Weigh the sodium hydroxide into your dry lye container.

Step 3: Following safety precautions, pour the sodium hydroxide into the water while stirring. Turn your head and lean away from the lye solution. Stir until all the granules have dissolved. Set aside.

Step 4: Weigh and melt the solid oils and butters.

Step 5: Weigh the liquid oils into the melted oils and butters.

Step 6: Add your essential oils to the prepared base oils.

Step 7: Check the temperature of your base oil mixture and lye solution. For swirling soap, a good range for both mixtures is between 80°F and 90°F.

Step 8: Pour the lye solution into your melted oils and mix to emulsion (for more details, refer to Recognizing Trace on page 34).

Step 9: Divide your soap evenly into containers for each color that you want in your swirl.

Step 10: Add colorant to each container, and mix using a spoon or a milk frother. Avoid using a stick blender, as it will thicken the soap further. At this point, your soap should be at light to medium trace.

Step 11: Rotating through each color, pour the soap in a single line right down the center of your mold, with each color on top of the next. If you pour heavy lines, you'll get thick stripes, and if you pour quick, light lines, you'll get thin stripes. Keep

→

Step 8

Step 10

Step 10, continued

Step 11

Step 12

Step 14

pouring right down the center of the mold. As you pour in the soap, it will look like it is getting muddied. But when you cut, you'll be surprised how crisp and beautiful the lines are.

Step 12: Pour until you have used up all the soap. You can swirl the top using a skewer, but don't push it deep into the soap or you will ruin the design. Push it down just enough to swirl the top.

Step 13: Allow the soap to saponify for 24 hours.

Step 14: Unmold your soap, cut into bars, and allow to cure in a cool, dry space for at least 4 weeks.

In-the-Mold Loaf Swirl

This design uses a loaf mold to create a beautiful swirl that you'll see once you cut your soap. For an in-the-pot swirl (page 40), you pour your colored soap back into your main soap pot and then pour it into your mold. For this swirl, you pour your colored soap into the base right in your mold. It creates bolder and crisper swirls than an in-the-pot swirl.

SAFETY FIRST: Remember to wear goggles and gloves. Mix the lye solution in a well-ventilated area with access to a sink for flushing with water if necessary. Keep your work space free from distractions, small children, and pets.

Prep ahead: Weigh your essential oils into a small glass container.

Step 1: Weigh the water into your lye solution container.

Step 2: Weigh the sodium hydroxide into your dry lye container.

Step 3: Following safety precautions, pour the sodium hydroxide into the water while stirring. Turn your head and lean away from the lye solution. Stir until all the granules have dissolved. Set aside.

Step 4: Weigh and melt the solid oils and butters.

Step 5: Weigh the liquid oils into the melted oils and butters.

Step 6: Add your essential oils to the prepared base oils.

Step 7: Check the temperature of your base oil mixture and lye solution. For swirling soap, a good range for both mixtures is between 80°F and 90°F.

Step 8: Pour the lye solution into your melted oils and mix to emulsion (for more details, refer to Recognizing Trace on page 34).

Step 9: Divide your soap into separate containers for each color that you want in your swirl. For this swirl, I like to keep at least one-half to two-thirds of my soap uncolored as a base, or colored white using zinc oxide powder, and then divide the rest into individual cups to color. How much soap you color is a matter of preference.

→

Step 8

Step 9

Step 10

Step 11

Step 10: Add colorant to each container, and mix using a spoon or a milk frother. Avoid using a stick blender, as it will thicken the soap further. At this point, your soap should be at light to medium trace.

Step 11: Pour your base soap into your mold.

Step 12: Rotating through each color, pour your colored soap into the base, moving down the length of the mold to ensure each color will show in each bar. Hold the colored soap up high as you pour to allow it to penetrate deeply into the base. Hold it close as you finish pouring to leave some soap on the surface.

Step 12

Step 12, continued

Step 12, continued

Step 13

Step 15

Step 13: You can swirl the top using a skewer, but don't push it deep down into the soap or you will ruin the design. Push it down just enough to swirl the top.

Step 14: Allow the soap to saponify for 24 hours.

Step 15: Unmold your soap, cut into bars, and allow to cure in a cool, dry space for at least 4 weeks.

Layers

Layering soap into a loaf mold is an easy way to create stunning designs. It is a great technique because it uses thicker soap. So, if your aim is to create a wispy swirl using fluid soap but your soap mixture gets too thick, you can always fall back on layering! Some soap artists use this technique to create intricate landscape designs. For example, you can create a beach design by layering a sand-colored soap, then blues for water, and then different blues and white for a sky and clouds.

SAFETY FIRST: Remember to wear goggles and gloves. Mix the lye solution in a well-ventilated area with access to a sink for flushing with water if necessary. Keep your work space free from distractions, small children, and pets.

Prep ahead: Weigh your essential oils into a small glass container.

Step 1: Weigh the water into your lye solution container.

Step 2: Weigh the sodium hydroxide into your dry lye container.

Step 3: Following safety precautions, pour the sodium hydroxide into the water while stirring. Turn your head and lean away from the lye solution. Stir until all the granules have dissolved. Set aside.

Step 4: Weigh and melt the solid oils and butters.

Step 5: Weigh the liquid oils into the melted oils and butters.

Step 6: Add your essential oils to the prepared base oils.

Step 7: Check the temperature of your base oil mixture and lye solution. For layering soap, a good range for both mixtures is between 80°F and 90°F.

Step 8

Step 9

Step 10

Step 11

Step 11, continued

Step 8: Pour the lye solution into your melted oils and mix to light trace (see Recognizing Trace, page 34).

Step 9: Divide your soap into separate containers for each color that you want to layer.

Step 10: Add colorant to each container, and mix using a spoon or a milk frother.

Step 11: Use your stick blender to thicken up your first layer. You want it to be really thick so it will support the next layer. Spoon this first layer into your mold. Bang the mold on a solid surface to help flatten the soap.

→

Layers, continued

Step 12

Step 13

Step 15

Step 12: If you are adding more than two layers, thicken up the next layer using your stick blender. Once thick, spoon it onto the first layer in the mold. Repeat this step for each additional layer in your design, except for the last layer.

Step 13: Pour the last layer into your mold (or second layer, if you're just doing two). The last layer doesn't need to be thickened because it doesn't have to support any other layers. You can leave it fluid.

Step 14: Allow the soap to saponify for 24 hours.

Step 15: Unmold your soap, cut into bars, and allow to cure in a cool, dry space for at least 4 weeks.

Adding a Charcoal Line Between Layers

A popular design technique when layering soap is to create a charcoal line between layers. To do this, put some charcoal into a tea strainer. After your layer has set up, dust a little charcoal on the surface. Leave some soap from the bottom layer peeking through—if you dust a solid layer, you'll risk your layers separating. Spoon the next layer over the charcoal-covered layer. Repeat the charcoal dusting between each layer.

Dusting charcoal on the surface.

Leave some soap peeking through.

Finished bar of soap.

Cold-Process Recipes

Basic Beginner Soap—Lard or Tallow

BODY

This simple recipe is perfect for the beginner soapmaker. It is a nice all-over body soap that includes three oils for simplicity. Lard makes a hard white soap, and beef tallow makes a similar soap with a more lotion-like lather. You can use either lard or beef tallow in this recipe without having to recalculate the lye amount.

YIELD: 1,290 grams | 10 bars (129 grams each)

START TO FINISH TIME: 1 hour to create soap, 24 to 48 hours to saponify, 4 weeks to cure

SCENT: Your choice

LYE DISCOUNT: 5%

SAFETY FIRST: Remember to wear goggles and gloves. Mix the lye solution in a well-ventilated area with access to a sink for flushing with water if necessary. Keep your work space free from distractions, small children, and pets.

EQUIPMENT

* Digital scale
* Glass container
* Lye solution container
* Dry lye container
* Silicone spatulas
* Microwave-safe batch container
* Infrared thermometer (optional)
* Stick blender
* 10-inch silicone loaf mold

INGREDIENTS

Scent

* 45 grams essential oil (single or a blend from page 22)

Lye Solution

* 260 grams distilled water
* 130 grams sodium hydroxide

Base Oils (900 grams)

* 297 grams (33%) lard or tallow
* 297 grams (33%) 76-degree coconut oil
* 306 grams (34%) olive oil

Prep ahead: Weigh the essential oils into a glass container; blend together if necessary. Set aside.

Step 1: Weigh the water into your lye solution container.

Step 2: Weigh the sodium hydroxide into your dry lye container.

Step 3: Following safety precautions, pour the sodium hydroxide into the water while stirring. Turn your head and lean away from the lye solution. Stir until all the granules have dissolved. Set aside to cool.

Step 4: Weigh and melt the lard or tallow and coconut oil into the microwave-safe batch container.

Step 5: Weigh the olive oil into the melted oils and butters.

Step 6: Add the essential oils to the prepared base oils.

Step 7: Check the temperature of your base oil mixture and lye solution. For a solid-colored soap, a good range for both mixtures is between 80°F and 110°F.

Step 8: Pour the lye solution into the melted oils and mix to trace.

Step 9: Once the soap has traced, pour it into the mold.

Step 10: Allow the soap to saponify for 24 to 48 hours.

Step 11: Unmold your soap, cut into bars, and allow to cure in a cool, dry space for at least 4 weeks.

Basic Beginner Soap—Vegan

VEGAN · BODY

This is one of my favorite basic vegan and palm oil-free soap formulas. It is another simple recipe, using only three base oils. It makes a hard white bar of soap that is easy to customize with your choice of essential oils and additives.

~~~~~~

YIELD: 1,290 grams | 10 bars (129 grams each)

START TO FINISH TIME: 1 hour to create soap, 24 to 48 hours to saponify, 4 weeks to cure

SCENT: Your choice

LYE DISCOUNT: 5%

SAFETY FIRST: Remember to wear goggles and gloves. Mix the lye solution in a well-ventilated area with access to a sink for flushing with water if necessary. Keep your work space free from distractions, small children, and pets.

~~~~~~

EQUIPMENT

* Digital scale
* Glass container
* Lye solution container
* Dry lye container
* Silicone spatulas
* Microwave-safe batch container
* Infrared thermometer (optional)
* Stick blender
* 10-inch silicone loaf mold

INGREDIENTS

Scent

* 45 grams essential oil (single or a blend from page 22)

Lye Solution

* 260 grams distilled water
* 130 grams sodium hydroxide

Base Oils (900 grams)

* 315 grams (35%) 76-degree coconut oil
* 135 grams (15%) cocoa butter
* 450 grams (50%) olive oil

Prep ahead: Weigh the essential oils into a glass container; blend together if necessary. Set aside.

Step 1: Weigh the water into your lye solution container.

Step 2: Weigh the sodium hydroxide into your dry lye container.

Step 3: Following safety precautions, pour the sodium hydroxide into the water while stirring. Turn your head and lean away from the lye solution. Stir until all the granules have dissolved. Set aside to cool.

Step 4: Weigh and melt the coconut oil and cocoa butter into the microwave-safe batch container.

Step 5: Weigh the olive oil into the melted oils and butters.

Step 6: Add your essential oils to the prepared base oils.

Step 7: Check the temperature of your base oil mixture and lye solution. For a solid-colored soap, a good range for both mixtures is between 80°F and 110°F.

Step 8: Pour the lye solution into your melted oils and mix to trace.

Step 9: Pour your soap into the mold.

Step 10: Allow the soap to saponify for 24 to 48 hours.

Step 11: Unmold your soap, cut into bars, and allow to cure in a cool, dry space for at least 4 weeks.

Castile Soap

VEGAN · BODY · FACE · GENTLE

Originating from the Castile region of Spain, this soap was traditionally made using 100 percent olive oil. These days, larger companies call any vegan soap made with a high amount of olive oil Castile soap. For the purposes of this book (and in the popular opinion of soapmakers), Castile soap is 100 percent olive oil soap. Once saponified, olive oil is very low-cleansing, meaning it doesn't strip your skin of all its natural oils. High olive oil soaps are great for sensitive skin. Olive oil soap doesn't lather very much, but that doesn't mean it isn't cleaning your skin. It's nourishing and gentle.

YIELD: 1,153 grams | 10 bars (115 grams each)

START TO FINISH TIME: 1 hour to create soap, 24 to 48 hours to saponify, 4 weeks to cure

SCENT: Your choice

LYE DISCOUNT: 5%

SAFETY FIRST: Remember to wear goggles and gloves. Mix the lye solution in a well-ventilated area with access to a sink for flushing with water if necessary. Keep your work space free from distractions, small children, and pets.

EQUIPMENT

* Digital scale
* Glass container
* Lye solution container
* Dry lye container
* Silicone spatulas
* Microwave-safe batch container
* Infrared thermometer (optional)
* Stick blender
* 10-inch silicone loaf mold

INGREDIENTS

Scent
* 45 grams essential oil (single or a blend from page 22)

Lye Solution
* 138 grams distilled water
* 115 grams sodium hydroxide

Base Oils (900 grams)
* 900 grams (100%) olive oil

Prep ahead: Weigh the essential oils into a glass container; blend together if necessary. Set aside.

Step 1: Weigh the water into your lye solution container.

Step 2: Weigh the sodium hydroxide into your dry lye container.

Step 3: Following safety precautions, pour the sodium hydroxide into the water while stirring. Turn your head and lean away from the lye solution. Stir until all the granules have dissolved. Set aside to cool.

Step 4: Weigh the olive oil into the microwave-safe batch container.

Step 5: Add your essential oils to the prepared olive oil.

Step 6: Check the temperature of your base oil mixture and lye solution. For a solid-colored soap, a good range for both mixtures is between 80°F and 110°F.

Step 7: Pour the lye solution into your oils and mix to trace.

Step 8: Once the soap has traced, pour it into your mold.

Step 9: Allow the soap to saponify for 24 to 48 hours.

Step 10: Unmold your soap, cut into bars, and allow to cure in a cool, dry space for at least 4 weeks.

Tip: *Olive oil creates a very soft soap that can be sticky upon unmolding. It also takes longer to cure into a hard bar. I normally use a 2:1 ratio of lye to water in regular bars of soap, but I use a ratio of 1.2:1 in Castile soap. This helps create a harder bar of soap that doesn't need a longer cure time. Castile soap gets better with age. Try a bar after the usual four-week cure, but tuck some away for several months and see how you like them.*

Bastile Soap with Coconut Oil

VEGAN · BODY · FACE · GENTLE

Bastile is a term coined by the soapmaking community for a soap that's high in olive oil but also includes a small percentage of other oils. With 80 to 95 percent olive oil, Bastile soap is still super gentle and nourishing. This recipe includes a little coconut oil to boost the lather a bit.

YIELD: 1,161 grams | 10 bars (116 grams each)

START TO FINISH TIME: 1 hour to create soap, 24 to 48 hours to saponify, 4 weeks to cure

SCENT: Your choice

LYE DISCOUNT: 5%

SAFETY FIRST: Remember to wear goggles and gloves. Mix the lye solution in a well-ventilated area with access to a sink for flushing with water if necessary. Keep your work space free from distractions, small children, and pets.

EQUIPMENT

* Digital scale
* Glass container
* Lye solution container
* Dry lye container
* Silicone spatulas
* Microwave-safe batch container
* Infrared thermometer (optional)
* Stick blender
* 10-inch silicone loaf mold

INGREDIENTS

Scent

* 45 grams essential oil (single or a blend from page 22)

Lye Solution

* 142 grams distilled water
* 119 grams sodium hydroxide

Base Oils (900 grams)

* 90 grams (10%) 76-degree coconut oil
* 810 grams (90%) olive oil

Prep ahead: Weigh the essential oils into a glass container; blend together if necessary. Set aside.

Step 1: Weigh the water into your lye solution container.

Step 2: Weigh the sodium hydroxide into your dry lye container.

Step 3: Following safety precautions, pour the sodium hydroxide into the water while stirring. Turn your head and lean away from the lye solution. Stir until all the granules have dissolved. Set aside to cool.

Step 4: Weigh and melt the coconut oil.

Step 5: Weigh the olive oil into the melted coconut oil.

Step 6: Add your essential oils to the prepared base oils.

Step 7: Check the temperature of your base oil mixture and lye solution. For a solid-colored soap, a good range for both mixtures is between 80°F and 110°F.

Step 8: Pour the lye solution into your melted oils and mix to trace.

Step 9: Pour your soap into the mold.

Step 10: Allow the soap to saponify for 24 to 48 hours.

Step 11: Unmold your soap, cut into bars, and allow to cure in a cool, dry space for at least 4 weeks.

Bastile Soap with Shea Butter

VEGAN · BODY · FACE · GENTLE

Shea butter increases the hardness of a high olive oil soap. This soap is still very gentle, perfect for sensitive skin. The shea butter creates a decadent lather, rich and creamy, almost lotion-like.

〜〜〜〜〜〜〜〜〜〜〜〜〜〜〜〜〜〜〜〜〜〜〜〜〜〜〜〜〜〜〜〜〜

YIELD: 1,150 grams | 10 bars (115 grams each)

START TO FINISH TIME: 1 hour to create soap, 24 to 48 hours to saponify, 4 weeks to cure

SCENT: Your choice

LYE DISCOUNT: 5%

SAFETY FIRST: Remember to wear goggles and gloves. Mix the lye solution in a well-ventilated area with access to a sink for flushing with water if necessary. Keep your work space free from distractions, small children, and pets.

〜〜〜〜〜〜〜〜〜〜〜〜〜〜〜〜〜〜〜〜〜〜〜〜〜〜〜〜〜〜〜〜〜

EQUIPMENT

* Digital scale
* Glass container
* Lye solution container
* Dry lye container
* Silicone spatulas
* Microwave-safe batch container
* Infrared thermometer (optional)
* Stick blender
* 10-inch silicone loaf mold

INGREDIENTS

Scent

* 45 grams essential oil (single or a blend from page 22; see tip)

Lye Solution

* 136 grams distilled water
* 114 grams sodium hydroxide

Base Oils (900 grams)

* 135 grams (15%) shea butter
* 765 grams (85%) olive oil

Prep ahead: Weigh the essential oils into a glass container; blend together if necessary. Set aside.

Step 1: Weigh the water into your lye solution container.

Step 2: Weigh the sodium hydroxide into your dry lye container.

Step 3: Following safety precautions, pour the sodium hydroxide into the water while stirring. Turn your head and lean away from the lye solution. Stir until all the granules have dissolved. Set aside to cool.

Step 4: Weigh and melt the shea butter.

Step 5: Weigh the olive oil into the melted shea butter.

Step 6: Add your essential oils to the prepared base oils.

Step 7: Check the temperature of your base oil mixture and lye solution. For a solid-colored soap, a good range for both mixtures is between 80°F and 110°F.

Step 8: Pour the lye solution into your melted oils and mix to trace.

Step 9: Pour your soap into the mold.

Step 10: Allow the soap to saponify for 24 to 48 hours.

Step 11: Unmold your soap, cut into bars, and allow to cure in a cool, dry space for at least 4 weeks.

Tip: *Bastile soap is great for babies or elder folks, both of whom will benefit from a gentle, low-cleansing soap that doesn't strip the skin of natural oils. With babies, take care when washing and rinsing their heads, as this soap can sting their eyes. Also, don't add any essential oils—leave the soap unscented.*

100% Coconut Oil Soap— 20% Superfat

VEGAN · BODY · ACNE-FIGHTING

This simple soap uses only coconut oil, which is traditionally drying if used at this high percentage. But by using a 20 percent superfat (see page 257), you can create a soap that isn't drying at all. The unsaponified oils in this soap make it easier on the skin.

~~~~~~

YIELD: 1,293 grams | 10 bars (129 grams each)

START TO FINISH TIME: 1 hour to create soap, 24 to 48 hours to saponify, 4 weeks to cure

SCENT: Your choice

LYE DISCOUNT: 5%

SAFETY FIRST: Remember to wear goggles and gloves. Mix the lye solution in a well-ventilated area with access to a sink for flushing with water if necessary. Keep your work space free from distractions, small children, and pets.

~~~~~~

EQUIPMENT

* Digital scale
* Glass container
* Lye solution container
* Dry lye container
* Silicone spatulas
* Microwave-safe batch container
* Infrared thermometer (optional)
* Stick blender
* 10-inch silicone loaf mold

INGREDIENTS

Scent
* 45 grams essential oil (single or a blend from page 22; see tip)

Lye Solution
* 262 grams distilled water
* 131 grams sodium hydroxide

Base Oils (900 grams)
* 900 grams (100%) 76-degree coconut oil

Prep ahead: Weigh the essential oils into a glass container; blend together if necessary. Set aside.

Step 1: Weigh the water into your lye solution container.

Step 2: Weigh the sodium hydroxide into your dry lye container.

Step 3: Following safety precautions, pour the sodium hydroxide into the water while stirring. Turn your head and lean away from the lye solution. Stir until all the granules have dissolved. Set aside to cool.

Step 4: Weigh and melt the coconut oil.

Step 5: Add your essential oils to the prepared coconut oil.

Step 6: Check the temperature of your base oil mixture and lye solution. For a solid soap, a good range for both mixtures is between 80°F and 110°F.

Step 7: Pour the lye solution into your melted coconut oil and mix to trace.

Step 8: Pour your soap into the mold.

Step 9: Allow the soap to saponify for 24 to 48 hours.

Step 10: Unmold your soap, cut into bars, and allow to cure in a cool, dry space for at least 4 weeks.

Tip: *If you're looking for a stark-white soap that shows true colors, try this soap.*

100% Coconut Oil Soap— Laundry Soap

HIGH-CLEANSING · HOUSEHOLD

This soap is made with 100 percent coconut oil and uses a 0 percent superfat to create a high-cleansing soap to use as a base for natural laundry soap. While it's great for cleaning clothes, this soap would be much too harsh to use on your skin.

~~~~~~

YIELD: 1,392 grams | 10 bars (139 grams each)

START TO FINISH TIME: 1 hour to create soap, 24 to 48 hours to saponify

SCENT: Your choice

LYE DISCOUNT: 0%

SAFETY FIRST: Remember to wear goggles and gloves. Mix the lye solution in a well-ventilated area with access to a sink for flushing with water if necessary. Keep your work space free from distractions, small children, and pets.

~~~~~~

EQUIPMENT

* Digital scale
* Lye solution container
* Dry lye container
* Silicone spatulas
* Microwave-safe batch container
* Infrared thermometer (optional)
* Stick blender
* 10-inch silicone loaf mold

INGREDIENTS

Lye Solution

* 328 grams distilled water
* 164 grams sodium hydroxide

Base Oils (900 grams)

* 900 grams (100%) 76-degree coconut oil

Step 1: Weigh the water into your lye solution container.

Step 2: Weigh the sodium hydroxide into your dry lye container.

Step 3: Following safety precautions, pour the sodium hydroxide into the water while stirring. Turn your head and lean away from the lye solution. Stir until all the granules have dissolved. Set aside to cool.

Step 4: Weigh and melt the coconut oil.

Step 5: Check the temperature of your base oil mixture and lye solution. For a solid soap, a good range for both mixtures is between 80°F and 110°F.

Step 6: Pour the lye solution into the melted coconut oil and mix to trace.

Step 7: Pour your soap into the mold.

Step 8: Allow the soap to saponify for 24 to 48 hours.

Step 9: Unmold your soap and cut into bars. It does not need to cure.

Tip: *To make natural laundry soap, shred this soap using a cheese grater or electric grater after you cut it into bars. Combine 1 cup soap shreds, 2 cups borax, 2 cups washing soda (look in the laundry aisle for sodium carbonate made by Arm & Hammer), and 2 milliliters of essential oil into a large glass jar. To use, add 1 tablespoon of your natural laundry soap directly to your clothes washer. Use vinegar in the rinse cycle to prevent soap buildup in your machine. You can also rub this bar directly on stains to pretreat.*

Oatmeal Soap

VEGAN · BODY · FACE · GENTLE · FLORAL

This is a simple oatmeal soap scented with lavender essential oil. Oatmeal is excellent for the skin and can help soothe it by reducing itching and inflammation. Lather up the soap and allow it to sit on your skin for a couple of minutes before rinsing to give the oatmeal time to work. In my soapmaking classes here in the US, oatmeal soap is a favorite among students.

YIELD: 1,269 grams | 10 bars (127 grams each)

START TO FINISH TIME: 1 hour to create soap, 24 to 48 hours to saponify, 4 weeks to cure

SCENT: Lavender

LYE DISCOUNT: 8%

SAFETY FIRST: Remember to wear goggles and gloves. Mix the lye solution in a well-ventilated area with access to a sink for flushing with water if necessary. Keep your work space free from distractions, small children, and pets.

EQUIPMENT

* Digital scale
* Glass container
* Lye solution container
* Dry lye container
* Silicone spatulas
* Microwave-safe batch container
* Measuring spoons
* Infrared thermometer (optional)
* Stick blender
* 10-inch silicone loaf mold

INGREDIENTS

Scent

* 45 grams lavender essential oil

Lye Solution

* 246 grams distilled water
* 123 grams sodium hydroxide

Base Oils (900 grams)

* 270 grams (30%) 76-degree coconut oil
* 45 grams (5%) shea butter
* 450 grams (50%) olive oil
* 135 grams (15%) avocado oil

Colorants/Additives

* 2 tablespoons ground oats (see tip)

Prep ahead: Weigh the lavender essential oil into a glass container. Set aside.

Step 1: Weigh the water into your lye solution container.

Step 2: Weigh the sodium hydroxide into your dry lye container.

Step 3: Following safety precautions, pour the sodium hydroxide into the water while stirring. Turn your head and lean away from the lye solution. Stir until all the granules have dissolved. Set aside to cool.

Step 4: Weigh and melt the coconut oil and shea butter.

Step 5: Weigh the olive and avocado oils into the melted coconut oil and shea butter.

Step 6: Add your essential oil and ground oats to the prepared base oils and blend.

Step 7: Check the temperature of your base oil mixture and lye solution. For a solid-colored soap, a good range for both mixtures is between 80°F and 110°F.

Step 8: Pour the lye solution into your melted oils and mix to trace.

Step 9: Pour your soap into the mold.

Step 10: Allow the soap to saponify for 24 to 48 hours.

Step 11: Unmold your soap, cut into bars, and allow to cure in a cool, dry space for at least 4 weeks.

Tip: Whole oats can be super scratchy in soap and very unpleasant to wash with. I like to grind my oats into a powder using a food processor before I add them to my soap.

Charcoal Soap

VEGAN · BODY · FACE · ACNE-FIGHTING · MINTY · HERBAL

The cosmetic charcoal powder in this simple soap is a great natural colorant for getting a stark black, and it's also good at tackling acne. Charcoal draws impurities and toxins from the skin. Tea tree essential oil is antibacterial and a natural acne treatment.

~~~~~~

YIELD: 1,278 grams | 10 bars (128 grams each)

START TO FINISH TIME: 1 hour to create soap, 24 to 48 hours to saponify, 4 weeks to cure

SCENT: Peppermint, tea tree, rosemary, and lavender

LYE DISCOUNT: 5%

SAFETY FIRST: Remember to wear goggles and gloves. Mix the lye solution in a well-ventilated area with access to a sink for flushing with water if necessary. Keep your work space free from distractions, small children, and pets.

~~~~~~

EQUIPMENT

* Digital scale
* Glass container
* Lye solution container
* Dry lye container
* Silicone spatulas
* Microwave-safe batch container
* Measuring spoons
* Infrared thermometer (optional)
* Stick blender
* 10-inch silicone loaf mold

INGREDIENTS

Scent

* 20 grams tea tree essential oil
* 10 grams rosemary essential oil
* 10 grams lavender essential oil
* 5 grams peppermint essential oil

Lye Solution

* 252 grams distilled water
* 126 grams sodium hydroxide

Base Oils (900 grams)

* 270 grams (30%) 76-degree coconut oil
* 63 grams (7%) shea butter
* 360 grams (40%) olive oil
* 135 grams (15%) avocado oil
* 72 grams (8%) castor oil

Colorants/Additives

* 2 tablespoons cosmetic charcoal powder

Prep ahead: Weigh the tea tree, rosemary, lavender, and peppermint essential oils into a glass container; blend together. Set aside.

Step 1: Weigh the water into your lye solution container.

Step 2: Weigh the sodium hydroxide into your dry lye container.

Step 3: Following safety precautions, pour the sodium hydroxide into the water while stirring. Turn your head and lean away from the lye solution. Stir until all the granules have dissolved. Set aside to cool.

Step 4: Weigh and melt the coconut oil and shea butter.

Step 5: Weigh the olive, avocado, and castor oils into the melted coconut oil and shea butter.

Step 6: Add your essential oils and charcoal to the prepared base oils, and blend together.

Step 7: Check the temperature of your base oil mixture and lye solution. For a solid-colored soap, a good range for both mixtures is between 80°F and 110°F.

Step 8: Pour the lye solution into your melted oils and mix to trace.

Step 9: Pour your soap into the mold.

Step 10: Allow the soap to saponify for 24 to 48 hours.

Step 11: Unmold your soap, cut into bars, and allow to cure in a cool, dry space for at least 4 weeks.

Tip: *Not everyone likes the medicinal smell of tea tree oil by itself. By combining it with other essential oils such as peppermint and lavender, you can create a very pleasant aroma.*

Rose Clay Soap

VEGAN · BODY · FACE · FLORAL · CITRUS

Rose clay is one of my favorite natural colorants to create a pink color in soap. This makes a nice face soap, and it also features geranium essential oil, known to reduce wrinkles and repair skin.

YIELD: 1,281 grams | 10 bars (128 grams each)

START TO FINISH TIME: 1 hour to create soap, 24 to 48 hours to saponify, 4 weeks to cure

SCENT: Geranium, litsea, and orange

LYE DISCOUNT: 5%

SAFETY FIRST: Remember to wear goggles and gloves. Mix the lye solution in a well-ventilated area with access to a sink for flushing with water if necessary. Keep your work space free from distractions, small children, and pets.

EQUIPMENT

* Digital scale
* Glass container
* Lye solution container
* Dry lye container
* Silicone spatulas
* Microwave-safe batch container
* Measuring spoons
* Infrared thermometer (optional)
* Stick blender
* 10-inch silicone loaf mold

INGREDIENTS

Scent

* 15 grams litsea essential oil
* 20 grams orange essential oil
* 10 grams geranium essential oil

Lye Solution

* 254 grams distilled water
* 127 grams sodium hydroxide

Base Oils (900 grams)

* 270 grams (30%) 76-degree coconut oil
* 90 grams (10%) mango butter
* 360 grams (40%) olive oil
* 135 grams (15%) avocado oil
* 45 grams (5%) rice bran oil

Colorants/Additives

* 1 teaspoon rose clay powder

Prep ahead: Weigh the litsea, orange, and geranium essential oils into a glass container; blend together. Set aside.

Step 1: Weigh the water into your lye solution container.

Step 2: Weigh the sodium hydroxide into your dry lye container.

Step 3: Following safety precautions, pour the sodium hydroxide into the water while stirring. Turn your head and lean away from the lye solution. Stir until all the granules have dissolved.

Step 4: Add the clay to the hot lye solution. Set aside to cool.

Step 5: Weigh and melt the coconut oil and mango butter.

Step 6: Weigh the olive, avocado, and rice bran oils into the melted coconut oil and mango butter.

Step 7: Add your essential oils to the prepared base oils and blend.

Step 8: Check the temperature of your base oil mixture and lye solution. For a solid-colored soap, a good range for both mixtures is between 80°F and 110°F.

Step 9: Pour the lye solution into your melted oils and mix to trace.

Step 10: Pour your soap into the mold.

Step 11: Allow the soap to saponify for 24 to 48 hours.

Step 12: Unmold your soap, cut into bars, and allow to cure in a cool, dry space for at least 4 weeks.

Tip: *If you're making a single-colored soap using clay, adding your clay to the lye water will help draw the color out. If you're using clay in a multicolored soap, add it to your traced soap as usual.*

Lavender Mint Soap

VEGAN · BODY · EXFOLIATING · FLORAL · MINTY

Lavender and mint essential oils are one of my favorite blends. The combination is simple and appeals to a wide variety of people.

~~~~~~

YIELD: 1,287 grams | 10 bars (129 grams each)

START TO FINISH TIME: 1 hour to create soap, 24 to 48 hours to saponify, 4 weeks to cure

SCENT: Lavender and mint

LYE DISCOUNT: 5%

SAFETY FIRST: Remember to wear goggles and gloves. Mix the lye solution in a well-ventilated area with access to a sink for flushing with water if necessary. Keep your work space free from distractions, small children, and pets.

~~~~~~

EQUIPMENT

* Digital scale
* Glass container
* Lye solution container
* Dry lye container
* Silicone spatulas
* Microwave-safe batch container
* Measuring spoons
* Infrared thermometer (optional)
* Stick blender
* 10-inch silicone loaf mold

INGREDIENTS

Scent

* 35 grams lavender essential oil
* 10 grams peppermint essential oil

Lye Solution

* 258 grams distilled water
* 129 grams sodium hydroxide

Base Oils (900 grams)

* 315 grams (35%) 76-degree coconut oil
* 45 grams (5%) cocoa butter
* 360 grams (40%) olive oil
* 135 grams (15%) avocado oil
* 45 grams (5%) castor oil

Colorants/Additives

* 1 tablespoon crushed dried mint

Prep ahead: Weigh the lavender and peppermint essential oils into a glass container; blend together. Set aside.

Step 1: Weigh the water into your lye solution container.

Step 2: Weigh the sodium hydroxide into your dry lye container.

Step 3: Following safety precautions, pour the sodium hydroxide into the water while stirring. Turn your head and lean away from the lye solution. Stir until all the granules have dissolved. Set aside to cool.

Step 4: Weigh and melt the coconut oil and cocoa butter.

Step 5: Weigh the olive, avocado, and castor oils into the melted coconut oil and cocoa butter.

Step 6: Add your essential oils and dried mint to the prepared base oils and blend.

Step 7: Check the temperature of your base oil mixture and lye solution. For a solid-colored soap, a good range for both mixtures is between 80°F and 110°F.

Step 8: Pour the lye solution into your melted oils and mix to trace.

Step 9: Pour your soap into the mold.

Step 10: Allow the soap to saponify for 24 to 48 hours.

Step 11: Unmold your soap, cut into bars, and allow to cure in a cool, dry space for at least 4 weeks.

> **Tip:** *You can purchase dried herbs for soapmaking or dry your own. My favorite herbs from my garden to use in soap include mint, basil, and rosemary. Just hang the fresh herbs to dry and then crush them.*

Neem Soap

VEGAN · BODY · FACE · GENTLE · FLORAL · CITRUS

Neem oil is great for combatting dry, itchy, and troublesome skin. Traditionally, both neem oil and leaves have been used in India to treat skin conditions. This oil is stinky, however, so use it at low percentages in your soap.

YIELD: 1,287 grams | 10 bars (129 grams each)

START TO FINISH TIME: 1 hour to create soap, 24 to 48 hours to saponify, 4 weeks to cure

SCENT: Lemongrass, vetiver, patchouli, and orange

LYE DISCOUNT: 5%

SAFETY FIRST: Remember to wear goggles and gloves. Mix the lye solution in a well-ventilated area with access to a sink for flushing with water if necessary. Keep your work space free from distractions, small children, and pets.

EQUIPMENT

* Digital scale
* Glass container
* Lye solution container
* Dry lye container
* Silicone spatulas
* Microwave-safe batch container
* Measuring spoons
* Infrared thermometer (optional)
* Stick blender
* 10-inch silicone loaf mold

INGREDIENTS

Scent
* 15 grams orange essential oil
* 10 grams lemongrass essential oil
* 10 grams vetiver essential oil
* 10 grams patchouli essential oil

Lye Solution
* 258 grams distilled water
* 129 grams sodium hydroxide

Base Oils (900 grams)
* 315 grams (35%) 76-degree coconut oil
* 45 grams (5%) cocoa butter
* 360 grams (40%) olive oil
* 135 grams (15%) avocado oil
* 45 grams (5%) neem oil

Colorants/Additives
* 2 tablespoons nettle leaf powder

Prep ahead: Weigh the orange, lemongrass, vetiver, and patchouli essential oils into a glass container; blend together. Set aside.

Step 1: Weigh the water into your lye solution container.

Step 2: Weigh the sodium hydroxide into your dry lye container.

Step 3: Following safety precautions, pour the sodium hydroxide into the water while stirring. Turn your head and lean away from the lye solution. Stir until all the granules have dissolved. Set aside to cool.

Step 4: Weigh and melt the coconut oil and cocoa butter.

Step 5: Weigh the olive, avocado, and neem oils into the melted coconut oil and cocoa butter.

Step 6: Add your essential oils and nettle powder to the prepared base oils and blend.

Step 7: Check the temperature of your base oil mixture and lye solution. For a solid-colored soap, a good range for both mixtures is between 80°F and 110°F.

Step 8: Pour the lye solution into your melted oils and mix to trace.

Step 9: Pour your soap into the mold.

Step 10: Allow the soap to saponify for 24 to 48 hours.

Step 11: Unmold your soap, cut into bars, and allow to cure in a cool, dry space for at least 4 weeks.

Tip: *Green is a hard color to achieve using natural colorants, as the hue tends to oxidize easily and fade. Nettle leaf is one natural green colorant that I have found to last a long time in soap.*

Juniper's Soap

VEGAN · BODY · FLORAL

This soap is named after my daughter, Juniper Blue. It features juniper berries and juniper essential oil. Juniper berries are used in the production of gin, and when you grind them up and inhale their aroma, you can smell a gin-like scent.

YIELD: 1,290 grams | 10 bars (129 grams each)

START TO FINISH TIME: 1 hour to create soap, 24 to 48 hours to saponify, 4 weeks to cure

SCENT: Juniper, ylang-ylang, and bergamot

LYE DISCOUNT: 5%

SAFETY FIRST: Remember to wear goggles and gloves. Mix the lye solution in a well-ventilated area with access to a sink for flushing with water if necessary. Keep your work space free from distractions, small children, and pets.

EQUIPMENT

* Digital scale
* Glass container
* Measuring spoons
* Coffee grinder (optional)
* Lye solution container
* Dry lye container
* Silicone spatulas
* Microwave-safe batch container
* Infrared thermometer (optional)
* Stick blender
* 10-inch silicone loaf mold

INGREDIENTS

Scent

* 15 grams juniper berry essential oil
* 10 grams ylang-ylang essential oil
* 10 grams bergamot essential oil
* 5 grams patchouli essential oil
* 5 grams clary sage essential oil

Lye Solution

* 260 grams distilled water
* 130 grams sodium hydroxide

Base Oils (900 grams)

* 315 grams (35%) 76-degree coconut oil
* 45 grams (5%) cocoa butter
* 360 grams (40%) olive oil
* 135 grams (15%) rice bran oil
* 45 grams (5%) sweet almond oil

Colorants/Additives

* 1 tablespoon dried juniper berries
* 2 tablespoons alkanet root powder

Prep ahead: Weigh the juniper berry, ylang-ylang, bergamot, patchouli, and clary sage essential oils into a glass container; blend together. Set aside. In a coffee grinder or with a mortar and pestle, grind the juniper berries as finely as you can. They are a bit sticky and will make a pasty powder.

Step 1: Weigh the water into your lye solution container.

Step 2: Weigh the sodium hydroxide into your dry lye container.

Step 3: Following safety precautions, pour the sodium hydroxide into the water while stirring. Turn your head and lean away from the lye solution. Stir until all the granules have dissolved.

Step 4: Add the ground juniper berries into the hot lye solution. (The lye solution will soften them, so there is no need to strain your lye solution before you make the soap.) Set aside to cool.

Step 5: Weigh and melt the coconut oil and cocoa butter.

Step 6: Add the alkanet root powder to the melted coconut oil and cocoa butter. Let sit and steep for about 10 minutes to draw the natural color out.

Step 7: Weigh the olive, rice bran, and sweet almond oils into the melted coconut oil and cocoa butter.

Step 8: Add your essential oils to the prepared base oils and blend.

Step 9: Check the temperature of your base oil mixture and lye solution. For a solid-colored soap, a good range for both mixtures is between 80°F and 110°F.

Step 10: Pour the lye solution into your melted oils and mix to trace.

Step 11: Pour your soap into the mold.

Step 12: Allow the soap to saponify for 24 to 48 hours.

Step 13: Unmold your soap, cut into bars, and allow to cure in a cool, dry space for at least 4 weeks.

Tip: *If you don't have the exact essential oils used for this (or any other) recipe, replace with 45 grams of your favorite essential oil or blend.*

Almond Orange Soap

VEGAN · BODY · GENTLE · CITRUS

When my husband, Benjamin, and I were teaching in Haiti, we asked our soapmaking students to bring anything that they thought might be useful to color the soap. They mentioned woukou, but we weren't sure what they meant. The next day they brought little pods filled with bright orange seeds. Benjamin's eyes lit up when he recognized annatto seeds, one of his favorite natural colorants. They grew there naturally, all over the place! Annatto seed gives this soap a beautiful orange color.

~~~~~~~~~~~~~~~~~~~~~~~~~~~~~~~~~~~~~~~

YIELD: 1,278 grams | 10 bars (128 grams each)

START TO FINISH TIME: 1 hour to create soap, 24 to 48 hours to saponify, 4 weeks to cure

SCENT: Almond and orange

LYE DISCOUNT: 5%

SAFETY FIRST: Remember to wear goggles and gloves. Mix the lye solution in a well-ventilated area with access to a sink for flushing with water if necessary. Keep your work space free from distractions, small children, and pets.

~~~~~~~~~~~~~~~~~~~~~~~~~~~~~~~~~~~~~~~

EQUIPMENT

* Digital scale
* Glass container
* Lye solution container
* Dry lye container
* Silicone spatulas
* Microwave-safe batch container
* Measuring spoons
* Infrared thermometer (optional)
* Stick blender
* 10-inch silicone loaf mold

INGREDIENTS

Scent
* 35 grams orange essential oil
* 10 grams bitter almond essential oil

Lye Solution
* 260 grams distilled water
* 130 grams sodium hydroxide

Base Oils (900 grams)
* 315 grams (35%) 76-degree coconut oil
* 135 grams (15%) cocoa butter
* 45 grams (5%) shea butter
* 360 grams (40%) olive oil
* 45 grams (5%) sweet almond oil

Colorants/Additives
* 2 tablespoons annatto seed powder

Prep ahead: Weigh the orange and bitter almond essential oils into a glass container; blend together. Set aside.

Step 1: Weigh the water into your lye solution container.

Step 2: Weigh the sodium hydroxide into your dry lye container.

Step 3: Following safety precautions, pour the sodium hydroxide into the water while stirring. Turn your head and lean away from the lye solution. Stir until all the granules have dissolved. Set aside to cool.

Step 4: Weigh and melt the coconut oil, cocoa butter, and shea butter.

Step 5: Weigh the olive and sweet almond oils into the melted coconut oil, cocoa butter, and shea butter.

Step 6: Add your essential oils and annatto seed powder to the prepared base oils and blend.

Step 7: Check the temperature of your base oil mixture and lye solution. For a solid-colored soap, a good range for both mixtures is between 80°F and 110°F.

Step 8: Pour the lye solution into your melted oils and mix to trace.

Step 9: Pour your soap into the mold.

Step 10: Allow the soap to saponify for 24 to 48 hours.

Step 11: Unmold your soap, cut into bars, and allow to cure in a cool, dry space for at least 4 weeks.

Tip: *Real bitter almond essential oil is usually sold as a blend in a base of sweet almond oil. It contains prussic acid, which is regulated by the US Drug Enforcement Administration, so it can't be sold without being diluted. It can be hard to find bitter almond essential oil at a decent price. I recommend Rainbow Meadow (see Essential Oil Suppliers, page 270).*

Bay Rum Soap

VEGAN · BODY · CITRUS · SPICY

Spice, pine, and citrus will make this soap popular with the men in your life. This aroma has been traditionally used in aftershaves and colognes. I taught a couples' soapmaking class once, and every single gentleman in the class wanted this premixed essential oil blend. It's a good one!

~~~~~~

YIELD: 1,290 grams | 10 bars (129 grams each)

START TO FINISH TIME: 1 hour to create soap, 24 to 48 hours to saponify, 4 weeks to cure

SCENT: Clove, cinnamon, pine, and orange

LYE DISCOUNT: 5%

SAFETY FIRST: Remember to wear goggles and gloves. Mix the lye solution in a well-ventilated area with access to a sink for flushing with water if necessary. Keep your work space free from distractions, small children, and pets.

~~~~~~

EQUIPMENT

* Digital scale
* Glass container
* Lye solution container
* Dry lye container
* Silicone spatulas
* Microwave-safe batch container
* Infrared thermometer (optional)
* Silicone or stainless-steel whisk
* 10-inch silicone loaf mold

INGREDIENTS

Scent

* 15 grams orange essential oil
* 14 grams pine essential oil
* 10 grams litsea essential oil
* 3 grams clove bud essential oil
* 3 grams cinnamon leaf essential oil

Lye Solution

* 260 grams distilled water
* 130 grams sodium hydroxide

Base Oils (900 grams)

* 315 grams (35%) 76-degree coconut oil
* 135 grams (15%) cocoa butter
* 45 grams (5%) shea butter
* 405 grams (45%) olive oil

Prep ahead: Weigh the orange, pine, litsea, clove bud, and cinnamon leaf essential oils into a glass container; blend together. Set aside.

Step 1: Weigh the water into your lye solution container.

Step 2: Weigh the sodium hydroxide into your dry lye container.

Step 3: Following safety precautions, pour the sodium hydroxide into the water while stirring. Turn your head and lean away from the lye solution. Stir until all the granules have dissolved. Set aside to cool.

Step 4: Weigh and melt the coconut oil, cocoa butter, and shea butter.

Step 5: Weigh the olive oil into the melted coconut oil, cocoa butter, and shea butter.

Step 6: Add your essential oils to the prepared base oils and blend.

Step 7: Check the temperature of your base oil mixture and lye solution. For a solid-colored soap, a good range for both mixtures is between 80°F and 110°F.

Step 8: Pour the lye solution into your melted oils, and mix to trace by hand using a silicone or stainless-steel whisk.

Step 9: Quickly pour your soap into the mold.

Step 10: Allow the soap to saponify for 24 to 48 hours.

Step 11: Unmold your soap, cut into bars, and allow to cure in a cool, dry space for at least 4 weeks.

Tip: *Spice essential oils are notorious for making soap trace quickly. Stir those recipes that contain spice essential oils by hand to ensure you have time to properly emulsify the soap. You'll need to work quickly to get it into your mold.*

Chamomile Tea Soap

VEGAN · BODY · FACE · FLORAL · CITRUS

Making tea is a great way to add herbs to your soap. Chamomile has long been used to soothe skin and relieve anxiety. Will soap relieve your anxiety? Probably not! But chamomile lovers will enjoy this soap featuring their favorite herb.

~~~~~~

YIELD: 1,278 grams | 10 bars (128 grams each)

START TO FINISH TIME: 1 hour to create soap, 24 to 48 hours to saponify, 4 weeks to cure

SCENT: Geranium, spruce, grapefruit, and litsea

LYE DISCOUNT: 5%

SAFETY FIRST: Remember to wear goggles and gloves. Mix the lye solution in a well-ventilated area with access to a sink for flushing with water if necessary. Keep your work space free from distractions, small children, and pets.

~~~~~~

EQUIPMENT

* Digital scale
* Glass container
* Lye solution container
* Dry lye container
* Silicone spatulas
* Microwave-safe batch container
* Measuring spoons
* Infrared thermometer (optional)
* Stick blender
* 10-inch silicone loaf mold

INGREDIENTS

Scent

* 20 grams grapefruit essential oil
* 10 grams black spruce essential oil
* 10 grams litsea essential oil
* 5 grams geranium essential oil

Lye Solution

* 300 grams distilled water
* 126 grams sodium hydroxide

Base Oils (900 grams)

* 225 grams (25%) 76-degree coconut oil
* 135 grams (15%) cocoa butter
* 360 grams (40%) olive oil
* 90 grams (10%) avocado oil
* 90 grams (10%) high oleic sunflower oil

Colorants/Additives

* 2 chamomile tea bags
* 1 teaspoon yellow silt clay powder

Prep ahead: Weigh the grapefruit, black spruce, litsea, and geranium essential oils into a glass container; blend together. Set aside. Boil the water and pour over your chamomile tea bags to make a tea. Allow it to steep for about 10 minutes. Refrigerate to cool completely until you are ready to make soap.

Step 1: Weigh 252 grams of chamomile tea into your lye solution container.

Step 2: Weigh the sodium hydroxide into your dry lye container.

Step 3: Following safety precautions, pour the sodium hydroxide into the tea while stirring. Turn your head and lean away from the lye solution. Stir until all the granules have dissolved.

Step 4: Add the yellow silt clay to your lye solution. Set aside to cool.

Step 5: Weigh and melt the coconut oil and cocoa butter.

Step 6: Weigh the olive, avocado, and sunflower oils into the melted coconut oil and cocoa butter.

Step 7: Add your essential oils to the prepared base oils and blend.

Step 8: Check the temperature of your base oil mixture and lye solution. For a solid-colored soap, a good range for both mixtures is between 80°F and 110°F.

Step 9: Pour the lye solution into your melted oils and mix to trace.

Step 10: Pour your soap into the mold.

Step 11: Allow the soap to saponify for 24 to 48 hours.

Step 12: Unmold your soap, cut into bars, and allow to cure in a cool, dry space for at least 4 weeks.

Tip: Chamomile essential oil is expensive. Instead, consider using chamomile tea, as in this recipe, or a chamomile-infused olive oil.

Coconut Milk & Cedarwood Soap

VEGAN · BODY · FACE · CITRUS · WOODSY

Coconut milk creates a soap with a lotion-like lather. You can substitute in any milk for the coconut milk. We taught soapmaking to women in a Tibetan village in China. They were traditional yak farmers, so we used—you guessed it—yak milk! Any milk will give a soap a creamy lather. This woodsy citrus essential oil blend is one of my favorites and appeals to both men and women.

YIELD: 1,269 grams | 10 bars (127 grams each)

START TO FINISH TIME: 1 hour to create soap, 24 to 48 hours to saponify, 4 weeks to cure

SCENT: Juniper, cedarwood, patchouli, orange, and lemongrass

LYE DISCOUNT: 5%

SAFETY FIRST: Remember to wear goggles and gloves. Mix the lye solution in a well-ventilated area with access to a sink for flushing with water if necessary. Keep your work space free from distractions, small children, and pets.

EQUIPMENT

* Digital scale
* Glass container
* Ice cube tray
* Lye solution container
* Dry lye container
* Measuring spoons
* Silicone spatulas
* Microwave-safe batch container
* Infrared thermometer (optional)
* Stick blender
* 10-inch silicone loaf mold

INGREDIENTS

Scent

* 15 grams cedarwood essential oil
* 10 grams orange essential oil
* 10 grams lemongrass essential oil
* 5 grams patchouli essential oil
* 5 grams juniper berry essential oil

Lye Solution

* 246 grams coconut milk
* 123 grams sodium hydroxide

Base Oils (900 grams)

* 225 grams (25%) 76-degree coconut oil
* 135 grams (15%) mango butter
* 405 grams (45%) olive oil
* 90 grams (10%) sweet almond oil
* 45 grams (5%) jojoba oil

Colorants/Additives

* 1 teaspoon French green clay powder

Prep ahead: Weigh the cedarwood, orange, lemongrass, patchouli, and juniper berry essential oils into a glass container; blend together. Set aside. Freeze the coconut milk in an ice cube tray.

Step 1: Weigh the frozen coconut milk into your lye solution container. If you need to break up the cubes or add water to get the last little bit needed, you can do so.

Step 2: Weigh the sodium hydroxide into your dry lye container.

Step 3: Following safety precautions, pour the sodium hydroxide into the coconut milk while stirring. Turn your head and lean away from the lye solution. Stir until all the granules have dissolved.

Step 4: Add the French green clay to the hot lye solution. Set aside to cool.

Step 5: Weigh and melt the coconut oil and mango butter.

Step 6: Weigh the olive, sweet almond, and jojoba oils into the melted coconut oil and mango butter.

Step 7: Add your essential oils to the prepared base oils and blend.

Step 8: Check the temperature of your base oil mixture and lye solution. For a solid-colored soap, a good range for both mixtures is between 80°F and 110°F.

Step 9: Pour the lye solution into your melted oils and mix to trace.

Step 10: Pour your soap into the mold.

Step 11: Allow the soap to saponify for 24 to 48 hours.

Step 12: Unmold your soap, cut into bars, and allow to cure in a cool, dry space for at least 4 weeks.

Tip: *When making soap with milk, I recommend freezing your milk in ice cube trays the night before. When you add your sodium hydroxide to the frozen milk, it will melt it and your lye solution will stay cool. Milk and lye solutions can turn different colors and get thick. Don't be alarmed—it's expected!*

Cocoa & Honey Soap

BODY · FLORAL · MINTY · CITRUS

Cocoa powder is one of my favorite natural brown colorants. Who doesn't want to bathe with chocolate? The essential oil blend in this soap is perfect for the holiday season, with notes of citrus, mint, and marzipan.

YIELD: 1,287 grams | 10 bars (129 grams each)

START TO FINISH TIME: 1 hour to create soap, 24 to 48 hours to saponify, 4 weeks to cure

SCENT: Peppermint, orange, lavender, and almond

LYE DISCOUNT: 5%

SAFETY FIRST: Remember to wear goggles and gloves. Mix the lye solution in a well-ventilated area with access to a sink for flushing with water if necessary. Keep your work space free from distractions, small children, and pets.

EQUIPMENT

* Digital scale
* Glass container
* Lye solution container
* Dry lye container
* Silicone spatulas
* Microwave-safe batch container
* Measuring spoons
* Infrared thermometer (optional)
* Stick blender
* 10-inch silicone loaf mold

INGREDIENTS

Scent

* 15 grams orange essential oil
* 10 grams lavender essential oil
* 8 grams peppermint essential oil
* 7 grams bitter almond essential oil
* 5 grams lemon essential oil

Lye Solution

* 258 grams distilled water
* 129 grams sodium hydroxide

Base Oils (900 grams)

* 315 grams (35%) 76-degree coconut oil
* 135 grams (15%) cocoa butter
* 315 grams (35%) olive oil
* 90 grams (10%) avocado oil
* 45 grams (5%) castor oil

Colorants/Additives

* 1 tablespoon honey
* ¼ cup cocoa powder

Prep ahead: Weigh the orange, lavender, peppermint, bitter almond, and lemon essential oils into a glass container; blend together. Set aside.

Step 1: Weigh the water into your lye solution container.

Step 2: Weigh the sodium hydroxide into your dry lye container.

Step 3: Following safety precautions, pour the sodium hydroxide into the water while stirring. Turn your head and lean away from the lye solution. Stir until all the granules have dissolved. Set aside to cool.

Step 4: Weigh and melt the coconut oil and cocoa butter.

Step 5: Add the honey to the warm coconut oil and cocoa butter and mix until completely dissolved. This will help ensure your soap doesn't end up with honey spots in it.

Step 6: Weigh the olive, avocado, and castor oils into the melted coconut oil and cocoa butter.

Step 7: Add your essential oils and cocoa powder to the prepared base oils and blend. Be sure to break up any cocoa powder clumps.

Step 8: Check the temperature of your base oil mixture and lye solution. For a solid-colored soap, a good range for both mixtures is between 80°F and 110°F.

Step 9: Pour the lye solution into your melted oils and mix to trace.

Step 10: Pour your soap into the mold.

Step 11: Allow the soap to saponify for 24 to 48 hours.

Step 12: Unmold your soap, cut into bars, and allow to cure in a cool, dry space for at least 4 weeks.

Tip: *Honey and other sugars can cause your soap to heat up. If your soap starts to crack, cool it down by placing it in the freezer.*

Dandelion, Nettle & Aloe Soap

VEGAN · BODY · FACE · HERBAL · CITRUS

Dandelion and nettle are two herbs known to soothe irritated skin. Though most people consider dandelion a weed, it has been used in traditional medicine for centuries for both its topical and internal benefits. Nettle gives this soap a beautiful green color. And, of course, the aloe is soothing and therapeutic.

YIELD: 1,290 grams | 10 bars (129 grams each)

START TO FINISH TIME: 1 hour to create soap, 24 to 48 hours to saponify, 4 weeks to cure

SCENT: Lime and rosemary

LYE DISCOUNT: 5%

SAFETY FIRST: Remember to wear goggles and gloves. Mix the lye solution in a well-ventilated area with access to a sink for flushing with water if necessary. Keep your work space free from distractions, small children, and pets.

EQUIPMENT

* Digital scale
* Glass container
* Lye solution container
* Dry lye container
* Silicone spatulas
* Microwave-safe batch container
* Measuring spoons
* Infrared thermometer (optional)
* Stick blender
* 10-inch silicone loaf mold

INGREDIENTS

Scent
* 30 grams lime essential oil
* 15 grams rosemary essential oil

Lye Solution
* 260 grams aloe vera liquid (see tip)
* 130 grams sodium hydroxide

Base Oils (900 grams)
* 315 grams (35%) 76-degree coconut oil
* 135 grams (15%) cocoa butter
* 450 grams (50%) olive oil

Colorants/Additives
* 1 tablespoon dandelion root powder
* 1 tablespoon nettle leaf powder

Prep ahead: Weigh the lime and rosemary essential oils into a glass container; blend together. Set aside.

Step 1: Weigh the aloe vera liquid into your lye solution container.

Step 2: Weigh the sodium hydroxide into your dry lye container.

Step 3: Following safety precautions, pour the sodium hydroxide into the aloe while stirring. Turn your head and lean away from the lye solution. Stir until all the granules have dissolved. Set aside to cool.

Step 4: Weigh and melt the coconut oil and cocoa butter.

Step 5: Weigh the olive oil into the melted coconut oil and cocoa butter.

Step 6: Add your essential oils and dandelion and nettle powders to the prepared base oils and blend.

Step 7: Check the temperature of your base oil mixture and lye solution. For a solid-colored soap, a good range for both mixtures is between 80°F and 110°F.

Step 8: Pour the lye solution into your melted oils and mix to trace.

Step 9: Pour your soap into the mold.

Step 10: Allow the soap to saponify for 24 to 48 hours.

Step 11: Unmold your soap, cut into bars, and allow to cure in a cool, dry space for at least 4 weeks.

Tip: *You can purchase aloe vera liquid or easily make your own. Using a sharp knife, remove the spines (sides) of the leaves. Remove the top and bottom skins. You're left with the solid aloe gel. Cut the gel into chunks and blend in a blender. Use this blended gel in your lye solution. If you don't have quite the amount called for here, add water until you get the total amount of liquid needed. Be aware that your lye solution might turn bright orange when you combine aloe and sodium hydroxide—this is expected. The orange will fade to a cream color or to the color of the natural colorant you use.*

Sea Clay & Eucalyptus Soap

VEGAN · BODY · FACE · EXFOLIATING · MINTY · HERBAL

Sea clay is a gentle exfoliant in soap. Like most clays, it draws impurities from the skin. Use this soap like a mask, allowing the lather to sit on your skin for a bit. The essential oil blend is minty and cool; it might tingle a bit.

YIELD: 1,287 grams | 10 bars (129 grams each)

START TO FINISH TIME: 1 hour to create soap, 24 to 48 hours to saponify, 4 weeks to cure

SCENT: Eucalyptus, peppermint, rosemary, and spearmint

LYE DISCOUNT: 5%

SAFETY FIRST: Remember to wear goggles and gloves. Mix the lye solution in a well-ventilated area with access to a sink for flushing with water if necessary. Keep your work space free from distractions, small children, and pets.

EQUIPMENT

* Digital scale
* Glass container
* Lye solution container
* Dry lye container
* Measuring spoons
* Silicone spatulas
* Microwave-safe batch container
* Infrared thermometer (optional)
* Stick blender
* 10-inch silicone loaf mold

INGREDIENTS

Scent

* 25 grams eucalyptus essential oil
* 10 grams peppermint essential oil
* 5 grams rosemary essential oil
* 5 grams spearmint essential oil

Lye Solution

* 258 grams distilled water
* 129 grams sodium hydroxide

Base Oils (900 grams)

* 315 grams (35%) 76-degree coconut oil
* 135 grams (15%) mango butter
* 270 grams (30%) rice bran oil
* 90 grams (10%) avocado oil
* 90 grams (10%) sweet almond oil

Colorants/Additives

* 1 tablespoon sea clay powder
* 1 teaspoon indigo root powder

Prep ahead: Weigh the eucalyptus, peppermint, rosemary, and spearmint essential oils into a glass container; blend together. Set aside.

Step 1: Weigh the water into your lye solution container.

Step 2: Weigh the sodium hydroxide into your dry lye container.

Step 3: Following safety precautions, pour the sodium hydroxide into the water while stirring. Turn your head and lean away from the lye solution. Stir until all the granules have dissolved.

Step 4: Add the sea clay and indigo root powders to your hot lye solution. Set aside to cool.

Step 5: Weigh and melt the coconut oil and mango butter.

Step 6: Weigh the rice bran, avocado, and sweet almond oils into the melted coconut oil and mango butter.

Step 7: Add your essential oils to the prepared base oils and blend.

Step 8: Check the temperature of your base oil mixture and lye solution. For a solid-colored soap, a good range for both mixtures is between 80°F and 110°F.

Step 9: Pour the lye solution into your melted oils and mix to trace.

Step 10: Pour your soap into the mold.

Step 11: Allow the soap to saponify for 24 to 48 hours.

Step 12: Unmold your soap, cut into bars, and allow to cure in a cool, dry space for at least 4 weeks.

> **Tip:** *Adding indigo root powder to the lye water really draws out the blue color. You can also use pre-reduced indigo crystals, which give a brighter blue color. If you use the crystals, only add about ⅛ teaspoon to the lye water and stir to dissolve. Strain the mixture to catch any crystals that don't dissolve.*

Lavender & Geranium Soap

VEGAN · BODY · FACE · GENTLE · FLORAL

The pairing of lavender and geranium is a classic combo for a facial soap. This floral soap is colored a bluish purple using alkanet root and indigo root powders.

~~~~~~

YIELD: 1,278 grams | 10 bars (128 grams each)

START TO FINISH TIME: 1 hour to create soap, 24 to 48 hours to saponify, 4 weeks to cure

SCENT: Lavender, geranium, and lemon

LYE DISCOUNT: 5%

SAFETY FIRST: Remember to wear goggles and gloves. Mix the lye solution in a well-ventilated area with access to a sink for flushing with water if necessary. Keep your work space free from distractions, small children, and pets.

~~~~~~

EQUIPMENT

* Digital scale
* Glass container
* Lye solution container
* Dry lye container
* Measuring spoons
* Silicone spatulas
* Microwave-safe batch container
* Infrared thermometer (optional)
* Stick blender
* 10-inch silicone loaf mold

INGREDIENTS

Scent

* 20 grams lavender essential oil
* 15 grams geranium essential oil
* 10 grams lemon essential oil

Lye Solution

* 252 grams distilled water
* 126 grams sodium hydroxide

Base Oils (900 grams)

* 315 grams (35%) 76-degree coconut oil
* 423 grams (47%) olive oil
* 72 grams (8%) high oleic sunflower oil
* 45 grams (5%) grapeseed oil
* 45 grams (5%) jojoba oil

Colorants/Additives

* ½ teaspoon indigo root powder
* 1 teaspoon alkanet root powder

Prep ahead: Weigh the lavender, geranium, and lemon essential oils into a glass container; blend together. Set aside.

Step 1: Weigh the water into your lye solution container.

Step 2: Weigh the sodium hydroxide into your dry lye container.

Step 3: Following safety precautions, pour the sodium hydroxide into the water while stirring. Turn your head and lean away from the lye solution. Stir until all the granules have dissolved.

Step 4: Add the indigo root powder to the hot lye solution. Set aside to cool.

Step 5: Weigh and melt the coconut oil.

Step 6: Weigh the olive, sunflower, grapeseed, and jojoba oils into the melted coconut oil.

Step 7: Add your essential oils and alkanet root powder to the prepared base oils and blend.

Step 8: Check the temperature of your base oil mixture and lye solution. For a solid-colored soap, a good range for both mixtures is between 80°F and 110°F.

Step 9: Pour the lye solution into your melted oils and mix to trace.

Step 10: Pour your soap into the mold.

Step 11: Allow the soap to saponify for 24 to 48 hours.

Step 12: Unmold your soap, cut into bars, and allow to cure in a cool, dry space for at least 4 weeks.

Tip: *Geranium essential oil can make soap thicken quickly. Be prepared to move fast to get this soap into your mold. It only needs a couple of blasts from the stick blender, and then you can finish mixing by hand.*

Coffee Scrub Soap

VEGAN · BODY · EXFOLIATING · MINTY · HERBAL · CITRUS · WOODSY

Coffee makes a wonderful exfoliant in soap, though a little goes a long way. I once had a student add about a cup of coffee to her soap before I could stop her. I joked that the soap would scrub her hide clean off! The essential oil blend is complex and perfect in this three-color swirled soap.

~~~~~~

YIELD: 1,296 grams | 10 bars (130 grams each)

START TO FINISH TIME: 1 hour to create soap, 24 to 48 hours to saponify, 4 weeks to cure

SCENT: Fir, basil, orange, spearmint, and almond

LYE DISCOUNT: 5%

SAFETY FIRST: Remember to wear goggles and gloves. Mix the lye solution in a well-ventilated area with access to a sink for flushing with water if necessary. Keep your work space free from distractions, small children, and pets.

~~~~~~

EQUIPMENT

* Digital scale
* Glass container
* Lye solution container
* Dry lye container
* Silicone spatulas
* Microwave-safe batch container
* Infrared thermometer (optional)
* Stick blender
* 3 mixing containers
* Measuring spoons
* 10-inch silicone loaf mold
* Skewer

INGREDIENTS

Scent

* 10 grams basil essential oil
* 10 grams orange essential oil
* 10 grams spearmint essential oil
* 9 grams fir needle essential oil
* 6 grams bitter almond essential oil

Lye Solution

* 264 grams distilled water
* 132 grams sodium hydroxide

Base Oils (900 grams)

* 360 grams (40%) 76-degree coconut oil
* 135 grams (15%) cocoa butter
* 405 grams (45%) olive oil

Colorants/Additives

* 1 tablespoon zinc oxide powder
* 1 teaspoon ground coffee
* 2 teaspoons cosmetic charcoal powder

Prep ahead: Weigh the basil, orange, spearmint, fir needle, and bitter almond essential oils into a glass container; blend together. Set aside.

Step 1: Weigh the water into your lye solution container.

Step 2: Weigh the sodium hydroxide into your dry lye container.

Step 3: Following safety precautions, pour the sodium hydroxide into the water while stirring. Turn your head and lean away from the lye solution. Stir until all the granules have dissolved. Set aside to cool.

Step 4: Weigh and melt the coconut oil and cocoa butter.

Step 5: Weigh the olive oil into the melted coconut oil and cocoa butter.

Step 6: Add your essential oils to the prepared base oils and blend.

Step 7: Check the temperature of your base oil mixture and lye solution. For a swirled soap, a good range for both mixtures is between 80°F and 90°F.

Step 8: Pour the lye solution into your melted oils and mix to emulsion or light trace.

Step 9: Divide your soap among the mixing containers into 3 equal parts to color.

Step 10: Add the zinc oxide to one container, the coffee to the second, and the charcoal powder to the third.

Step 11: Using the tiger stripe swirl technique (page 47), pour a portion of each color in straight lines down the center of the mold. Rotate through the colors 4 to 6 times each.

Step 12: Use a skewer to swirl the very top of the soap.

Step 13: Allow the soap to saponify for 24 to 48 hours.

Step 14: Unmold your soap, cut into bars, and allow to cure in a cool, dry space for at least 4 weeks.

Tip: *Coffee grounds can be quite scratchy in soap. I grind mine for a long time to get a fine powder. It will still be exfoliating in your soap.*

Apple Cider Vinegar Soap

VEGAN · BODY · FACE · FLORAL · CITRUS

Apple cider vinegar is so popular these days as a natural health tonic. In soap, it neutralizes a bit of the lye, leaving you with a super-moisturizing bar. Apple cider vinegar has traditionally been used to help ease troublesome skin conditions, including eczema and psoriasis.

YIELD: 1,281 grams | 10 bars (128 grams each)

START TO FINISH TIME: 1 hour to create soap, 24 to 48 hours to saponify, 4 weeks to cure

SCENT: Lavender, patchouli, grapefruit, and amyris

LYE DISCOUNT: 5%

SAFETY FIRST: Remember to wear goggles and gloves. Mix the lye solution in a well-ventilated area with access to a sink for flushing with water if necessary. Keep your work space free from distractions, small children, and pets.

EQUIPMENT

* Digital scale
* Glass container
* Lye solution container
* Dry lye container
* Silicone spatulas
* Microwave-safe batch container
* Infrared thermometer (optional)
* Stick blender
* 3 mixing containers
* Measuring spoons
* 10-inch silicone loaf mold
* Skewer

INGREDIENTS

Scent

* 20 grams lavender essential oil
* 10 grams patchouli essential oil
* 10 grams grapefruit essential oil
* 5 grams amyris essential oil

Lye Solution

* 254 grams apple cider vinegar
* 127 grams sodium hydroxide

Base Oils (900 grams)

* 270 grams (30%) 76-degree coconut oil
* 45 grams (5%) kokum butter
* 405 grams (45%) olive oil
* 135 grams (15%) high oleic sunflower oil
* 45 grams (5%) castor oil

Colorants/Additives

* 1 tablespoon zinc oxide powder
* 1 tablespoon turmeric powder
* 1 tablespoon madder root powder

Prep ahead: Weigh the lavender, patchouli, grapefruit, and amyris essential oils into a glass container; blend together. Set aside.

Step 1: Weigh the apple cider vinegar into your lye solution container.

Step 2: Weigh the sodium hydroxide into your dry lye container.

Step 3: Following safety precautions, pour the sodium hydroxide into the apple cider vinegar while stirring. Turn your head and lean away from the lye solution. Stir until all the granules have dissolved. Set aside to cool.

Step 4: Weigh and melt the coconut oil and kokum butter.

Step 5: Weigh the olive, sunflower, and castor oils into the melted coconut oil and kokum butter.

Step 6: Add your essential oils to the prepared base oils and blend.

Step 7: Check the temperature of your base oil mixture and lye solution. For a swirled soap, a good range for both mixtures is between 80°F and 90°F.

Step 8: Pour the lye solution into your melted oils and mix to emulsion or light trace.

Step 9: Divide your soap among the mixing containers into 3 equal parts to color.

Step 10: Add the zinc oxide to one container, the turmeric powder to another, and the madder root powder to the third.

Step 11: Using the tiger stripe swirl technique (page 47), pour a portion of each color in straight lines down the center of the mold. Rotate through the colors 4 to 6 times each.

Step 12: Use a skewer to swirl the very top of the soap.

Step 13: Allow the soap to saponify for 24 to 48 hours.

Step 14: Unmold your soap, cut into bars, and allow to cure in a cool, dry space for at least 4 weeks.

Tip: *Since the apple cider vinegar neutralizes a small percentage of the sodium hydroxide, many soapmakers make this type of soap with excellent results. You're left with a higher superfat amount, creating a very nourishing bar of soap.*

Cypress, Lavender & Sage Soap

VEGAN · BODY · FACE · GENTLE · FLORAL · WOODSY

This beautiful purple and green swirled soap has a floral and woodsy scent. It includes jojoba oil, which is a liquid wax that mirrors the sebum of our skin and is a great ingredient for natural skin care.

~~~~~~

YIELD: 1,269 grams | 10 bars (127 grams each)

START TO FINISH TIME: 1 hour to create soap, 24 to 48 hours to saponify, 4 weeks to cure

SCENT: Cypress, lavender, sage, and bergamot

LYE DISCOUNT: 5%

SAFETY FIRST: Remember to wear goggles and gloves. Mix the lye solution in a well-ventilated area with access to a sink for flushing with water if necessary. Keep your work space free from distractions, small children, and pets.

~~~~~~

EQUIPMENT

* Digital scale
* Glass container
* Lye solution container
* Dry lye container
* Silicone spatulas
* Microwave-safe batch container
* Infrared thermometer (optional)
* Stick blender
* 2 mixing containers
* Measuring spoons
* 10-inch silicone loaf mold
* Skewer

INGREDIENTS

Scent

* 20 grams lavender essential oil
* 10 grams cypress essential oil
* 10 grams bergamot essential oil
* 5 grams clary sage essential oil

Lye Solution

* 246 grams distilled water
* 123 grams sodium hydroxide

Base Oils (900 grams)

* 270 grams (30%) 76-degree coconut oil
* 72 grams (8%) shea butter
* 405 grams (45%) olive oil
* 90 grams (10%) avocado oil
* 63 grams (7%) jojoba oil

Colorants/Additives

* 2 tablespoons zinc oxide powder
* 1 tablespoon alkanet root powder
* 1 tablespoon nettle leaf powder

Prep ahead: Weigh the lavender, cypress, bergamot, and clary sage essential oils into a glass container; blend together. Set aside.

Step 1: Weigh the water into your lye solution container.

Step 2: Weigh the sodium hydroxide into your dry lye container.

Step 3: Following safety precautions, pour the sodium hydroxide into the water while stirring. Turn your head and lean away from the lye solution. Stir until all the granules have dissolved. Set aside to cool.

Step 4: Weigh and melt the coconut oil and shea butter.

Step 5: Weigh the olive, avocado, and jojoba oils into the melted coconut oil and shea butter.

Step 6: Add your essential oils to the prepared base oils and blend.

Step 7: Check the temperature of your base oil mixture and lye solution. For a swirled soap, a good range for both mixtures is between 80°F and 90°F.

Step 8: Pour the lye solution into your melted oils and mix to emulsion or light trace.

Step 9: Pour a quarter of the mixture into one mixing container, a quarter into the other, and then leave the rest in the main container.

Step 10: Add the zinc oxide to the base, the alkanet root powder to one container, and the nettle powder to the last container; blend well.

Step 11: Using the in-the-pot swirl technique (page 40), pour the alkanet root and nettle soap mixtures back into the zinc-colored soap base, rotating through each color at least 3 times. Use a small silicone spatula to give the soap one swirl in the pot.

Step 12: Pour the soap into your mold. It will swirl more as you pour.

Step 13: Use a skewer to swirl the very top of the soap.

Step 14: Allow the soap to saponify for 24 to 48 hours.

Step 15: Unmold your soap, cut into bars, and allow to cure in a cool, dry space for at least 4 weeks.

Tip: Remember to keep your temperatures cool when swirling. The hotter the soap, the faster it thickens.

Lemon Turmeric Soap

VEGAN · BODY · FACE · CITRUS

Turmeric is an easy natural colorant for a yellow or bright orange soap, and it pairs well with lemon essential oil. Turmeric is used in India to treat troublesome skin. This bright essential oil blend matches the vibrant coloring.

~~~~~~

YIELD: 1,284 grams | 10 bars (128 grams each)

START TO FINISH TIME: 1 hour to create soap, 24 to 48 hours to saponify, 4 weeks to cure

SCENT: Lemon and litsea

LYE DISCOUNT: 5%

SAFETY FIRST: Remember to wear goggles and gloves. Mix the lye solution in a well-ventilated area with access to a sink for flushing with water if necessary. Keep your work space free from distractions, small children, and pets.

~~~~~~

EQUIPMENT

* Digital scale
* Glass container
* Lye solution container
* Dry lye container
* Silicone spatulas
* Microwave-safe batch container
* 2 mixing containers
* Measuring spoons
* Infrared thermometer (optional)
* Stick blender
* 10-inch silicone loaf mold
* Skewer

INGREDIENTS

Scent

* 30 grams lemon essential oil
* 15 grams litsea essential oil

Lye Solution

* 256 grams distilled water
* 128 grams sodium hydroxide

Base Oils (900 grams)

* 270 grams (30%) 76-degree coconut oil
* 90 grams (10%) mango butter
* 405 grams (45%) olive oil
* 135 grams (15%) apricot kernel oil

Colorants/Additives

* 2 tablespoons zinc oxide powder
* 1 tablespoon turmeric powder
* 1 tablespoon annatto seed powder

Prep ahead: Weigh the lemon and litsea essential oils into a glass container; blend together. Set aside.

Step 1: Weigh the water into your lye solution container.

Step 2: Weigh the sodium hydroxide into your dry lye container.

Step 3: Following safety precautions, pour the sodium hydroxide into the water while stirring. Turn your head and lean away from the lye solution. Stir until all the granules have dissolved. Set aside to cool.

Step 4: Weigh and melt the coconut oil and mango butter.

Step 5: Weigh the olive and apricot kernel oils into the melted coconut oil and mango butter.

Step 6: Add your essential oils to the prepared base oils and blend.

Step 7: Check the temperature of your base oil mixture and lye solution. For a swirled soap, a good range for both mixtures is between 80°F and 90°F.

Step 8: Pour the lye solution into your melted oils and mix to emulsion or light trace.

Step 9: Pour a quarter of the mixture into one mixing container, a quarter into the other, and then leave the rest in the main container as the base.

Step 10: Add the zinc oxide to the base, the turmeric powder to one container, and the annatto seed powder to the last container; blend well.

Step 11: Using the in-the-pot swirl technique (page 40), pour the turmeric and annatto soap mixtures back into the zinc-colored soap, rotating through each color at least 3 times. Use a small silicone spatula to give the soap one swirl in the pot.

Step 12: Pour the soap into your mold. It will swirl more as you pour.

Step 13: Use a skewer to swirl the very top of the soap.

Step 14: Allow the soap to saponify for 24 to 48 hours.

Step 15: Unmold your soap, cut into bars, and allow to cure in a cool, dry space for at least 4 weeks.

Tip: *When creating a swirl, don't overmix your soap. By the time you pour it to swirl, it should be at light to medium trace.*

Kombucha Soap

VEGAN · BODY · FACE · GENTLE · ACNE-FIGHTING
FLORAL · HERBAL · CITRUS

Kombucha is all the rage. It is a fermented tea containing beneficial bacteria, yeast, and probiotics, and it boasts numerous health benefits. Make this soap for the kombucha lover in your life.

YIELD: 1,284 grams | 10 bars (128 grams each)

START TO FINISH TIME: 1 hour to create soap, 24 to 48 hours to saponify, 4 weeks to cure

SCENT: Lemongrass, cedarwood, lavender, and orange

LYE DISCOUNT: 5%

SAFETY FIRST: Remember to wear goggles and gloves. Mix the lye solution in a well-ventilated area with access to a sink for flushing with water if necessary. Keep your work space free from distractions, small children, and pets.

EQUIPMENT

* Digital scale
* Glass container
* Lye solution container
* Dry lye container
* Silicone spatulas
* Microwave-safe batch container
* Infrared thermometer (optional)
* Stick blender
* 3 mixing containers
* Measuring spoons
* 10-inch silicone loaf mold
* Skewer

INGREDIENTS

Scent

* 10 grams lemongrass essential oil
* 10 grams cedarwood essential oil
* 10 grams lavender essential oil
* 10 grams orange essential oil
* 5 grams basil essential oil

Lye Solution

* 256 grams kombucha
* 128 grams sodium hydroxide

Base Oils (900 grams)

* 270 grams (30%) 76-degree coconut oil
* 90 grams (10%) mango butter
* 405 grams (45%) olive oil
* 135 grams (15%) apricot kernel oil

Colorants/Additives

* 2 tablespoons zinc oxide powder
* 1 teaspoon pink clay powder
* 1 teaspoon orange clay powder
* 1 teaspoon red clay powder

Prep ahead: Weigh the lemongrass, cedarwood, lavender, orange, and basil essential oils into a glass container; blend together. Set aside.

Step 1: Weigh the kombucha into your lye solution container.

Step 2: Weigh the sodium hydroxide into your dry lye container.

Step 3: Following safety precautions, pour the sodium hydroxide into the kombucha while stirring. Turn your head and lean away from the lye solution. Stir until all the granules have dissolved. Set aside to cool.

Step 4: Weigh and melt the coconut oil and mango butter.

Step 5: Weigh the olive and apricot kernel oils into the melted coconut oil and mango butter.

Step 6: Add your essential oils to the prepared base oils and blend.

Step 7: Check the temperature of your base oil mixture and lye solution. For a swirled soap, a good range for both mixtures is between 80°F and 90°F.

Step 8: Pour the lye solution into your melted oils and mix to emulsion or light trace.

Step 9: Divide your soap to color. For this design, leave half the soap in the main container as the base. Divide the other half of the soap among the 3 smaller containers to color. You don't have to be exact; just eyeball it.

Step 10: Add the zinc oxide to the base, the pink clay to the first container, the orange clay to the second, and the red clay to the third. Blend each color well.

→

Step 11: Using the in-the-mold loaf swirl technique (page 49), pour the zinc-colored base into your mold. Rotating through each of the clay-colored soaps at least four times, pour the colored soap into the base, moving up and down the length of the mold.

Step 12: Use a skewer to swirl the very top of the soap.

Step 13: Allow the soap to saponify for 24 to 48 hours.

Step 14: Unmold your soap, cut into bars, and allow to cure in a cool, dry space for at least 4 weeks.

TIP: *You can use home-brewed kombucha or any unflavored kombucha from the grocery store. Some soapmakers even purée their kombucha scoby and include it in their soap as an additive.*

Egg & Turmeric Soap

BODY · FACE · HERBAL · CITRUS

It might sound a little weird to incorporate egg into soap, but many soapmakers do it. Eggs are full of vitamins and protein and leave skin feeling smooth. Create this soap for the chicken lover in your life!

~~~~~~

YIELD: 1,287 grams | 10 bars (129 grams each)

START TO FINISH TIME: 1 hour to create soap, 24 to 48 hours to saponify, 4 weeks to cure

SCENT: Lemongrass, orange, rosemary, and lime

LYE DISCOUNT: 5%

SAFETY FIRST: Remember to wear goggles and gloves. Mix the lye solution in a well-ventilated area with access to a sink for flushing with water if necessary. Keep your work space free from distractions, small children, and pets.

~~~~~~

EQUIPMENT

* Digital scale
* Glass container
* 2 mixing containers
* Lye solution container
* Dry lye container
* Silicone spatulas
* Microwave-safe batch container
* Measuring spoons
* Infrared thermometer (optional)
* Stick blender
* 10-inch silicone loaf mold
* Skewer

INGREDIENTS

Scent

* 20 grams rosemary essential oil
* 10 grams lemongrass essential oil
* 10 grams orange essential oil
* 5 grams lime essential oil

Lye Solution

* 258 grams distilled water
* 129 grams sodium hydroxide

Base Oils (900 grams)

* 315 grams (35%) 76-degree coconut oil
* 135 grams (15%) cocoa butter
* 315 grams (35%) olive oil
* 90 grams (10%) avocado oil
* 45 grams (5%) castor oil

Colorants/Additives

* 1 medium egg
* 3 tablespoons zinc oxide powder
* 1 teaspoon yellow clay powder
* 1 teaspoon turmeric powder

→

Prep ahead: Weigh all of the essential oils into a glass container; blend together. Set aside. Crack an egg into a soap-safe container and whisk.

Step 1: Weigh the water into your lye solution container.

Step 2: Weigh the sodium hydroxide into your dry lye container.

Step 3: Following safety precautions, pour the sodium hydroxide into the water while stirring. Turn your head and lean away from the lye solution. Stir until all the granules have dissolved. Set aside to cool.

Step 4: Weigh and melt the coconut oil and cocoa butter.

Step 5: Weigh the olive, avocado, and castor oils into the melted coconut oil and cocoa butter.

Step 6: Add your essential oils to the prepared base oils and blend.

Step 7: Check the temperature of your base oil mixture and lye solution. For a swirled soap, a good range for both mixtures is between 80°F and 90°F.

Step 8: Pour the lye solution into your melted oils and mix to emulsion or light trace.

Step 9: Pour about a cup of your traced soap into the container with the egg and blend. Pour this mixture back into your main container of soap and blend to fully incorporate the egg.

Step 10: Divide your soap to color. For this design, leave three-quarters of the soap in the main container as the base. Divide the other quarter of the soap between two smaller containers to color. You don't have to be exact; just eyeball it.

Step 11: Add the zinc oxide to the base, the yellow clay to one container, and the annatto seed powder to the other. Blend each color well.

Step 12: Using the in-the-mold loaf swirl technique (page 49), pour the zinc-colored base into your mold. Alternating between the two colored soaps at least four times, pour the colored soap into the base, moving up and down the length of the mold.

Step 13: Use a skewer to swirl the very top of the soap.

Step 14: Allow the soap to saponify for 24 to 48 hours.

Step 15: Unmold your soap, cut into bars, and allow to cure in a cool, dry space for at least 4 weeks.

Tip: *Follow step 9 to temper the egg into your soap, or you could end up with scrambled eggs. Your soap might be green when you cut it, but that will go away as it cures.*

Tomato & Herb Soap

VEGAN · BODY · GENTLE · HERBAL · CITRUS

This wonderful soap includes tomato in the lye solution. When combined with
herbs, this soap evokes the feel of a summer garden.

YIELD: 1,290 grams | 10 bars (129 grams each)

START TO FINISH TIME: 1 hour to create soap, 24 to 48 hours to saponify, 4 weeks to cure

SCENT: Basil, lemon, orange, and sage

LYE DISCOUNT: 5%

SAFETY FIRST: Remember to wear goggles and gloves. Mix the lye solution in a
well-ventilated area with access to a sink for flushing with water if necessary. Keep
your work space free from distractions, small children, and pets.

EQUIPMENT

* Digital scale
* Glass container
* 3 mixing containers
* Stick blender
* Lye solution container
* Dry lye container
* Silicone spatulas
* Microwave-safe batch container
* Measuring spoons
* Infrared thermometer (optional)
* 10-inch silicone loaf mold
* Skewer

INGREDIENTS

Scent
* 10 grams orange essential oil
* 10 grams lemon essential oil
* 10 grams litsea essential oil
* 5 grams basil essential oil
* 5 grams clary sage essential oil
* 5 grams vetiver essential oil

Lye Solution
* 2 large tomatoes
* 130 grams sodium hydroxide

Base Oils (900 grams)
* 315 grams (35%) 76-degree coconut oil
* 135 grams (15%) kokum butter
* 450 grams (50%) olive oil

Colorants/Additives
* 1 tablespoon crushed dried basil
* 2 tablespoons zinc oxide powder
* 1 teaspoon red clay powder
* 1 teaspoon nettle leaf powder

Prep ahead: Weigh the orange, lemon, litsea, basil, clary sage, and vetiver essential oils into a glass container; blend together. Set aside. Purée the tomatoes and set aside.

Step 1: Weigh 260 grams of tomato purée into your lye solution container. If you don't have enough tomato purée, add water until you reach 260 grams.

Step 2: Weigh the sodium hydroxide into your dry lye container.

Step 3: Following safety precautions, pour the sodium hydroxide into the tomato purée while stirring. Turn your head and lean away from the lye solution. Stir until all the granules have dissolved. Set aside to cool.

Step 4: Weigh and melt the coconut oil and kokum butter.

Step 5: Weigh the olive oil into the melted coconut oil and kokum butter.

Step 6: Add your essential oils and crushed dried basil to the prepared base oils and blend.

Step 7: Check the temperature of your base oil mixture and lye solution. For a swirled soap, a good range for both mixtures is between 80°F and 90°F.

Step 8: Pour the lye solution into your melted oils and mix to emulsion or light trace.

Step 9: Leave three-quarters of the soap in the main container as the base. Divide the other quarter of the soap between the two smaller containers to color. You don't have to be exact; just eyeball it.

Step 10: Add zinc oxide to the base, red clay to one container, and nettle leaf powder to the other. Blend each color well.

Step 11: Using the in-the-mold loaf swirl technique (page 49), pour the zinc-colored base into your mold. Alternating between the two other colored soaps at least four times, pour the colored soap into the base, moving up and down the length of the mold.

Step 12: Use a skewer to swirl the very top of the soap.

Step 13: Allow the soap to saponify for 24 to 48 hours.

Step 14: Unmold your soap, cut into bars, and allow to cure in a cool, dry space for at least 4 weeks.

Tip: *Other popular fruits and vegetables to purée for soap include cucumber, pumpkin, sweet potato, carrot, spinach, and avocado. You might think that these purées would get moldy in soap, but they don't. Soap has a high pH, and as long as fruits and vegetables are completely liquefied, they will not grow nasties.*

Sea Clay & Avocado Soap

VEGAN · BODY · FACE · FLORAL · MINTY

This is one of my favorite face soaps. Sea clay draws impurities from the skin, and avocado oil is high in vitamin E and other beneficial vitamins, as well as great for older skin or skin that needs repair. When using this soap, let the lather sit on your face like a mask before rinsing off. If you'd like to add a black charcoal line between layers, refer to page 55.

YIELD: 1,287 grams | 10 bars (129 grams each)

START TO FINISH TIME: 1 hour to create soap, 24 to 48 hours to saponify, 4 weeks to cure

SCENT: Peppermint, spearmint, and lavender

LYE DISCOUNT: 5%

SAFETY FIRST: Remember to wear goggles and gloves. Mix the lye solution in a well-ventilated area with access to a sink for flushing with water if necessary. Keep your work space free from distractions, small children, and pets.

EQUIPMENT

* Digital scale
* Glass container
* Small mixing container
* Stick blender
* Lye solution container
* Dry lye container
* Silicone spatulas
* Microwave-safe batch container
* Large mixing container
* Measuring spoons
* Infrared thermometer (optional)
* 10-inch silicone loaf mold

INGREDIENTS

Scent
* 25 grams lavender essential oil
* 10 grams peppermint essential oil
* 10 grams spearmint essential oil

Lye Solution
* 158 grams distilled water
* 129 grams sodium hydroxide

Base Oils (900 grams)
* 306 grams (34%) 76-degree coconut oil
* 90 grams (10%) cocoa butter
* 414 grams (46%) olive oil
* 90 grams (10%) avocado oil

Colorants/Additives
* 1 tablespoon sea clay powder
* 1 large avocado
* 1 teaspoon French green clay powder
* ½ teaspoon nettle leaf powder

→

Prep ahead: Weigh the lavender, peppermint, and spearmint essential oils into a glass container; blend together. Set aside. Immediately before making the soap, peel and purée the avocado, discarding the peel and pit. Weigh out 100 grams and set aside.

Step 1: Weigh the distilled water into your lye solution container.

Step 2: Weigh the sodium hydroxide into your dry lye container.

Step 3: Following safety precautions, pour the sodium hydroxide into the water while stirring. Turn your head and lean away from the lye solution. Stir until all the granules have dissolved.

Step 4: Add the sea clay to the lye solution and set aside to cool.

Step 5: Weigh and melt the coconut oil and cocoa butter.

Step 6: Weigh the olive and avocado oils into the melted coconut oil and cocoa butter.

Step 7: Add your essential oils and the avocado purée to the prepared base oils, and blend using your stick blender to ensure the avocado is completely incorporated.

Step 8: Check the temperature of your base oil mixture and lye solution. For a layered soap, a good range for both mixtures is between 80°F and 90°F.

Step 9: Pour the lye solution into your melted oils and mix to light trace.

Step 10: Divide your soap into 2 equal parts to color. You can leave half in the batch container and pour half into the large mixing container. One half will have the natural color from the sea clay, and one will be green.

Step 11: Add the French green clay and nettle powder to one half of the soap and blend well.

Step 12: Thicken the green layer to a medium to thick trace. Pour into your mold and bang your mold down onto a hard surface to flatten.

Step 13: Spoon the natural-colored soap gently over the green layer. If you notice it sinks into the green layer, let your soap sit for a bit longer to thicken.

Step 14: Allow the soap to saponify for 24 to 48 hours.

Step 15: Unmold your soap, cut into bars, and allow to cure in a cool, dry space for at least 4 weeks.

Tip: *I used 100 grams of avocado purée in this soap and reduced the water by 100 grams. Most purées should be treated as liquid, even if they are added to the base oils and not the lye solution.*

Garden Herb Soap

VEGAN · BODY · EXFOLIATING · FLORAL · MINTY · HERBAL

I encourage students to bring herbs into class so we can share and go over how to use them. One student brought in a trash bag full of peppermint that she harvested. She chuckled at how little you need for soap (1 teaspoon to 1 tablespoon). There was plenty to go around! This beautiful layered soap includes crushed dried peppermint to make it exfoliating. Use this soap after a day in the garden to scrub away the dirt from your hands. If you'd like to add a black charcoal line between layers, refer to page 55.

YIELD: 1,287 grams | 10 bars (129 grams each)

START TO FINISH TIME: 1 hour to create soap, 24 to 48 hours to saponify, 4 weeks to cure

SCENT: Rosemary, spearmint, lavender, and eucalyptus

LYE DISCOUNT: 5%

SAFETY FIRST: Remember to wear goggles and gloves. Mix the lye solution in a well-ventilated area with access to a sink for flushing with water if necessary. Keep your work space free from distractions, small children, and pets.

EQUIPMENT

* Digital scale
* Glass container
* Lye solution container
* Dry lye container
* Silicone spatulas
* Microwave-safe batch container
* Measuring spoons
* Infrared thermometer (optional)
* Stick blender
* Large mixing container
* 10-inch silicone loaf mold

INGREDIENTS

Scent

* 20 grams rosemary essential oil
* 10 grams spearmint essential oil
* 10 grams lavender essential oil
* 5 grams eucalyptus essential oil

Lye Solution

* 258 grams distilled water
* 129 grams sodium hydroxide

Base Oils (900 grams)

* 306 grams (34%) 76-degree coconut oil
* 45 grams (5%) cocoa butter
* 45 grams (5%) shea butter
* 414 grams (46%) olive oil
* 90 grams (10%) sweet almond oil

Colorants/Additives

* 1 teaspoon crushed dried peppermint
* 1 teaspoon indigo root powder

Prep ahead: Weigh the rosemary, spearmint, lavender, and eucalyptus essential oils into a glass container; blend together. Set aside.

Step 1: Weigh the distilled water into your lye solution container.

Step 2: Weigh the sodium hydroxide into your dry lye container.

Step 3: Following safety precautions, pour the sodium hydroxide into the water while stirring. Turn your head and lean away from the lye solution. Stir until all the granules have dissolved. Set aside to cool.

Step 4: Weigh and melt the coconut oil, cocoa butter, and shea butter.

Step 5: Weigh the olive and sweet almond oils into the melted coconut oil, cocoa butter, and shea butter.

Step 6: Add your essential oils and crushed dried peppermint to the prepared base oils and blend.

Step 7: Check the temperature of your base oil mixture and lye solution. For a layered soap, a good range for both mixtures is between 80°F and 90°F.

Step 8: Pour the lye solution into your melted oils and mix to light trace.

Step 9: Divide your soap into 2 equal parts to color. You can leave half in the batch container and pour half into the large mixing container.

→

Step 10: Leave one half of the soap uncolored, and add the indigo to the other half; blend well.

Step 11: Thicken the indigo layer to a thick trace. Pour into your mold and bang your mold down onto a hard surface to flatten.

Step 12: Spoon the rest of the soap gently over the indigo layer. If you notice it sinks into the indigo layer, let your soap sit for a bit longer to thicken.

Step 13: Allow the soap to saponify for 24 to 48 hours.

Step 14: Unmold your soap, cut into bars, and allow to cure in a cool, dry space for at least 4 weeks.

Tip: Indigo root powder can be tricky. First, be sure you're getting blue indigo and not green. For a really stunning blue, try using pre-reduced indigo crystals dissolved in water. You might need less of the pre-reduced indigo crystals. Start by dissolving ¼ teaspoon of crystals in 1 teaspoon of water. Add drop by drop to your soap until you get the desired color.

Basil, Lavender & Mint Soap

VEGAN · BODY · MINTY · HERBAL

With a whopping six-layer design, this artistic bar is sure to impress your family and friends with its intricacy. The scent is both minty and herbal, a classic combination. If you'd like to add a black charcoal line between layers, refer to page 55.

YIELD: 1,284 grams | 10 bars (128 grams each)

START TO FINISH TIME: 1 hour to create soap, 24 to 48 hours to saponify, 4 weeks to cure

SCENT: Peppermint, lavender, and basil

LYE DISCOUNT: 5%

SAFETY FIRST: Remember to wear goggles and gloves. Mix the lye solution in a well-ventilated area with access to a sink for flushing with water if necessary. Keep your work space free from distractions, small children, and pets.

EQUIPMENT

* Digital scale
* Glass container
* Lye solution container
* Dry lye container
* Silicone spatulas
* Microwave-safe batch container
* Infrared thermometer (optional)
* Stick blender
* 3 mixing containers
* Measuring spoons
* 10-inch silicone loaf mold

INGREDIENTS

Scent

* 30 grams lavender essential oil
* 10 grams peppermint essential oil
* 5 grams basil essential oil

Lye Solution

* 256 grams distilled water
* 128 grams sodium hydroxide

Base Oils (900 grams)

* 270 grams (30%) 76-degree coconut oil
* 126 grams (14%) mango butter
* 360 grams (40%) olive oil
* 144 grams (16%) high oleic sunflower oil

Colorants/Additives

* 1 teaspoon alkanet root powder
* 1 teaspoon nettle leaf powder
* 1 teaspoon indigo root powder

→

Prep ahead: Weigh the lavender, peppermint, and basil essential oils into a glass container; blend together. Set aside.

Step 1: Weigh the distilled water into your lye solution container.

Step 2: Weigh the sodium hydroxide into your dry lye container.

Step 3: Following safety precautions, pour the sodium hydroxide into the water while stirring. Turn your head and lean away from the lye solution. Stir until all the granules have dissolved. Set aside to cool.

Step 4: Weigh and melt the coconut oil and mango butter.

Step 5: Weigh the olive and sunflower oils into the melted coconut oil and mango butter.

Step 6: Add your essential oils to the prepared base oils and blend.

Step 7: Check the temperature of your base oil mixture and lye solution. For a layered soap, a good range for both mixtures is between 80°F and 90°F.

Step 8: Pour the lye solution into your melted oils and mix to light trace.

Step 9: Divide your soap into the 3 mixing containers.

Step 10: Add the alkanet powder to the first container, the nettle powder to the second, and the indigo powder to the third. Blend each one well.

Step 11: Thicken up the alkanet soap and spoon half of it into your mold.

Step 12: Thicken up the nettle soap and spoon half of it over your first layer.

Step 13: Thicken up the indigo soap and spoon half of it over your second layer.

Step 14: Repeat steps 12 to 14 a second time for a total of 6 layers.

Step 15: Allow the soap to saponify for 24 to 48 hours.

Step 16: Unmold your soap, cut into bars, and allow to cure in a cool, dry space for at least 4 weeks.

Tip: *If making six layers feels intimidating, feel free to only do three layers, using all of each color each time you pour.*

Patchouli Orange Soap

VEGAN · BODY · FLORAL · CITRUS

Patchouli is one of those essential oils that people either love or hate. Even if you typically don't like patchouli, I highly recommend trying this essential oil blend. Combining patchouli with orange creates a wonderful aroma that is bright and pleasing. If you'd like to add a black charcoal line between layers, refer to page 55.

YIELD: 1,275 grams | 10 bars (127 grams each)

START TO FINISH TIME: 1 hour to create soap, 24 to 48 hours to saponify, 4 weeks to cure

SCENT: Patchouli and orange

LYE DISCOUNT: 5%

SAFETY FIRST: Remember to wear goggles and gloves. Mix the lye solution in a well-ventilated area with access to a sink for flushing with water if necessary. Keep your work space free from distractions, small children, and pets.

EQUIPMENT

* Digital scale
* Glass container
* Lye solution container
* Dry lye container
* Silicone spatulas
* Microwave-safe batch container
* Infrared thermometer (optional)
* Stick blender
* Large mixing container
* Measuring spoons
* 10-inch silicone loaf mold

INGREDIENTS

Scent

* 30 grams orange essential oil
* 15 grams patchouli essential oil

Lye Solution

* 250 grams distilled water
* 125 grams sodium hydroxide

Base Oils (900 grams)

* 270 grams (30%) 76-degree coconut oil
* 90 grams (10%) kokum butter
* 360 grams (40%) olive oil
* 72 grams (8%) avocado oil
* 72 grams (8%) rice bran oil
* 36 grams (4%) jojoba oil

Colorants/Additives

* 1 teaspoon annatto seed powder
* 2 teaspoons yellow dock root powder

Prep ahead: Weigh the orange and patchouli essential oils into a glass container; blend together. Set aside.

Step 1: Weigh the distilled water into your lye solution container.

Step 2: Weigh the sodium hydroxide into your dry lye container.

Step 3: Following safety precautions, pour the sodium hydroxide into the water while stirring. Turn your head and lean away from the lye solution. Stir until all the granules have dissolved. Set aside to cool.

Step 4: Weigh and melt the coconut oil and kokum butter.

Step 5: Weigh the olive, avocado, rice bran, and jojoba oils into the melted coconut oil and kokum butter.

Step 6: Add your essential oils to the prepared base oils and blend.

Step 7: Check the temperature of your base oil mixture and lye solution. For a layered soap, a good range for both mixtures is between 80°F and 90°F.

Step 8: Pour the lye solution into your melted oils and mix to light trace.

Step 9: Divide your soap into 2 equal parts to color. You can leave half in the batch container and pour half into the large mixing container.

Step 10: Add the annatto seed powder to one container, and add the yellow dock root powder to the other; blend well.

Step 11: Blend the annatto layer to a thick trace. Pour into the mold and bang your mold down onto a hard surface to flatten.

Step 12: Spoon the yellow dock–colored soap gently over the first layer. If you notice it sinks into the annatto layer, let your soap sit for a bit longer to thicken.

Step 13: Allow the soap to saponify for 24 to 48 hours.

Step 14: Unmold your soap, cut into bars, and allow to cure in a cool, dry space for at least 4 weeks.

Tip: *You might think that yellow dock turns yellow in soap. But this yellow herbal powder reacts to the high pH of soap and, surprisingly, turns into a beautiful mauve or crimson red, depending on how much you use.*

Plantain-Infused Lavender Soap

VEGAN · BODY · FACE · GENTLE · FLORAL

Plantain—the herb, not the banana-like fruit—is a wonderfully healing natural remedy. You may have some growing in your backyard. It is edible and tastes like spinach, but more bitter. It's skin-soothing and perfect for a gentle bar of soap. If you'd like to add a black charcoal line between layers, refer to page 55.

YIELD: 1,293 grams | 10 bars (129 grams each)

START TO FINISH TIME: 1 hour to create soap, 24 to 48 hours to saponify, 4 weeks to cure

SCENT: Lavender

LYE DISCOUNT: 5%

SAFETY FIRST: Remember to wear goggles and gloves. Mix the lye solution in a well-ventilated area with access to a sink for flushing with water if necessary. Keep your work space free from distractions, small children, and pets.

EQUIPMENT

* Digital scale
* 2 large mixing containers
* Glass container
* Lye solution container
* Dry lye container
* Silicone spatulas
* Microwave-safe batch container
* Measuring spoons
* Infrared thermometer (optional)
* Stick blender
* 10-inch silicone loaf mold

INGREDIENTS

* 400 grams olive oil

Scent
* 45 grams lavender essential oil

Lye Solution
* 262 grams distilled water
* 131 grams sodium hydroxide

Base Oils (900 grams)
* 360 grams (40%) 76-degree coconut oil
* 360 grams (40%) plantain-infused olive oil
* 90 grams (10%) avocado oil
* 90 grams (10%) rice bran oil

Colorants/Additives
* 1 cup dried plantain
* 2 teaspoons purple Brazilian clay powder

Prep ahead: Create a warm infusion of the olive oil and dried plantain (see Creating an Oil Infusion, page 19). Strain and discard the solids. Weigh the lavender essential oil into a glass container. Set aside.

Step 1: Weigh the distilled water into your lye solution container.

Step 2: Weigh the sodium hydroxide into your dry lye container.

Step 3: Following safety precautions, pour the sodium hydroxide into the water while stirring. Turn your head and lean away from the lye solution. Stir until all the granules have dissolved. Set aside to cool.

Step 4: Weigh and melt the coconut oil.

Step 5: Weigh the plantain-infused olive, avocado, and rice bran oils into the melted coconut oil.

Step 6: Add your essential oils to the prepared base oils and blend.

Step 7: Check the temperature of your base oil mixture and lye solution. For a layered soap, a good range for both mixtures is between 80°F and 90°F.

Step 8: Pour the lye solution into your melted oils and mix to light trace.

Step 9: Divide your soap into 2 equal parts to color. You can leave half in the batch container and pour half into the large mixing container.

Step 10: Add the purple clay to one half and blend well.

Step 11: Blend the purple clay layer to a thick trace. Pour into the mold and bang your mold down onto a hard surface to flatten.

Step 12: Spoon the uncolored soap gently over the first layer. If it sinks into the purple clay layer, let your soap sit for a bit longer to thicken.

Step 13: Allow the soap to saponify for 24 to 48 hours.

Step 14: Unmold your soap, cut into bars, and allow to cure in a cool, dry space for at least 4 weeks.

Tip: *You start with 400 grams of olive oil but only use 360 grams after infusing it with the plantain. That's because the powder absorbs some of the liquid from the oil; by starting with a little extra, you'll be able to weigh out exactly what you need.*

Carrot & Honey Soap

BODY · FACE · GENTLE · MINTY · CITRUS

This soap is great on the face. It is colored using carrot purée, which is full of vitamins and minerals. I included orange clay for its ability to draw out toxins. Let this soap sit on your face like a mask before rinsing off. If you'd like to add a black charcoal line between layers, refer to page 55.

~~~~~~

YIELD: 1,284 grams | 10 bars (128 grams each)

START TO FINISH TIME: 1 hour to create soap, 24 to 48 hours to saponify, 4 weeks to cure

SCENT: Spearmint, orange, and clary sage

LYE DISCOUNT: 5%

SAFETY FIRST: Remember to wear goggles and gloves. Mix the lye solution in a well-ventilated area with access to a sink for flushing with water if necessary. Keep your work space free from distractions, small children, and pets.

~~~~~~

EQUIPMENT

* Digital scale
* Glass container
* Medium mixing container
* Stick blender
* Lye solution container
* Dry lye container
* Silicone spatulas
* Microwave-safe batch container
* Infrared thermometer (optional)
* Measuring spoons
* Large mixing container
* 10-inch silicone loaf mold

INGREDIENTS

Scent
* 30 grams orange essential oil
* 10 grams spearmint essential oil
* 5 grams clary sage essential oil

Lye Solution
* 256 grams distilled water
* 128 grams sodium hydroxide

Base Oils (900 grams)
* 306 grams (34%) 76-degree coconut oil
* 90 grams (10%) shea butter
* 360 grams (40%) olive oil
* 144 grams (16%) avocado oil

Colorants/Additives
* 2 large carrots
* 1 tablespoon honey
* 1 teaspoon orange clay powder

Prep ahead: Weigh the orange, spearmint, and clary sage essential oils into a glass container; blend together. Set aside. Peel and trim the carrots, then steam and purée them.

Step 1: Weigh the distilled water and 100 grams of carrot purée into your lye solution container.

Step 2: Weigh the sodium hydroxide into your dry lye container.

Step 3: Following safety precautions, pour the sodium hydroxide into the liquid while stirring. Turn your head and lean away from the lye solution. Stir until all the granules have dissolved. Set aside to cool.

Step 4: Weigh and melt the coconut oil and shea butter.

Step 5: Add the honey to the hot melted coconut oil and shea butter. This will help dissolve the honey and prevent honey spots in your soap.

Step 6: Weigh the olive and avocado oils into the melted coconut oil and shea butter.

Step 7: Add your essential oils to the prepared base oils and blend.

Step 8: Check the temperature of your base oil mixture and lye solution. For a layered soap, a good range for both mixtures is between 80°F and 90°F.

Step 9: Pour the lye solution into your melted oils and mix to light trace.

Step 10: Divide your soap into 2 equal parts to color. You can leave half in the batch container and pour half into the large mixing container.

Step 11: Add the orange clay to one half and blend well.

Step 12: Blend the orange clay layer to a thick trace. Pour into the mold and bang your mold down onto a hard surface to flatten.

Step 13: Spoon the uncolored soap gently over the first layer. If you notice it sinks into the orange layer, let your soap sit for a bit longer to thicken.

Step 14: Allow the soap to saponify for 24 to 48 hours.

Step 15: Unmold your soap, cut into bars, and allow to cure in a cool, dry space for at least 4 weeks.

Ocean Breeze Soap

VEGAN · BODY · MINTY

Ready to be transported? This summery design features a combination of layering and swirling techniques. The brown layer represents the sandy beach, and the blue and light blue swirl layer represents the ocean.

~~~~~~

YIELD: 1,284 grams | 10 bars (128 grams each)

START TO FINISH TIME: 1 hour to create soap, 24 to 48 hours to saponify, 4 weeks to cure

SCENT: Peppermint

LYE DISCOUNT: 5%

SAFETY FIRST: Remember to wear goggles and gloves. Mix the lye solution in a well-ventilated area with access to a sink for flushing with water if necessary. Keep your work space free from distractions, small children, and pets.

~~~~~~

EQUIPMENT

* Digital scale
* Glass container
* Lye solution container
* Dry lye container
* Silicone spatulas
* Microwave-safe batch container
* Infrared thermometer (optional)
* Stick blender
* 3 mixing containers
* Measuring spoons
* 10-inch silicone loaf mold

INGREDIENTS

Scent
* 20 grams peppermint essential oil

Lye Solution
* 256 grams distilled water
* 128 grams sodium hydroxide

Base Oils (900 grams)
* 297 grams (33%) 76-degree coconut oil
* 45 grams (5%) cocoa butter
* 45 grams (5%) shea butter
* 468 grams (52%) olive oil
* 45 grams (5%) castor oil

Colorants/Additives
* 1 teaspoon yellow clay powder
* 1 teaspoon ground black walnut hulls
* 1 tablespoon zinc oxide powder
* 1 teaspoon indigo root powder

Prep ahead: Weigh the peppermint essential oil into a glass container. Set aside.

Step 1: Weigh the distilled water into your lye solution container.

Step 2: Weigh the sodium hydroxide into your dry lye container.

Step 3: Following safety precautions, pour the sodium hydroxide into the distilled water while stirring. Turn your head and lean away from the lye solution. Stir until all the granules have dissolved. Set aside to cool.

Step 4: Weigh and melt the coconut oil, cocoa butter, and shea butter.

Step 5: Weigh the olive and castor oils into the melted coconut oil, cocoa butter, and shea butter.

Step 6: Add your essential oils to the prepared base oils and blend.

Step 7: Check the temperature of your base oil mixture and lye solution. For a layered soap, a good range for both mixtures is between 80°F and 90°F.

Step 8: Pour the lye solution into your melted oils and mix to light trace.

Step 9: Divide your soap equally between two of the mixing containers to color.

Step 10: Add the yellow clay and ground walnut hulls to one container and blend well to make a sandy brown soap.

Step 11: Add the indigo root to the other container and blend well.

Step 12: Pour half of the indigo root soap into the third mixing container.

Step 13: Add the zinc oxide to the third container to create a lighter blue.

Step 14: Thicken up the sandy brown soap and pour it into your mold.

Step 15: Pour the light blue into the regular blue container using the in-the-pot swirl technique (page 40).

Step 16: Pour the swirled blue mixture over the sandy-colored layer in the mold. As you pour, it will swirl more.

Step 17: Allow the soap to saponify for 24 to 48 hours.

Step 18: Unmold your soap, cut into bars, and allow to cure in a cool, dry space for at least 4 weeks.

Tip: *Peppermint essential oil is strong when used alone in soap. Normally we would use 45 grams total essential oil, but when it comes to peppermint, I use just 20 grams for this size batch.*

Lavender Soap, page 178

Red Wine Soap, page 156

Clay & Agave Swirled Soap, page 174

Orange Spice Soap, page 152

Lemon & Poppy Seed Soap, page 166

O4

Hot-Process Soapmaking

Ready to move on to hot-process? Hot-process soapmaking is like cold-process, all the way through mixing to trace. Once at trace, hot-process soap is cooked until it's neutral—this means the saponification process has occurred and there is no longer active lye in your soap. Hot-process soap is ready to use right away, but it does benefit from a bit of a cure.

Recipes

* Citrus Zest Kitchen Soap 148

* Nourishing Oatmeal
  & Honey Soap 150

* Orange Spice Soap 152

* Peppermint Lime Soap 154

* Red Wine Soap 156

* Honey & Clove Soap 158

* Seaweed & Pumice Soap 160

* Herb & Hemp Soap 162

* Pumpkin Purée Soap 164

* Lemon & Poppy Seed Soap 166

* Cucumber Scrub Soap 169

* Shea Butter & Geranium Soap 172

* Clay & Agave Swirled Soap 174

* Mocha Mint Soap 176

* Lavender Soap 178

Hot-Process Soapmaking Step-by-Step

Before we get started with the step-by-step, I'd like to introduce a few different process variations on cooking your soap and adding colorants and additives.

Cook Your Soap

Hot-process soap can be cooked using two different methods:

Slow cooker: The most common method for cooking hot-process soap is to use a slow cooker. This method allows for gentle and even cooking. Be sure to cover it to prevent evaporation. This is the process used throughout this section.

Oven: You can also put your soap in a covered stainless-steel pot and cook in the oven on the lowest setting, usually around 170°F.

Color Your Soap

When making hot-process soap, you can add color and additives in two different ways:

To base oils: If you are making a single-color soap, you can add your colors and additives directly to the oils before adding your lye solution. This ensures that everything is mixed well.

To cooked soap: If you want to divide your soap to swirl, you can divide your cooked soap and add colors and additives at that point. It's harder to mix colors and additives into cooked soap because it's thick and gloppy. Disperse powdered herbs and spices in a base oil (such as olive oil) to help them mix in more easily.

Cold-Process to Hot-Process

Most cold-process soap recipes can be modified slightly to be hot-processed. The main concern to watch for is evaporation and your soap drying out during cooking.

Most of the cold-process soap recipes in this book have a 2:1 water-to-lye ratio, but for hot-process soap, I recommend using a 2.5:1 water-to-lye ratio. For example, if a cold-process recipe calls for 128 grams of lye, you would use 320 grams of water with the hot-process method.

Any recipe made using the hot-process method comes out thick and gloppy; however, there are some loosening additives that you can use to create a more fluid hot-process soap.

- **SODIUM LACTATE:** Sodium lactate is a liquid salt. It helps loosen the soap as it cooks and makes it more fluid when swirled or poured into the mold. Add 1 teaspoon per 450 grams of base oils to the warm lye solution.

- **SUGAR:** Sugar helps with fluidity and acts as a lather booster. You can use any type of sugar, including regular white sugar, brown sugar, agave, honey, or maple syrup. I add 1 teaspoon per 450 grams of base oils to the warm lye solution to dissolve.

- **YOGURT:** Yogurt contains lactic acid and helps loosen the soap as it cooks. Add 1 teaspoon per 450 grams of base oils to the warm lye solution.

You can use one loosening additive or all three. Don't be afraid to experiment to get your desired consistency.

Make Your Soap

Let's make hot-process soap!

Step 1: Prepare your lye solution. Weigh the water by placing a lye solution container on the scale and hitting tare to zero the scale. Weigh the water and set aside.

Step 2: Weigh the sodium hydroxide by placing another container on the scale and hitting the tare button to zero the scale. Weigh the sodium hydroxide.

Step 3: Following safety precautions, pour the sodium hydroxide into the water while stirring. Turn your head and lean away from the lye solution. Stir until all the granules have dissolved. Set your lye solution aside to cool.

Step 4: Prepare the base oils. Place a microwave-safe bowl on the scale and hit tare to zero the scale. Weigh each oil from your recipe into the bowl, pressing the tare button in between oils to zero the scale.

Step 5: Heat the base oils in the microwave until all are melted.

Step 6: Pour the oils into your slow cooker, carefully scraping the bowl with a silicone spatula. You can also

Step 3

Step 4

Step 6

Step 8

Step 9

Step 9, continued

Step 9, continued

Step 9, continued

weigh the oils into your slow cooker on medium to melt, but microwaving is much faster.

Step 7: Add any loosening ingredients, such as sugar solution, sodium lactate, or yogurt, to your cooled lye solution.

Step 8: If you are creating a single-colored soap, add your colors and additives to the oils now. If you are dividing your soap to swirl, wait until the soap is cooked. This is further explained in the Decorative Techniques section (see page 142).

Step 9: Pour the lye solution into your melted oils and mix to trace (see Recognizing Trace, page 34).

Step 11

Step 12

Step 14

Step 10: Let your soap cook until it is neutral, which means it's done. This can take 30 minutes to 1 hour. To know when hot-process soap is done, test by checking for the following signs:

* It should all be translucent.
* See if your soap zaps. Grab a bit of soap paste on a spoon. Blow on it to cool it down. Touch it to your tongue. If it zaps (feels like an electric shock), that means that it has active lye in it, so you'll need to keep cooking.
* Phenolphthalein drops can be used to test the pH. Rub a bit of soap onto a paper towel. Drop a couple drops of phenolphthalein solution on it. If it turns pink, keep cooking.

→

Step 11: Once your soap is cooked, add your essential oil blend, colors, and additives, and mix well.

Step 12: Spoon your soap into your mold.

Step 13: Allow the soap to harden completely. This will usually take 4 to 6 hours.

Step 14: Once hard, unmold and cut your soap.

Step 15: Hot-process soap is safe to use right away, but I still prefer to cure mine for 2 weeks. This allows for more water to evaporate, leaving you with a soap that lasts longer in the shower.

Hot-Process Soap Pro Tips

- No matter how you cook your soap, be sure to keep it covered while cooking to prevent evaporation. Usually the lid that comes with your slow cooker or stainless-steel pot works just fine, but you can also use Press'n Seal (a more leakproof plastic film) for a more airtight option.

- Resist the urge to stir your soap more than once or twice. Stirring will cause water to evaporate. I usually check on my soap for doneness after 30 minutes, and give it one good stir.

- Cook your soap on low or medium heat. Using high heat might cause your soap to dry out before it is fully cooked.

- If you are using milk or other ingredients with sugar that might burn, cook on the lowest setting available.

- Soap expands as it cooks, so make sure that your soap mixture only fills your slow cooker or stainless-steel pot halfway. Give it room to rise a bit.

Hot-Process Soap Troubleshooting

Issue: Soap has hard, lumpy bits in it when you spoon it into the mold.

CAUSE/WAYS TO PREVENT: This is usually from overheating. Soap that touches the sides of the slow cooker overheats and dehydrates. Turn your slow cooker down next time.

FIX: This is an aesthetic issue, and the soap can be used as is.

Issue: Soap zaps when you test it. This means that you have active lye in your soap.

CAUSE/WAYS TO PREVENT: If you measured everything correctly, this means that your soap needs to cook longer. If you have been cooking your soap for hours and it is still zapping, then you probably mismeasured your lye, adding too much.

FIX: If soap has too much lye in it, I would probably toss it and start over. You can try adding oil by the tablespoon until your soap tests neutral. It can be hard to know exactly how much to add, but if you have time to experiment, go for it.

Issue: Soap mixture separates during cooking.

CAUSE/WAYS TO PREVENT: Be sure that you are at true trace before you set your soap to cook.

FIX: Emulsify it back together using a stick blender.

Issue: Soap mixture volcanoes out of cooking container.

CAUSE/WAYS TO PREVENT: Your slow cooker or oven might have been set too hot. Reduce heat.

FIX: If you're able, scoop everything back into your cooking container.

Layering Hot-Process Soap

One of my favorite ways to create a decorative hot-process soap is to divide the cooked soap into different containers, add color, and then layer into the mold. You can create an easy two-layer soap, or you can create four to six layers for a more colorful and complex design.

SAFETY FIRST: Remember to wear goggles and gloves. Mix the lye solution in a well-ventilated area with access to a sink for flushing with water if necessary. Keep your work space free from distractions, small children, and pets. Hot-process soap is hot during cooking and molding.

Prep ahead: Weigh the essential oils into a glass container; blend together. Disperse the colorants by mixing them in small plastic or glass cups.

Step 1: Prepare your lye solution by weighing the water into your lye solution container.

Step 2: Weigh the sodium hydroxide into your dry lye container.

Step 3: Following safety precautions, pour the sodium hydroxide into the water while stirring. Turn your head and lean away from the lye solution. Stir until all the granules have dissolved. Set aside.

Step 4: Weigh all the base oils into a microwave-safe container.

Step 5: Heat the base oils in the microwave until melted.

Step 6: Pour the oils into your slow cooker, carefully scraping the bowl with a silicone spatula.

Step 7: Add the sugar, sodium lactate, and/or yogurt to your cooled lye solution.

Step 8: Pour the lye solution into your melted oils and mix to trace using a stick blender.

Step 9: Let the soap cook until it tests neutral.

Step 10: Once your soap is cooked, add your essential oil blend and mix.

Step 9

Step 12

Step 13

Step 13, continued

Step 15

Step 11: Divide your soap into containers, one for each color.

Step 12: Add a dispersed colorant to each container and blend. You'll need to work quickly, as your soap will start to harden as it cools.

Step 13: Spoon the first layer into your mold. Bang the mold down onto a firm surface to flatten the soap. Repeat for each additional layer, moving quickly. You don't want the layers drying in between or your layers won't stick. You can moisten them with a spray of alcohol if they dry out.

Step 14: Allow the soap to harden completely. This will usually take 4 to 6 hours.

Step 15: Once hard, unmold and cut your soap.

Step 16: Allow your soap to cure for a minimum of 2 weeks.

Swirling Hot-Process Soap

Swirling hot-process soap is a bit different than swirling cold-process soap. Cold-process soap is nice and fluid, whereas hot-process soap is thick and gloppy. You won't get nice wispy and delicate swirls by swirling hot-process soap, but you'll get some interesting designs. Once you spoon the different colored soaps into your mold, you can run a chopstick through the soap to swirl together. Just as with layering, you can swirl two colors together—or as many as you're brave enough to try.

SAFETY FIRST: Remember to wear goggles and gloves. Mix the lye solution in a well-ventilated area with access to a sink for flushing with water if necessary. Keep your work space free from distractions, small children, and pets. Hot-process soap is hot during cooking and molding.

Prep ahead: Weigh the essential oils into a glass container; blend together. Disperse the colorants by mixing them in the small plastic or glass cups.

Step 1: Prepare your lye solution by weighing the water into your lye solution container.

Step 2: Weigh the sodium hydroxide into your dry lye container.

Step 3: Following safety precautions, pour the sodium hydroxide into the water while stirring. Turn your head and lean away from the lye solution. Stir until all the granules have dissolved. Set aside.

Step 4: Weigh all your base oils into a microwave-safe container.

Step 5: Heat the base oils in the microwave until melted.

Step 6: Pour the oils into your slow cooker, carefully scraping the bowl with a silicone spatula.

Step 7: Add the sugar, sodium lactate, and/or yogurt to your cooled lye solution.

Step 8: Pour the lye solution into your melted oils and mix to trace using a stick blender.

Step 9: Let your soap cook until it tests neutral.

Step 10: Once your soap is cooked, add your essential oil blend and mix.

Step 11: Divide your soap into containers, one for each color.

Step 9

Step 12

Step 13

Step 13, continued

Step 15

Step 12: Add a dispersed colorant to each container and blend. You'll need to work quickly, as your soap will start to harden as it cools.

Step 13: Rotating colors, use a spoon to scoop soap into the mold. Run a chopstick through the soap to swirl.

Step 14: Allow your soap to harden completely. This will usually take 4 to 6 hours.

Step 15: Once hard, unmold and cut your soap.

Step 16: Allow your soap to cure for a minimum of 2 weeks.

In-the-Pot Hot-Process Soap Swirl

This is an alternative way to swirl hot-process soap. I sometimes call it the lazy soapmaker's hot-process swirl. You place a cardboard divider into the cooked soap in the slow cooker, then add color to each side, give it a quick swirl, and spoon it into your mold.

SAFETY FIRST: Remember to wear goggles and gloves. Mix the lye solution in a well-ventilated area with access to a sink for flushing with water if necessary. Keep your work space free from distractions, small children, and pets. Hot-process soap is hot during cooking and molding.

Prep ahead: Weigh the essential oils into a glass container; blend together. Disperse the colorants by mixing them in small plastic or glass cups.

Step 1: Prepare your lye solution by weighing the water into your lye solution container.

Step 2: Weigh the sodium hydroxide into your dry lye container.

Step 3: Following safety precautions, pour the sodium hydroxide into the water while stirring. Turn your head and lean away from the lye solution. Stir until all the granules have dissolved. Set aside.

Step 4: Weigh all your base oils into a microwave-safe container.

Step 5: Heat the base oils in the microwave until melted.

Step 6: Pour the oils into your slow cooker, carefully scraping the bowl with a silicone spatula.

Step 7: Add the sugar, sodium lactate, and/or yogurt to your cooled lye solution.

Step 8: Pour the lye solution into your melted oils and mix to trace using a stick blender.

Step 9: Let your soap cook until it tests neutral.

Step 11

Step 12

Step 13

Step 14

Step 14, continued

Step 16

Step 10: Once your soap is cooked, add your essential oil blend and mix.

Step 11: Place a cardboard divider into the soap, dividing it in half.

Step 12: Add a dispersed colorant to each side and blend as best you can.

Step 13: Remove the divider from the soap. Swirl the soap a bit using a spatula or spoon.

Step 14: Spoon it into your mold.

Step 15: Allow your soap to harden completely. This will usually take 4 to 6 hours.

Step 16: Once hard, unmold and cut your soap.

Step 17: Allow your soap to cure for a minimum of 2 weeks.

Hot-Process Recipes
Citrus Zest Kitchen Soap

VEGAN · BODY · EXFOLIATING · CITRUS

This soap has a bright citrus scent. Keep it by the kitchen sink for a light, exfoliating hand wash.

~~~~~~

YIELD: 1,371 grams | 10 bars (137 grams each)

START TO FINISH TIME: 1 to 2 hours to create soap, 4 to 6 hours to harden and unmold, 2 weeks to cure

SCENT: Orange and lemon

LYE DISCOUNT: 5%

SAFETY FIRST: Remember to wear goggles and gloves. Mix the lye solution in a well-ventilated area with access to a sink for flushing with water if necessary. Keep your work space free from distractions, small children, and pets. Hot-process soap is hot during cooking and molding.

~~~~~~

EQUIPMENT

* Digital scale
* Glass container
* Lye solution container
* Dry lye container
* Microwave-safe batch container
* Slow cooker
* Measuring spoons
* Silicone spatulas
* Stick blender
* 10-inch silicone loaf mold

INGREDIENTS

Scent

* 15 grams orange essential oil
* 10 grams litsea essential oil
* 5 grams lemon essential oil

Lye Solution

* 322 grams distilled water
* 129 grams sodium hydroxide

Base Oils (900 grams)

* 306 grams (34%) 76-degree coconut oil
* 90 grams (10%) cocoa butter
* 504 grams (56%) olive oil

Colorants/Additives

* 2 teaspoons sugar
* 2 teaspoons sodium lactate
* 2 teaspoons yogurt
* 1 teaspoon orange peel powder

Prep ahead: Weigh the orange, litsea, and lemon essential oils into a glass container; blend together. Set aside.

Step 1: Prepare your lye solution by weighing the water into your lye solution container.

Step 2: Weigh the sodium hydroxide into your dry lye container.

Step 3: Following safety precautions, pour the sodium hydroxide into the water while stirring. Turn your head and lean away from the lye solution. Stir until all the granules have dissolved. Set aside.

Step 4: Weigh the coconut oil, cocoa butter, and olive oil into the microwave-safe container.

Step 5: Heat the oils in the microwave until melted.

Step 6: Pour the oil mixture into your slow cooker, carefully scraping the bowl with a silicone spatula.

Step 7: Add the sugar, sodium lactate, and yogurt to your cooled lye solution.

Step 8: Add the orange peel powder to the base oils.

Step 9: Pour the lye solution into your melted oils and mix to trace using a stick blender.

Step 10: Let your soap cook until it tests neutral.

Step 11: Once your soap is cooked, add your essential oil blend and mix.

Step 12: Spoon your soap into the mold.

Step 13: Allow your soap to harden completely. This will usually take 4 to 6 hours.

Step 14: Once hard, unmold and cut your soap.

Step 15: Allow your soap to cure for a minimum of 2 weeks.

Nourishing Oatmeal & Honey Soap

BODY · GENTLE · CITRUS · SPICY

This recipe has a large amount of olive oil, making a soap that's gentle on the skin. Oatmeal is also known to soothe troubled skin.

～～～～～～～～～～～～～～～～～～～～～～～～～～～～～

YIELD: 1,351 grams | 10 bars (135 grams each)

START TO FINISH TIME: 1 to 2 hours to create soap, 4 to 6 hours to harden and unmold, 2 weeks to cure

SCENT: Grapefruit, cinnamon, and clove

LYE DISCOUNT: 5%

SAFETY FIRST: Remember to wear goggles and gloves. Mix the lye solution in a well-ventilated area with access to a sink for flushing with water. Keep your work space free from distractions, small children, and pets. Hot-process soap is hot during cooking and molding.

～～～～～～～～～～～～～～～～～～～～～～～～～～～～～

EQUIPMENT

* Digital scale
* Glass container
* Lye solution container
* Dry lye container
* Microwave-safe batch container
* Slow cooker
* Measuring spoons
* Silicone spatulas
* Stick blender
* 10-inch silicone loaf mold

INGREDIENTS

Scent

* 24 grams grapefruit essential oil
* 3 grams cinnamon leaf essential oil
* 3 grams clove essential oil

Lye Solution

* 322 grams distilled water
* 129 grams sodium hydroxide

Base Oils (900 grams)

* 315 grams (35%) 76-degree coconut oil
* 540 grams (60%) olive oil
* 45 grams (5%) castor oil

Colorants/Additives

* 2 teaspoons honey
* 2 teaspoons sodium lactate
* 2 teaspoons yogurt
* 1 teaspoon ground oats

Prep ahead: Weigh the grapefruit, cinnamon leaf, and clove essential oils into a glass container; blend together. Set aside.

Step 1: Prepare your lye solution by weighing the water into your lye solution container.

Step 2: Weigh the sodium hydroxide into your dry lye container.

Step 3: Following safety precautions, pour the sodium hydroxide into the water while stirring. Turn your head and lean away from the lye solution. Stir until all the granules have dissolved. Set aside.

Step 4: Weigh the coconut, olive, and castor oils into the microwave-safe container.

Step 5: Heat the oils in the microwave until melted.

Step 6: Pour the oil mixture into your slow cooker, carefully scraping the bowl with a silicone spatula.

Step 7: Add the honey, sodium lactate, and yogurt to your cooled lye solution.

Step 8: Add the ground oats to the base oils and blend.

Step 9: Pour the lye solution into your melted oils and mix to trace using a stick blender.

Step 10: Let your soap cook until it tests neutral.

Step 11: Once your soap is cooked, add your essential oil blend and mix.

Step 12: Spoon your soap into the mold.

Step 13: Allow your soap to harden completely. This will usually take 4 to 6 hours.

Step 14: Once hard, unmold and cut your soap.

Step 15: Allow your soap to cure for a minimum of 2 weeks.

> **Tip:** *Adding honey to your lye solution might make it turn bright orange! Don't worry, once your soap is unmolded, the color will have faded. Adding whole oats will create a super-scratchy soap. You can grind oats to a powder using a coffee grinder or food processor.*

Orange Spice Soap

VEGAN · BODY · CITRUS · SPICY

Orange and cinnamon warm up the holiday season. That's why this soap makes a perfect gift for friends and family.

~~~~~~

YIELD: 1,351 grams | 10 bars (135 grams each)

START TO FINISH TIME: 1 to 2 hours to create soap, 4 to 6 hours to harden and unmold, 2 weeks to cure

SCENT: Orange and cinnamon

LYE DISCOUNT: 5%

SAFETY FIRST: Remember to wear goggles and gloves. Mix the lye solution in a well-ventilated area with access to a sink for flushing with water. Keep your work space free from distractions, small children, and pets. Hot-process soap is hot during cooking and molding.

~~~~~~

EQUIPMENT

* Digital scale
* Glass container
* Lye solution container
* Dry lye container
* Microwave-safe batch container
* Slow cooker
* Measuring spoons
* Silicone spatulas
* Stick blender
* 10-inch silicone loaf mold

INGREDIENTS

Scent

* 25 grams orange essential oil
* 5 grams cinnamon leaf essential oil

Lye Solution

* 322 grams distilled water
* 129 grams sodium hydroxide

Base Oils (900 grams)

* 315 grams (35%) 76-degree coconut oil
* 468 grams (52%) olive oil
* 72 grams (8%) high oleic sunflower oil
* 45 grams (5%) grapeseed oil

Colorants/Additives

* 2 teaspoons sugar
* 2 teaspoons sodium lactate
* 2 teaspoons yogurt
* 1 tablespoon turmeric powder
* ⅛ teaspoon clove powder
* ⅛ teaspoon cinnamon powder

Prep ahead: Weigh the orange and cinnamon leaf essential oils into a glass container; blend together. Set aside.

Step 1: Prepare your lye solution by weighing the water into your lye solution container.

Step 2: Weigh the sodium hydroxide into your dry lye container.

Step 3: Following safety precautions, pour the sodium hydroxide into the water while stirring. Turn your head and lean away from the lye solution. Stir until all the granules have dissolved. Set aside.

Step 4: Weigh the coconut, olive, sunflower, and grapeseed oils into the microwave-safe container.

Step 5: Heat the oils in the microwave until melted.

Step 6: Pour the oil mixture into your slow cooker, carefully scraping the bowl with a silicone spatula.

Step 7: Add the sugar, sodium lactate, and yogurt to your cooled lye solution.

Step 8: Add the turmeric, clove, and cinnamon powders to the base oils and mix.

Step 9: Pour the lye solution into your melted oils and mix to trace using a stick blender.

Step 10: Let your soap cook until it tests neutral.

Step 11: Once your soap is cooked, add your essential oil blend and mix.

Step 12: Spoon your soap into your mold.

Step 13: Allow your soap to harden completely. This will usually take 4 to 6 hours.

Step 14: Once hard, unmold and cut your soap.

Step 15: Allow your soap to cure for a minimum of 2 weeks.

Peppermint Lime Soap

VEGAN · BODY · FACE · GENTLE · MINTY

This peppermint and lime scent combo creates a soap that men love. Nettles have a long history in traditional medicine, and they work wonders on troubled skin.

~~~~~~

YIELD: 1,358 grams | 10 bars (136 grams each)

START TO FINISH TIME: 1 to 2 hours to create soap, 4 to 6 hours to harden and unmold, 2 weeks to cure

SCENT: Peppermint and lime

LYE DISCOUNT: 5%

SAFETY FIRST: Remember to wear safety gear, especially goggles and gloves. Mix the lye solution in a well-ventilated area with access to a sink for flushing with water. Keep your work space free from distractions, especially small children, and pets. Hot-process soap is hot during cooking and molding.

~~~~~~

EQUIPMENT

* Digital scale
* Glass container
* Lye solution container
* Dry lye container
* Microwave-safe batch container
* Slow cooker
* Measuring spoons
* Silicone spatulas
* Stick blender
* 10-inch silicone loaf mold

INGREDIENTS

Scent

* 15 grams lime essential oil
* 10 grams peppermint essential oil
* 5 grams litsea essential oil

Lye Solution

* 327 grams distilled water
* 131 grams sodium hydroxide

Base Oils (900 grams)

* 342 grams (38%) 76-degree coconut oil
* 468 grams (52%) olive oil
* 90 grams (10%) rice bran oil

Colorants/Additives

* 2 teaspoons sugar
* 2 teaspoons sodium lactate
* 2 teaspoons yogurt
* 1 tablespoon nettle leaf powder
* 1 tablespoon zinc oxide powder

Prep ahead: Weigh the lime, peppermint, and litsea essential oils into a glass container; blend together. Set aside.

Step 1: Prepare your lye solution by weighing the water into your lye solution container.

Step 2: Weigh the sodium hydroxide into your dry lye container.

Step 3: Following safety precautions, pour the sodium hydroxide into the water while stirring. Turn your head and lean away from the lye solution. Stir until all the granules have dissolved. Set aside.

Step 4: Weigh the coconut, olive, and rice bran oils into the microwave-safe container.

Step 5: Heat the oils in the microwave until melted.

Step 6: Pour the oil mixture into your slow cooker, carefully scraping the bowl with a silicone spatula.

Step 7: Add the sugar, sodium lactate, and yogurt to your cooled lye solution.

Step 8: Add the nettle powder and zinc oxide to the base oils and stir.

Step 9: Pour the lye solution into your melted oils and mix to trace using a stick blender.

Step 10: Let your soap cook until it tests neutral.

Step 11: Once your soap is cooked, add your essential oil blend and mix.

Step 12: Spoon your soap into your mold.

Step 13: Allow your soap to harden completely. This will usually take 4 to 6 hours.

Step 14: Once hard, unmold and cut your soap.

Step 15: Allow your soap to cure for a minimum of 2 weeks.

Tip: *Litsea essential oil is found in many of my essential oil blends containing citrus oils. It is used to anchor citrus oils, whose scents can be fleeting.*

Red Wine Soap

VEGAN · BODY · GENTLE · FLORAL · HERBAL

This soap is perfect to make after a dinner party that leaves you with leftover wine. Wine contains lather-boosting sugar. You'll love this bubbly soap!

YIELD: 1,344 grams | 10 bars (134 grams each)

START TO FINISH TIME: 1 to 2 hours to create soap, 4 to 6 hours to harden and unmold, 2 weeks to cure

SCENT: Lavender, rosemary, and clary sage

LYE DISCOUNT: 5%

SAFETY FIRST: Remember to wear goggles and gloves. Mix the lye solution in a well-ventilated area with access to a sink for flushing with water. Keep your work space free from distractions, small children, and pets. Hot-process soap is hot during cooking and molding.

EQUIPMENT

* Digital scale
* Pot for boiling wine
* Glass container
* Lye solution container
* Dry lye container
* Microwave-safe batch container
* Slow cooker
* Measuring spoons
* Silicone spatulas
* Stick blender
* 10-inch silicone loaf mold

INGREDIENTS

* 634 grams red wine

Scent

* 10 grams lavender essential oil
* 10 grams rosemary essential oil
* 5 grams patchouli essential oil
* 5 grams clary sage essential oil

Lye Solution

* 317 grams reduced red wine
* 127 grams sodium hydroxide

Base Oils (900 grams)

* 270 grams (30%) 76-degree coconut oil
* 72 grams (8%) shea butter
* 513 grams (57%) olive oil
* 45 grams (5%) castor oil

Colorants/Additives

* 2 teaspoons sugar
* 2 teaspoons sodium lactate
* 2 teaspoons yogurt
* 1 tablespoon yellow dock root powder

Prep ahead: The day before you make soap, reduce your wine by 50 percent by carefully boiling it. You'll need 317 grams once reduced. Refrigerate the wine reduction overnight so it is chilled when you're ready to use it. When you're ready to make soap, weigh the lavender, rosemary, patchouli, and clary sage essential oils into a glass container; blend together. Set aside.

Step 1: Prepare your lye solution by weighing the chilled wine into your lye solution container.

Step 2: Weigh the sodium hydroxide into your dry lye container.

Step 3: Following safety precautions, pour the sodium hydroxide into the wine while stirring. Turn your head and lean away from the lye solution. Stir until all the granules have dissolved. Set aside.

Step 4: Weigh the coconut oil, shea butter, olive oil, and castor oil into the microwave-safe container.

Step 5: Heat the oils in the microwave until melted.

Step 6: Pour the oil mixture into your slow cooker, carefully scraping the bowl with a silicone spatula.

Step 7: Add the sugar, sodium lactate, and yogurt to your cooled lye solution.

Step 8: Add the yellow dock powder to the base oils and stir.

Step 9: Pour the lye solution into your melted oils and mix to trace using a stick blender.

Step 10: Let your soap cook until it tests neutral.

Step 11: Once your soap is cooked, add your essential oil blend and mix.

Step 12: Spoon your soap into your mold.

Step 13: Allow your soap to harden completely. This will usually take 4 to 6 hours.

Step 14: Once hard, unmold and cut your soap.

Step 15: Allow your soap to cure for a minimum of 2 weeks.

Tip: *Yellow dock root powder is a yellow powder, but when it reacts with the high pH environment of soap, it turns a dark crimson red. Boiling the alcohol out of your wine before you soap with it helps ensure that a negative reaction does not occur when mixing it with lye. Just to be on the safe side, mix your wine and lye solution in a sink in case it bubbles up a bit.*

Honey & Clove Soap

BODY · FLORAL · CITRUS · SPICY

Cloves have been used in cooking and traditional medicine for centuries. Clove essential oil is warming and comforting.

~~~~~~

YIELD: 1,341 grams | 10 bars (134 grams each)

START TO FINISH TIME: 1 to 2 hours to create soap, 4 to 6 hours to harden and unmold, 2 weeks to cure

SCENT: Clove, clary sage, and bergamot

LYE DISCOUNT: 5%

SAFETY FIRST: Remember to wear goggles and gloves. Mix the lye solution in a well-ventilated area with access to a sink for flushing with water. Keep your work space free from distractions, small children, and pets. Hot-process soap is hot during cooking and molding.

~~~~~~

EQUIPMENT

* Digital scale
* Glass container
* Lye solution container
* Dry lye container
* Microwave-safe batch container
* Slow cooker
* Measuring spoons
* Silicone spatulas
* Stick blender
* 10-inch silicone loaf mold

INGREDIENTS

Scent

* 10 grams litsea essential oil
* 5 grams clary sage essential oil
* 5 grams clove essential oil
* 5 grams bergamot essential oil
* 5 grams grapefruit essential oil

Lye Solution

* 315 grams distilled water
* 126 grams sodium hydroxide

Base Oils (900 grams)

* 315 grams (35%) 76-degree coconut oil
* 468 grams (52%) olive oil
* 72 grams (8%) apricot kernel oil
* 45 grams (5%) castor oil

Colorants/Additives

* 2 teaspoons honey
* 2 teaspoons sodium lactate
* 2 teaspoons yogurt

Prep ahead: Weigh the litsea, clary sage, clove, bergamot, and grapefruit essential oils into a glass container; blend together. Set aside.

Step 1: Prepare your lye solution by weighing the water into your lye solution container.

Step 2: Weigh the sodium hydroxide into your dry lye container.

Step 3: Following safety precautions, pour the sodium hydroxide into the water while stirring. Turn your head and lean away from the lye solution. Stir until all the granules have dissolved. Set aside.

Step 4: Weigh the coconut, olive, apricot kernel, and castor oils into the microwave-safe container.

Step 5: Heat the oils in the microwave until melted.

Step 6: Pour the oil mixture into your slow cooker, carefully scraping the bowl with a silicone spatula.

Step 7: Add the honey, sodium lactate, and yogurt to your cooled lye solution.

Step 8: Pour the lye solution into your melted oils and mix to trace using a stick blender.

Step 9: Let your soap cook until it tests neutral.

Step 10: Once your soap is cooked, add your essential oil blend and mix.

Step 11: Spoon your soap into your mold.

Step 12: Allow your soap to harden completely. This will usually take 4 to 6 hours.

Step 13: Once hard, unmold and cut your soap.

Step 14: Allow your soap to cure for a minimum of 2 weeks.

Tip: *If you don't have clove essential oil, cinnamon leaf essential oil is a good substitute, giving similar warmth to this blend. Spice essential oils can be irritating to the skin, so be sure to use them in small amounts, as I do in the recipes here.*

Seaweed & Pumice Soap

VEGAN · BODY · EXFOLIATING · MINTY · CITRUS

Seaweed is rich in nutrients and makes for a wonderful soap additive. It gives soap a natural green color and lightly exfoliates the skin. Pumice is powdered volcanic rock and is a popular exfoliant in soap.

~~~~~~

YIELD: 1,341 grams | 10 bars (134 grams each)

START TO FINISH TIME: 1 to 2 hours to create soap, 4 to 6 hours to harden and unmold, 2 weeks to cure

SCENT: Peppermint, spearmint, and lime

LYE DISCOUNT: 5%

SAFETY FIRST: Remember to wear goggles and gloves. Mix the lye solution in a well-ventilated area with access to a sink for flushing with water. Keep your work space free from distractions, small children, and pets. Hot-process soap is hot during cooking and molding.

~~~~~~

EQUIPMENT

* Digital scale
* Glass container
* Lye solution container
* Dry lye container
* Microwave-safe batch container
* Slow cooker
* Measuring spoons
* Silicone spatulas
* Stick blender
* 10-inch silicone loaf mold

INGREDIENTS

Scent

* 10 grams peppermint essential oil
* 10 grams lime essential oil
* 5 grams spearmint essential oil
* 5 grams lemongrass essential oil

Lye Solution

* 315 grams distilled water
* 126 grams sodium hydroxide

Base Oils (900 grams)

* 270 grams (30%) 76-degree coconut oil
* 126 grams (14%) shea butter
* 360 grams (40%) olive oil
* 72 grams (8%) rice bran oil
* 72 grams (8%) high oleic sunflower oil

Colorants/Additives

* 2 teaspoons sugar
* 2 teaspoons sodium lactate
* 2 teaspoons yogurt
* 1 teaspoon seaweed (kelp) powder
* ¼ cup pumice powder

Prep ahead: Weigh the peppermint, lime, spearmint, and lemongrass essential oils into a glass container; blend together. Set aside.

Step 1: Prepare your lye solution by weighing the water into your lye solution container.

Step 2: Weigh the sodium hydroxide into your dry lye container.

Step 3: Following safety precautions, pour the sodium hydroxide into the water while stirring. Turn your head and lean away from the lye solution. Stir until all the granules have dissolved. Set aside.

Step 4: Weigh the coconut oil, shea butter, olive oil, rice bran oil, and sunflower oil into the microwave-safe container.

Step 5: Heat the oils in the microwave until melted.

Step 6: Pour the oil mixture into your slow cooker, carefully scraping the bowl with a silicone spatula.

Step 7: Add the sugar, sodium lactate, and yogurt to your cooled lye solution.

Step 8: Add the seaweed powder and pumice to the base oils and mix.

Step 9: Pour the lye solution into your melted oils and mix to trace using a stick blender.

Step 10: Let your soap cook until it tests neutral.

Step 11: Once your soap is cooked, add your essential oil blend and mix.

Step 12: Spoon your soap into your mold.

Step 13: Allow your soap to harden completely. This will usually take 4 to 6 hours.

Step 14: Once hard, unmold and cut your soap.

Step 15: Allow your soap to cure for a minimum of 2 weeks.

Tip: *The amount of pumice you add is a matter of preference. If you want a more exfoliating soap, add more pumice. Seaweed powder can have an unpleasant smell. I like to combine it with strong essential oils such as peppermint and spearmint to overpower it.*

Herb & Hemp Soap

VEGAN · BODY · GENTLE · EXFOLIATING · FLORAL · HERBAL

Hemp seeds are pressed to make hemp seed oil. This herbaceous essential oil blend is paired with exfoliating dried peppermint leaves to make a soap that any horticulturist would love.

~~~~~~

YIELD: 1,351 grams | 10 bars (135 grams each)

START TO FINISH TIME: 1 to 2 hours to create soap, 4 to 6 hours to harden and unmold, 2 weeks to cure

SCENT: Ginger grass, spearmint, and lavender

LYE DISCOUNT: 5%

SAFETY FIRST: Remember to wear goggles and gloves. Mix the lye solution in a well-ventilated area with access to a sink for flushing with water. Keep your work space free from distractions, small children, and pets. Hot-process soap is hot during cooking and molding.

~~~~~~

EQUIPMENT

* Digital scale
* Glass container
* Lye solution container
* Dry lye container
* Microwave-safe batch container
* Slow cooker
* Measuring spoons
* Silicone spatulas
* Stick blender
* 10-inch silicone loaf mold

INGREDIENTS

Scent

* 5 grams ginger grass essential oil
* 5 grams spearmint essential oil
* 5 grams lemongrass essential oil
* 15 grams lavender essential oil

Lye Solution

* 322 grams distilled water
* 129 grams sodium hydroxide

Base Oils (900 grams)

* 315 grams (35%) 76-degree coconut oil
* 342 grams (38%) olive oil
* 135 grams (15%) high oleic canola oil
* 45 grams (5%) hemp seed oil
* 63 grams (7%) castor oil

Colorants/Additives

* 2 teaspoons sugar
* 2 teaspoons sodium lactate
* 2 teaspoons yogurt
* 1 tablespoon crushed dried peppermint

Prep ahead: Weigh the ginger grass, spearmint, lemongrass, and lavender essential oils into a glass container; blend together. Set aside.

Step 1: Prepare your lye solution by weighing the water into your lye solution container.

Step 2: Weigh the sodium hydroxide into your dry lye container.

Step 3: Following safety precautions, pour the sodium hydroxide into the water while stirring. Turn your head and lean away from the lye solution. Stir until all the granules have dissolved. Set aside.

Step 4: Weigh the coconut, olive, canola, hemp seed, and castor oils into the microwave-safe container.

Step 5: Heat the oils in the microwave until melted.

Step 6: Pour the oil mixture into your slow cooker, carefully scraping the bowl with a silicone spatula.

Step 7: Add the sugar, sodium lactate, and yogurt to your cooled lye solution.

Step 8: Add the dried peppermint to the base oils and mix.

Step 9: Pour the lye solution into your melted oils and mix to trace using a stick blender.

Step 10: Let your soap cook until it tests neutral.

Step 11: Once your soap is cooked, add your essential oil blend and mix.

Step 12: Spoon your soap into your mold.

Step 13: Allow your soap to harden completely. This will usually take 4 to 6 hours.

Step 14: Once hard, unmold and cut your soap.

Step 15: Allow your soap to cure for a minimum of 2 weeks.

Tip: *I use peppermint in this recipe, but you can use any dried herb, such as spearmint, nettle leaf, basil, lemon balm, rosemary, etc. Hemp oil is high in linolenic and linoleic fatty acids. Because oils high in these fatty acids are prone to rancidity, keep the use of hemp oil to 5 percent or less in your formula.*

Pumpkin Purée Soap

VEGAN · BODY · MINTY · CITRUS · SPICY

This soap uses fresh pumpkin purée in place of water, creating a soap that's perfect for the fall season. The orange, peppermint, and spice essential oil blend will warm up your home right through the holidays.

~~~~~~

YIELD: 1,348 grams | 10 bars (135 grams each)

START TO FINISH TIME: 1 to 2 hours to create soap, 4 to 6 hours to harden and unmold, 2 weeks to cure

SCENT: Orange, peppermint, and cinnamon

LYE DISCOUNT: 5%

SAFETY FIRST: Remember to wear goggles and gloves. Mix the lye solution in a well-ventilated area with access to a sink for flushing with water. Keep your work space free from distractions, small children, and pets. Hot-process soap is hot during cooking and molding.

~~~~~~

EQUIPMENT

* Digital scale
* Glass container
* Lye solution container
* Dry lye container
* Microwave-safe batch container
* Slow cooker
* Measuring spoons
* Silicone spatulas
* Stick blender
* 10-inch silicone loaf mold

INGREDIENTS

Scent

* 15 grams orange essential oil
* 5 grams grapefruit essential oil
* 5 grams cinnamon leaf essential oil
* 5 grams peppermint essential oil

Lye Solution

* 320 grams pumpkin purée
* 128 grams sodium hydroxide

Base Oils (900 grams)

* 297 grams (33%) 76-degree coconut oil
* 45 grams (5%) shea butter
* 45 grams (5%) cocoa butter
* 468 grams (52%) olive oil
* 45 grams (5%) castor oil

Colorants/Additives

* 2 teaspoons sugar
* 2 teaspoons sodium lactate
* 2 teaspoons yogurt
* ½ tablespoon annatto seed powder

Prep ahead: Weigh the orange, grapefruit, cinnamon leaf, and peppermint essential oils into a glass container; blend together. Set aside.

Step 1: Prepare your lye solution by weighing the pumpkin purée into your lye solution container.

Step 2: Weigh the sodium hydroxide into your dry lye container.

Step 3: Following safety precautions, pour the sodium hydroxide into the pumpkin purée while stirring. Turn your head and lean away from the lye solution. Stir until all the granules have dissolved. Set aside.

Step 4: Weigh the coconut oil, shea butter, cocoa butter, olive oil, and castor oil into the microwave-safe container.

Step 5: Heat the oils in the microwave until melted.

Step 6: Pour the oil mixture into your slow cooker, carefully scraping the bowl with a silicone spatula.

Step 7: Add the sugar, sodium lactate, and yogurt to your cooled lye solution.

Step 8: Add the annatto seed power to the base oils.

Step 9: Pour the lye solution into your melted oils and mix to trace using a stick blender.

Step 10: Let your soap cook until it tests neutral.

Step 11: Once your soap is cooked, add your essential oil blend and mix.

Step 12: Spoon your soap into your mold.

Step 13: Allow your soap to harden completely, usually 4 to 6 hours.

Step 14: Once hard, unmold and cut your soap.

Step 15: Allow your soap to cure for a minimum of 2 weeks.

Tip: You can either buy canned pumpkin or make your own purée. If you purchase canned pumpkin, be sure it is 100 percent pumpkin and not pumpkin pie filling. Pumpkin pie filling contains a ton of sugar, which can cause issues with your soap.

Lemon & Poppy Seed Soap

VEGAN · BODY · EXFOLIATING · CITRUS

Lemon poppy seed cake is one of my favorite desserts. Poppy seeds make this soap smoothly exfoliating. The lemon essential oil gives it a bright, tart scent.

~~~~~~

YIELD: 1,348 grams | 10 bars (135 grams each)

START TO FINISH TIME: 1 to 2 hours to create soap, 4 to 6 hours to harden and unmold, 2 weeks to cure

SCENT: Lemon and litsea

LYE DISCOUNT: 5%

SAFETY FIRST: Remember to wear goggles and gloves. Mix the lye solution in a well-ventilated area with access to a sink for flushing with water. Keep your work space free from distractions, small children, and pets. Hot-process soap is hot during cooking and molding.

~~~~~~

EQUIPMENT

* Digital scale
* Glass container
* Small plastic or glass cup
* Lye solution container
* Dry lye container
* Microwave-safe batch container
* Slow cooker
* Measuring spoons
* Silicone spatulas
* Stick blender
* 2 mixing containers
* 10-inch silicone loaf mold

INGREDIENTS

Scent
* 25 grams lemon essential oil
* 5 grams litsea essential oil

Lye Solution
* 320 grams distilled water
* 128 grams sodium hydroxide

Base Oils (900 grams)
* 306 grams (34%) 76-degree coconut oil
* 90 grams (10%) shea butter
* 414 grams (46%) olive oil
* 90 grams (10%) avocado oil

Colorants/Additives
* 2 teaspoons sugar
* 2 teaspoons sodium lactate
* 2 teaspoons yogurt
* 1 teaspoon poppy seeds
* 1 teaspoon ground turmeric
* 1 teaspoon olive oil

→

Prep ahead: Weigh the lemon and litsea essential oils into a glass container; blend together. Set aside. In the small cup, mix the turmeric into the 1 teaspoon of olive oil.

Step 1: Prepare your lye solution by weighing the water into your lye solution container.

Step 2: Weigh the sodium hydroxide into your dry lye container.

Step 3: Following safety precautions, pour the sodium hydroxide into the water while stirring. Turn your head and lean away from the lye solution. Stir until all the granules have dissolved. Set aside.

Step 4: Weigh the coconut oil, shea butter, olive oil, and avocado oil into the microwave-safe container.

Step 5: Heat the oils in the microwave until melted.

Step 6: Pour the oil mixture into your slow cooker, carefully scraping the bowl with a silicone spatula.

Step 7: Add the sugar, sodium lactate, and yogurt to your cooled lye solution.

Step 8: Pour the lye solution into your melted oils and mix to trace using a stick blender.

Step 9: Let your soap cook until it tests neutral.

Step 10: Once your soap is cooked, add your essential oil blend and mix.

Step 11: Divide your soap between the two mixing containers.

Step 12: Add the poppy seeds to one container and mix well. Add the turmeric–olive oil mixture to the other and mix well.

Step 13: Spoon the poppy seed soap into your mold. Bang the mold down onto a solid surface to flatten the layer.

Step 14: Immediately spoon the turmeric-colored soap into the mold.

Step 15: Allow your soap to harden completely, usually 4 to 6 hours.

Step 16: Once hard, unmold and cut your soap.

Step 17: Allow your soap to cure for a minimum of 2 weeks.

Tip: *When layering hot-process soap, you must move quickly or your soap will dry between layers and won't stick together.*

Cucumber Scrub Soap

VEGAN · BODY · FACE · EXFOLIATING · FLORAL · MINTY · SPICY

This soap uses cucumber purée in place of water. Cucumber is known to soothe itchy or inflamed skin. Nettle leaf and French green clay lightly exfoliate.

~~~~~~

YIELD: 1,348 grams | 10 bars (135 grams each)

START TO FINISH TIME: 1 to 2 hours to create soap, 4 to 6 hours to harden and unmold, 2 weeks to cure

SCENT: Spearmint, lavender, and cinnamon

LYE DISCOUNT: 5%

SAFETY FIRST: Remember to wear goggles and gloves. Mix the lye solution in a well-ventilated area with access to a sink for flushing with water. Keep your work space free from distractions, small children, and pets. Hot-process soap is hot during cooking and molding.

~~~~~~

EQUIPMENT

* Digital scale
* Glass container
* 2 small plastic or glass cups
* Stick blender
* Lye solution container
* Dry lye container
* Microwave-safe batch container
* Slow cooker
* Measuring spoons
* Silicone spatulas
* 2 mixing containers
* 10-inch silicone loaf mold
* Chopstick

INGREDIENTS

Scent

* 10 grams spearmint essential oil
* 10 grams lavender essential oil
* 5 grams patchouli essential oil
* 5 grams cinnamon leaf essential oil

Lye Solution

* 2 medium cucumbers
* 128 grams sodium hydroxide

Base Oils (900 grams)

* 306 grams (34%) 76-degree coconut oil
* 90 grams (10%) shea butter
* 360 grams (40%) olive oil
* 90 grams (10%) avocado oil
* 54 grams (6%) rice bran oil

Colorants/Additives

* 2 teaspoons sugar
* 2 teaspoons sodium lactate
* 2 teaspoons yogurt
* 1 teaspoon nettle leaf powder
* 1 teaspoon French green clay powder
* 4 teaspoons olive oil, divided
* 2 teaspoons zinc oxide

→

Prep ahead: Weigh the spearmint, lavender, patchouli, and cinnamon leaf essential oils into a glass container; blend together. Set aside. In one small cup or glass, disperse the nettle leaf powder and French green clay in 2 teaspoons of the olive oil. In the second cup or glass, disperse the zinc oxide in the remaining 2 teaspoons of olive oil. Peel and purée the cucumbers.

Step 1: Prepare your lye solution by weighing 320 grams of cucumber purée into your lye solution container. If the puréed cucumber doesn't reach 320 grams, add enough water to make up the difference.

Step 2: Weigh the sodium hydroxide into your dry lye container.

Step 3: Following safety precautions, pour the sodium hydroxide into the cucumber purée while stirring. Turn your head and lean away from the lye solution. Stir until all the granules have dissolved. Set aside.

Step 4: Weigh the coconut oil, shea butter, olive oil, avocado oil, and rice bran oil into the microwave-safe container.

Step 5: Heat the base oils in the microwave until melted.

Step 6: Pour the oil mixture into your slow cooker, carefully scraping the bowl with a silicone spatula.

Step 7: Add the sugar, sodium lactate, and yogurt to your cooled lye solution.

Step 8: Pour the lye solution into your melted oils and mix to trace using a stick blender.

Step 9: Let your soap cook until it tests neutral.

Step 10: Once your soap is cooked, add your essential oil blend and mix.

Step 11: Divide your soap between the two mixing containers.

Step 12: Add the nettle and French green clay–olive oil mixture to one container and mix well. Add the zinc oxide–olive oil mixture to the other container and mix well.

Step 13: Alternating colors, scoop spoonfuls into the mold. Use a chopstick to swirl by dragging it through the soap.

Step 14: Allow your soap to harden completely, usually 4 to 6 hours.

Step 15: Once hard, unmold and cut your soap.

Step 16: Allow your soap to cure for a minimum of 2 weeks.

Tip: *Purée the cucumber using a food processor or blender. If it's thick, just add water to thin it down to blend it completely.*

Shea Butter & Geranium Soap

VEGAN · BODY · FACE · GENTLE · FLORAL

This gentle geranium-scented soap uses an alkanet infusion to color it purple.
Geranium essential oil makes for a delicate facial soap.

~~~~~~

YIELD: 1,351 grams | 10 bars (135 grams each)

START TO FINISH TIME: 1 to 2 hours to create soap, 4 to 6 hours to harden and unmold, 2 weeks to cure

SCENT: Geranium and lavender

LYE DISCOUNT: 5%

SAFETY FIRST: Remember to wear goggles and gloves. Mix the lye solution in a well-ventilated area with access to a sink for flushing with water. Keep your work space free from distractions, small children, and pets. Hot-process soap is hot during cooking and molding.

~~~~~~

EQUIPMENT

* Digital scale
* Mixing container
* Glass container
* Lye solution container
* Dry lye container
* Microwave-safe batch container
* Slow cooker
* Measuring spoons
* Silicone spatulas
* Stick blender
* 2 mixing containers
* 10-inch silicone loaf mold
* Chopstick

INGREDIENTS

Scent

* 20 grams lavender essential oil
* 10 grams geranium essential oil

Lye Solution

* 322 grams distilled water
* 129 grams sodium hydroxide

Base Oils (900 grams)

* 200 grams (22%) alkanet-infused olive oil
* 160 grams (18%) olive oil
* 306 grams (34%) 76-degree coconut oil
* 90 grams (10%) shea butter
* 144 grams (16%) sweet almond oil

Colorants/Additives

* ½ teaspoon alkanet powder
* 210 grams and 2 teaspoons olive oil, divided
* 2 teaspoons sugar
* 2 teaspoons sodium lactate
* 2 teaspoons yogurt
* 2 teaspoons zinc oxide powder
* 2 teaspoons olive oil

Prep ahead: Create a warm infusion using the alkanet powder and 210 grams of olive oil (see Creating an Oil Infusion, page 19). Let sit overnight. When you're ready to make the soap, weigh the lavender and geranium essential oils into a glass container; blend together. Set aside. In one small cup, disperse the zinc oxide in 2 teaspoons of olive oil.

Step 1: Prepare your lye solution by weighing the water into your lye solution container.

Step 2: Weigh the sodium hydroxide into your dry lye container.

Step 3: Following safety precautions, pour the sodium hydroxide into the water while stirring. Turn your head and lean away from the lye solution. Stir until all the granules have dissolved. Set aside.

Step 4: Strain the alkanet-infused olive oil and weigh 200 grams of it into the microwave-safe container. Add 160 grams of regular, uninfused olive oil. Weigh the coconut oil, shea butter, and sweet almond oil into the same container.

Step 5: Heat the oils in the microwave until melted.

Step 6: Pour the oil mixture into your slow cooker, carefully scraping the bowl with a silicone spatula.

Step 7: Add the sugar, sodium lactate, and yogurt to your cooled lye solution.

Step 8: Pour the lye solution into your melted oils and mix to trace using a stick blender.

Step 9: Let your soap cook until it tests neutral.

Step 10: Once your soap is cooked, add your essential oil blend and mix.

Step 11: Divide your soap between the two mixing containers.

Step 12: Add the zinc oxide dispersed in olive oil to one container and mix well. Don't add anything to the other container.

Step 13: Alternating colors, scoop spoonfuls into the mold. Use a chopstick to swirl by dragging it through the soap.

Step 14: Allow your soap to harden completely, usually 4 to 6 hours.

Step 15: Once hard, unmold and cut your soap.

Step 16: Allow your soap to cure for a minimum of 2 weeks.

Clay & Agave Swirled Soap

VEGAN · BODY · FACE · FLORAL · HERBAL

Clays are a wonderful additive for soap, lending their bright colors and light exfoliation to gently scrub your skin. Use this soap like a mask, allowing it to sit on your face for a few minutes to absorb impurities and toxins.

~~~~~~

YIELD: 1,348 grams | 10 bars (135 grams each)

START TO FINISH TIME: 1 to 2 hours to create soap, 4 to 6 hours to harden and unmold, 2 weeks to cure

SCENT: Lavender, rosemary, and peppermint

LYE DISCOUNT: 5%

SAFETY FIRST: Remember to wear goggles and gloves. Mix the lye solution in a well-ventilated area with access to a sink for flushing with water. Keep your work space free from distractions, small children, and pets. Hot-process soap is hot during cooking and molding.

~~~~~~

EQUIPMENT

* Digital scale
* Glass container
* 3 small plastic or glass cups
* Lye solution container
* Dry lye container
* Microwave-safe batch container
* Slow cooker
* Measuring spoons
* Silicone spatulas
* Stick blender
* 3 mixing containers
* 10-inch silicone loaf mold
* Chopstick

INGREDIENTS

Scent

* 16 grams lavender essential oil
* 8 grams rosemary essential oil
* 4 grams peppermint essential oil
* 2 grams lemongrass essential oil

Lye Solution

* 320 grams distilled water
* 128 grams sodium hydroxide

Base Oils (900 grams)

* 270 grams (30%) 76-degree coconut oil
* 126 grams (14%) mango butter
* 360 grams (40%) olive oil
* 144 grams (16%) high oleic sunflower oil

Colorants/Additives

* 2 teaspoons agave nectar
* 2 teaspoons sodium lactate
* 2 teaspoons yogurt
* 2 teaspoons zinc oxide powder
* 2 teaspoons olive oil
* 2 teaspoons purple Brazilian clay powder
* 2 teaspoons French green clay powder
* 4 tablespoons water, divided

Prep ahead: Weigh the essential oils into a glass container and blend together. Set aside. Disperse your colorants. In the first small cup, mix the purple clay with 2 tablespoons of the water. In the second small cup, mix the green clay and the remaining 2 tablespoons of water. In the third small cup, mix the zinc oxide with the 2 teaspoons of olive oil.

Step 1: Prepare your lye solution by weighing the water into your lye solution container.

Step 2: Weigh the sodium hydroxide into your dry lye container.

Step 3: Following safety precautions, pour the sodium hydroxide into the water while stirring. Turn your head and lean away from the lye solution. Stir until all the granules have dissolved. Set aside.

Step 4: Weigh the coconut oil, mango butter, olive oil, and sunflower oil into the microwave-safe container.

Step 5: Heat the oils in the microwave until melted.

Step 6: Pour the oil mixture into your slow cooker, carefully scraping the bowl with a silicone spatula.

Step 7: Add the agave, sodium lactate, and yogurt to your cooled lye solution.

Step 8: Pour the lye solution into your melted oils and mix to trace using a stick blender.

Step 9: Let your soap cook until it tests neutral.

Step 10: Once your soap is cooked, add your essential oil blend and mix.

Step 11: Divide your soap among the three mixing containers.

Step 12: Add one dispersed color to each container of soap and mix well.

Step 13: Rotating colors, scoop spoonfuls of soap into the mold. Use a chopstick to swirl by dragging it through the soap.

Step 14: Allow your soap to harden completely, usually 4 to 6 hours.

Step 15: Once hard, unmold and cut your soap.

Step 16: Allow your soap to cure for a minimum of 2 weeks.

Tip: Because clays absorb water easily, they are best dispersed in water before mixing into soap. Add as much liquid as needed to make the mixture watery, not pasty.

Mocha Mint Soap

VEGAN · BODY · EXFOLIATING · MINTY

What goes together better than cocoa, coffee, and mint? Peppermint essential oil gives this soap the perfect pick-me-up scent for your morning shower. Cocoa powder is one of my favorite natural brown colorants in soap.

~~~~~~

YIELD: 1,344 grams | 10 bars (134 grams each)

START TO FINISH TIME: 1 to 2 hours to create soap, 4 to 6 hours to harden and unmold, 2 weeks to cure

SCENT: Peppermint

LYE DISCOUNT: 5%

SAFETY FIRST: Remember to wear goggles and gloves. Mix the lye solution in a well-ventilated area with access to a sink for flushing with water. Keep your work space free from distractions, small children, and pets. Hot-process soap is hot during cooking and molding.

~~~~~~

EQUIPMENT

* Digital scale
* Glass container
* Small plastic or glass cup
* Lye solution container
* Dry lye container
* Microwave-safe batch container
* Slow cooker
* Measuring spoons
* Silicone spatulas
* Stick blender
* 2 mixing containers
* 10-inch silicone loaf mold

INGREDIENTS

Scent

* 15 grams peppermint essential oil

Lye Solution

* 317 grams distilled water
* 127 grams sodium hydroxide

Base Oils (900 grams)

* 270 grams (30%) 76-degree coconut oil
* 90 grams (10%) shea butter
* 450 grams (50%) olive oil
* 45 grams (5%) high oleic safflower oil
* 45 grams (5%) avocado oil

Colorants/Additives

* 2 teaspoons sugar
* 2 teaspoons sodium lactate
* 2 teaspoons yogurt
* 2 teaspoons crushed dried peppermint leaves
* 1 tablespoon unsweetened cocoa powder
* 1 teaspoon espresso powder
* 1 tablespoon olive oil

Prep ahead: Weigh the peppermint essential oil into a glass container. Set aside. In the small cup, mix the cocoa and espresso powders with the 1 tablespoon of olive oil.

Step 1: Prepare your lye solution by weighing the water into your lye solution container.

Step 2: Weigh the sodium hydroxide into your dry lye container.

Step 3: Following safety precautions, pour the sodium hydroxide into the water while stirring. Turn your head and lean away from the lye solution. Stir until all the granules have dissolved. Set aside.

Step 4: Weigh the coconut oil, shea butter, olive oil, safflower oil, and avocado oil into the microwave-safe container.

Step 5: Heat the oils in the microwave until melted.

Step 6: Pour the oil mixture into your slow cooker, carefully scraping the bowl with a silicone spatula.

Step 7: Add the sugar, sodium lactate, and yogurt to your cooled lye solution.

Step 8: Pour the lye solution into your melted oils and mix to trace using a stick blender.

Step 9: Let your soap cook until it tests neutral.

Step 10: Once your soap is cooked, add your essential oil blend and mix.

Step 11: Divide your soap between the two mixing containers.

Step 12: Add the dried peppermint to one container and mix well. Add the cocoa and espresso powders dispersed in olive oil to the other and mix well.

Step 13: Spoon the cocoa and espresso powder soap into your mold. Bang the mold down onto a solid surface to flatten the layer.

Step 14: Immediately spoon the peppermint leaf soap into the mold.

Step 15: Allow your soap to harden completely, usually 4 to 6 hours.

Step 16: Once hard, unmold and cut your soap.

Step 17: Allow your soap to cure for a minimum of 2 weeks.

Tip: *Peppermint essential oil is strong. As you can see, I used half the usual amount of essential oil in this recipe. When it comes to peppermint, a little goes a long way.*

Lavender Soap

VEGAN · BODY · FACE · GENTLE · FLORAL

Lavender is a timeless scent in soap. It is both relaxing and balancing. Use this soap right before bed for a restful night's sleep.

~~~~~~

YIELD: 1,337 grams | 10 bars (134 grams each)

START TO FINISH TIME: 1 to 2 hours to create soap, 4 to 6 hours to harden and unmold, 2 weeks to cure

SCENT: Lavender

LYE DISCOUNT: 5%

SAFETY FIRST: Remember to wear goggles and gloves. Mix the lye solution in a well-ventilated area with access to a sink for flushing with water. Keep your work space free from distractions, small children, and pets. Hot-process soap is hot during cooking and molding.

~~~~~~

EQUIPMENT

* Digital scale
* Glass container
* Small plastic or glass cup
* Lye solution container
* Dry lye container
* Microwave-safe batch container
* Slow cooker
* Measuring spoons
* Silicone spatulas
* Stick blender
* 2 mixing containers
* 10-inch silicone loaf mold

INGREDIENTS

Scent
* 30 grams lavender essential oil

Lye Solution
* 312 grams distilled water
* 125 grams sodium hydroxide

Base Oils (900 grams)
* 270 grams (30%) 76-degree coconut oil
* 90 grams (10%) kokum butter
* 360 grams (40%) olive oil
* 72 grams (8%) avocado oil
* 72 grams (8%) rice bran oil
* 36 grams (4%) jojoba oil

Colorants/Additives
* 2 teaspoons sugar
* 2 teaspoons sodium lactate
* 2 teaspoons yogurt
* 1 teaspoon alkanet root powder
* 1 teaspoon madder root powder
* 2 teaspoons olive oil

Prep ahead: Weigh the lavender essential oil into a glass container. Set aside. In the small cup, mix the alkanet and madder root powders together into the 2 teaspoons of olive oil.

Step 1: Prepare your lye solution by weighing the water into your lye solution container.

Step 2: Weigh the sodium hydroxide into your dry lye container.

Step 3: Following safety precautions, pour the sodium hydroxide into the water while stirring. Turn your head and lean away from the lye solution. Stir until all the granules have dissolved. Set aside.

Step 4: Weigh the coconut oil, kokum butter, olive oil, avocado oil, rice bran oil, and jojoba oil into the microwave-safe container.

Step 5: Heat the oils in the microwave until melted.

Step 6: Pour the oil mixture into your slow cooker, carefully scraping the bowl with a silicone spatula.

Step 7: Add the sugar, sodium lactate, and yogurt to your cooled lye solution.

Step 8: Pour the lye solution into your melted oils and mix to trace using a stick blender.

Step 9: Let your soap cook until it tests neutral.

Step 10: Once your soap is cooked, add your essential oil blend and mix.

Step 11: Divide your soap between the two mixing containers.

Step 12: Add the alkanet and madder combination to one container and mix well. Leave the other uncolored.

Step 13: Spoon the colored soap into your mold. Bang the mold down onto a solid surface to flatten the layer.

Step 14: Immediately spoon the uncolored soap into the mold.

Step 15: Allow your soap to harden completely, usually 4 to 6 hours.

Step 16: Once hard, unmold and cut your soap.

Step 17: Allow your soap to cure for a minimum of 2 weeks.

Tip: *Don't be afraid to mix natural colorants to get new, unique colors. Alkanet root and madder root combine to make a pinkish-purple color.*

O5

Liquid Soapmaking

Making liquid soap is a little more involved than any other soapmaking process, but it is worth the effort, for sure. Liquid soap is inexpensive to make, as it is mostly water, and stores easily in jugs until you're ready to bottle it. Younger people tend to prefer liquid to bar soap; so, if you're selling your soap, offering liquid soap might help you attract a younger crowd. It's also perfect for guest bathrooms, where visitors might not want to touch a "used" bar of soap.

Recipes

* Olive Oil Liquid Soap Base 193

* Coconut Oil Cleaning Liquid Soap Base 196

* Sunflower Oil Liquid Soap Base 198

* Jojoba Oil Liquid Soap Base 200

* Avocado Oil Liquid Soap Base 202

Liquid Soapmaking
Step-by-Step

Before we go through the process of making liquid soap, here are a couple of considerations.

Liquid soap is made with a different type of lye than cold-process and hot-process soaps, which both use sodium hydroxide. Here, you'll use potassium hydroxide to make a soap paste that is then diluted down into liquid soap. You don't have to cure liquid soap like you do hot-process or cold-process; it's ready to use right away.

Some soapmakers want crystal-clear liquid soap, and so they formulate recipes using a lye excess (extra lye). Unsaponified oils are what cloud liquid soap, so using extra lye ensures that every single oil molecule is saponified. The lye excess is then neutralized, and you're left with a crystal-clear soap. To be honest, I find this type of soap drying to the skin, and the process is very intimidating, with extra steps, measurements, and ingredients.

I prefer to make a liquid soap that has a bit of a superfat (free-floating oils). I enter my recipes into a lye calculator that takes into account that potassium hydroxide is only about 90 percent pure. I then choose a 3 percent superfat. It feels more nourishing and gentle on the skin. The soap is a bit cloudy, but I liken it to natural apple cider vinegar. Natural and unprocessed apple cider vinegar is cloudy and has "the mother" in it, which contains lots of nutrients, good bacteria, and acetic acid. The same can be said for cloudy liquid soap. It has some superfat in it, which makes a more nourishing soap. The cloudiness looks natural to me.

I'm hoping that after you read this section on liquid soapmaking, you'll be able to confidently create a beautiful liquid soap that you can be very proud of.

Cook Your Soap

Liquid soap can be cooked using two different methods.

Slow cooker: This common method for cooking liquid soap allows for gentle and even cooking. Be sure to cover the slow cooker to prevent evaporation. This is the process that I use throughout this section.

Oven: You can also put your soap in a covered stainless-steel pot and cook in the oven on the lowest setting, usually around 170°F.

Make Your Soap

Let's make liquid soap!

SAFETY FIRST: Remember to wear goggles and gloves. Mix the lye solution in a well-ventilated area with access to a sink for flushing with water. Keep your work space free from distractions, small children, and pets.

Step 1: Prepare the base oils. Place a microwave-safe bowl on the scale and hit tare to zero the scale. Weigh each oil from your recipe into the bowl, pressing the tare button in between oils to zero the scale.

Step 2: Heat the bowl in the microwave until all the oils are melted.

Step 3: Pour the oils into your slow cooker, carefully scraping the bowl with a silicone spatula. You can also weigh the oils into your slow cooker on medium to melt, but microwaving is much quicker.

Step 4: Weigh the water by placing a lye solution container on the scale and hitting tare to zero the scale. Weigh the water and set aside.

Step 5: Weigh the potassium hydroxide by placing another container on the scale and hitting the tare button to zero the scale. Weigh the potassium hydroxide.

Step 6: Following safety precautions, pour the potassium hydroxide into the water while stirring. Turn your head and lean away from the lye solution. Stir until all the granules have

Step 1

Step 2

Step 5

Step 6

Step 6, continued

Step 7

Step 8

Step 8, continued

Step 8, continued

dissolved. Let the lye solution sit until it has cleared up, about 5 minutes.

Step 7: Pour the lye solution into your melted oils. You don't have to let the lye solution cool like you do for cold-process soap. In fact, a hot lye solution helps liquid soap emulsify and trace faster.

Step 8: Mix your soap paste to thick trace using a stick blender. It might go through some stages during the blending, including thickening to a pudding stage, liquefying again, and then getting to hard trace. Hard trace is like thick taffy, so thick and hard that you can't even stir it. It might take 10 to 20 minutes of mixing to get to this stage.

→

Step 9

Step 9, continued

Step 9: Cook your soap paste on medium for an hour. During the cook, it might start rising up a bit around the outside. You'll notice that it is starting to turn translucent. After 1 hour, give it a good stir and check to see if it is done. To know when liquid soap is done, check for the following signs:

* It should all be translucent.
* See if it zaps. Grab a bit of soap paste on a spoon. Blow on it to cool it down. Touch it to your tongue. If it zaps (feels like an electric shock), that means that it has active lye in it, so you'll need to keep cooking.
* Condensation will form on the lid and drop down onto the soap, diluting it a bit. If this diluted soap is clear, your soap is usually done. If it's cloudy, your soap needs to keep cooking.

Step 10: If your soap is not done after 1 hour, keep cooking for another hour, then test again. Liquid soap can take anywhere from 1 to 3 hours to cook. It all depends on your oils, lye solution temperatures, and slow cooker temperatures.

Step 11: Once you're done cooking, you'll have a soap paste that can be diluted to make liquid soap. You have two options: you can store the paste in an airtight container, or dilute it right away. You can also store half of your soap paste and dilute half now. It's completely up to you!

Diluting Your Liquid Soap

When you're just starting out, diluting liquid soap takes some trial and error. You'll need different amounts of water depending on your oil combination. Start with less water than you think you'll need for dilution, and go up from there. You don't want to thin out your liquid soap too much; it can be hard to thicken it back up.

I like to start dilution with 75 percent of my paste weight in water. So, if I have 1,200 grams of paste, I'll add 900 grams of water to dilute.

Step 1: Weigh your soap paste into a stainless-steel pot. Note the weight in grams.

Step 2: Multiply your total soap paste weight by 0.75. This will tell you how much distilled water to add for dilution.

Step 3: Add your water to the pot with the paste and set your burner to medium-high heat. Break up your paste a bit using a spoon or spatula. Smaller pieces of soap paste will dissolve more quickly. Heat until the soap starts to boil. Don't leave your soap unattended or it could boil over!

Step 4: Turn off the heat and cover the pot with a lid. Allow this mixture to sit overnight to dissolve. Liquid soap takes time to dissolve and dilute. The soap particles must absorb the water. When I make liquid soap, I set it to dilute before I go to bed. When I wake up, it has absorbed most of the water. Stirring does not help. Some people think they can use a stick blender to break up the clumps, but that usually just adds bubbles and creates a thick foam that doesn't dissolve.

Step 1

Step 3

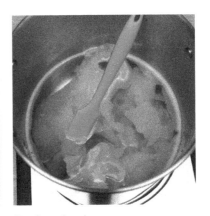
Step 3, continued

→

Step 5: If the soap has not fully dissolved overnight, you can add more water. You'll know that you need more water to dissolve your paste if your liquid soap has a thick skin on top of it and chunks of soap paste down below. Add water in 100- to 150-gram increments. If you add too much, you'll get thin, runny soap.

Heat your soap back up before you add water, following the instructions in step 3, and allow it to sit again to dissolve more paste. I usually find that soap paste needs around 75 to 100 percent of the paste weight in water to fully dissolve without thinning out too much.

Liquid Soap Pro Tips

- A salt solution can be used to thicken liquid soap that is too thin. Dissolve 5 grams of fine sea salt in 25 grams of hot distilled water. Add this salt solution to 1,000 grams of heated liquid soap and stir well. As it cools, the soap should thicken up.

- If your liquid soap separates during the cook, no big deal! Mix it back to emulsion using your stick blender, or mix by hand.

- You can thin your liquid soap down for foaming pump bottles by mixing equal parts liquid soap and distilled water.

- Generally, liquid soap does not need a preservative because of the high pH. If you thin your liquid soap down for foaming pump bottles, however, I recommend adding a preservative, such as Phenonip, as high dilution greatly lowers the pH. Follow the supplier's recommended usage rates.

- Store your liquid soap in a cool, dry area away from direct sunlight.

- When bottling your liquid soap, cool it completely before putting the cap on, or condensation will form inside the bottle.

Liquid Soap Troubleshooting

Issue: Your liquid soap won't trace.

CAUSE/WAYS TO PREVENT: Make sure your oils and lye solution are heated to between 120°F and 160°F. Heat helps the process. Room-temperature oils and lye solution will take much longer to trace.

FIX: Turn your slow cooker on, if you haven't already, and allow the mixture to heat up. Once hot, start mixing again.

Issue: Soap zaps when you test it. This means that you have active lye in your soap.

CAUSE/WAYS TO PREVENT: If you measured everything correctly, this means that your soap needs to cook longer.

FIX: Keep cooking your soap.

Issue: Soap mixture separates during the cook.

CAUSE/WAYS TO PREVENT: Be sure that you are at true trace before you set your soap to cook.

FIX: Emulsify it back together using a stick blender.

Issue: Soap paste won't dissolve.

CAUSE/WAYS TO PREVENT: N/A

FIX: It takes gentle heat and time for soap paste to dissolve. Heat up your soap and water mixture, turn off the heat, and allow it to sit overnight.

Adding Essential Oil Blends to Liquid Soap

The fun thing about liquid soap is that you can test out many different blends in a single batch of soap. You don't have to scent the whole batch using the same essential oils. Below are some of my favorite essential oil blends.

Essential oils are added to liquid soap at a rate of 1 percent of total diluted soap. That means if you have 1,000 grams of diluted liquid soap, you'll add 10 grams total of essential oils. The below blends can be added to 1,000 grams of liquid soap, but I've also provided the percentages in case you need to modify the amount you use. Here's a step-by-step process for adding these oils to your soap.

Step 1: Place a stainless-steel pot on a scale and hit the tare button to zero the scale.

Step 2: Weigh out 1,000 grams of liquid soap.

Step 3: Warm the liquid soap on low heat to between 90°F and 110°F. Warming the liquid soap helps it to blend with the essential oils more easily.

Step 4: Weigh your essential oils into a glass jar while your soap is warming.

Step 5: Remove your soap from the heat, add the essential oils, and mix well.

Step 6: You can now bottle your liquid soap. Use a funnel to pour it into bottles. Wait to cap the bottles until the liquid soap has cooled completely.

FAVORITE ESSENTIAL OIL BLENDS FOR LIQUID SOAP

You can certainly experiment, but here are some great blends to start with. Add any of these blends to the liquid soap base recipes in section two.

WOODS

* 6 grams (60%) lemon essential oil
* 2 grams (20%) spruce essential oil
* 2 grams (20%) cedarwood essential oil

HARMONY

* 4 grams (40%) lavender essential oil
* 2 grams (20%) patchouli essential oil
* 2 grams (20%) lime essential oil
* 2 grams (20%) ylang-ylang essential oil

RELAX AND BALANCE

* 4 grams (40%) lavender essential oil
* 3 grams (30%) geranium essential oil
* 3 grams (30%) clary sage essential oil

CITRUS MORNING

* 5 grams (50%) orange essential oil
* 3 grams (30%) lemon essential oil
* 2 grams (20%) litsea essential oil

SWEET EARTH

* 3 grams (30%) lavender essential oil
* 2 grams (20%) geranium essential oil
* 2 grams (20%) patchouli essential oil
* 2 grams (20%) lemongrass essential oil
* 1 gram (10%) juniper berry essential oil

ALMOND ORANGE

* 7 grams (70%) orange essential oil
* 3 grams (30%) bitter almond essential oil

CITRUS MINT

* 5 grams (50%) orange essential oil
* 3 grams (30%) peppermint essential oil
* 2 grams (20%) litsea essential oil

GARDEN BLEND

* 5 grams (50%) lavender essential oil
* 2 grams (20%) spearmint essential oil
* 2 grams (20%) peppermint essential oil
* 1 gram (10%) sweet basil essential oil

MINT-GRAPEFRUIT

* 6 grams (60%) grapefruit essential oil
* 3 grams (30%) peppermint essential oil
* 1 gram (10%) ylang-ylang essential oil

WARM WINTER

* 4 grams (40%) ginger grass essential oil
* 3 grams (30%) orange essential oil
* 2 grams (20%) lemon essential oil
* 1 gram (10%) clove essential oil

MORNING WAKE-UP

* 4 grams (40%) lemon essential oil
* 3 grams (30%) rosemary essential oil
* 2 grams (20%) lavender essential oil
* 1 gram (10%) peppermint essential oil

LAVENDER-PEPPERMINT

* 7 grams (70%) lavender essential oil
* 3 grams (30%) peppermint essential oil

TEA TREE BLEND

* 5 grams (50%) tea tree essential oil
* 2 grams (20%) lavender essential oil
* 2 grams (20%) peppermint essential oil
* 1 gram (10%) rosemary essential oil

CINNAMON-ORANGE

* 8 grams (80%) orange essential oil
* 2 grams (20%) cinnamon leaf essential oil

ALMOND

* 4 grams (40%) bitter almond essential oil
* 4 grams (40%) lavender essential oil
* 2 grams (20%) ylang-ylang essential oil

Olive Oil Liquid Soap Base

VEGAN

This is a gentle liquid soap base that is made mostly of olive oil. It is low-cleansing, meaning it doesn't strip your skin of natural oils, and it's great for those with sensitive skin. It's also a low-lather liquid soap.

YIELD: 1,967 to 2,248 grams of diluted liquid soap

START TO FINISH TIME: 2 to 3 hours to create soap paste, 24 hours to dilute

LYE DISCOUNT: 3%

SAFETY FIRST: Remember to wear goggles and gloves. Mix the lye solution in a well-ventilated area with access to a sink for flushing with water. Keep your work space free from distractions, small children, and pets.

EQUIPMENT

* Digital scale
* Microwave-safe batch container
* Slow cooker
* Silicone spatulas
* Lye solution container
* Dry lye container
* Stick blender

INGREDIENTS

Base Oils (600 grams)

* 420 grams (80%) olive oil
* 180 grams (20%) 76-degree coconut oil

Lye Solution

* 393 grams distilled water
* 131 grams potassium hydroxide

Water for Dilution

* 843 to 1,124 grams distilled water

→

Step 1: Weigh the olive and coconut oils into the microwave-safe container.

Step 2: Heat the oils in the microwave until melted.

Step 3: Pour the oil mixture into your slow cooker, carefully scraping the bowl with a silicone spatula. Set your slow cooker to medium heat.

Step 4: Prepare your lye solution by weighing the water into your lye solution container.

Step 5: Weigh the potassium hydroxide into your dry lye container.

Step 6: Following safety precautions, pour the potassium hydroxide into the water while stirring. Turn your head and lean away from the lye solution. Stir until all the granules have dissolved.

Step 7: As soon as your lye solution has started to clear up, pour it into your melted oils and use a stick blender to mix until you reach a taffy-like trace. This can take up to 20 minutes.

Step 8: Let your soap cook on medium heat until it tests neutral.

Step 9: Once your paste is done, you can dilute it using the 843 to 1,124 grams of water (see directions, page 187).

Step 10: Once diluted, choose a blend from Favorite Essential Oil Blends for Liquid Soap (page 191) to scent your soap.

Coconut Oil Cleaning Liquid Soap Base

VEGAN

This is a liquid soap suitable for use in DIY household cleaners. It has a 0 percent superfat, so it's too harsh to use on the skin. Instead, combine it with vinegar and essential oils for a natural household cleaner.

~~~~~~

YIELD: 2,247 to 2,568 grams of diluted liquid soap

START TO FINISH TIME: 2 to 3 hours to create soap paste, 24 hours to dilute

LYE DISCOUNT: 0%

SAFETY FIRST: Remember to wear goggles and gloves. Mix the lye solution in a well-ventilated area with access to a sink for flushing with water. Keep your work space free from distractions, small children, and pets.

~~~~~~

EQUIPMENT

* Digital scale
* Microwave-safe batch container
* Slow cooker
* Silicone spatulas
* Lye solution container
* Dry lye container
* Stick blender

INGREDIENTS

Base Oils (600 grams)

* 600 grams (100%) 76-degree coconut oil

Lye Solution

* 513 grams distilled water
* 171 grams potassium hydroxide

Water for Dilution

* 963 to 1,284 grams distilled water

Step 1: Weigh the coconut oil into the microwave-safe container.

Step 2: Heat the coconut oil in the microwave until melted.

Step 3: Pour the coconut oil into your slow cooker, carefully scraping the bowl with a silicone spatula. Set your slow cooker to medium heat.

Step 4: Prepare your lye solution by weighing the water into your lye solution container.

Step 5: Weigh the potassium hydroxide into your dry lye container.

Step 6: Following safety precautions, pour the potassium hydroxide into the water while stirring. Turn your head and lean away from the lye solution. Stir until all the granules have dissolved.

Step 7: As soon as your lye solution has started to clear up, pour it into your melted oils and use a stick blender to mix until you reach a taffy-like trace. This can take up to 20 minutes.

Step 8: Let your soap cook on medium heat until it tests neutral.

Step 9: Once your paste is done, you can dilute it using the 963 to 1,284 grams of water (see directions, page 187).

> **Tip:** *Once diluted, combine 2 cups of white vinegar, 2 tablespoons of this liquid soap, and 15 drops of essential oils (see page 191 for possible combinations) into a spray bottle for an all-purpose surface cleaner.*

Sunflower Oil Liquid Soap Base

VEGAN

Sunflower oil is one of my favorite oils to use in liquid soap. It is high in oleic acid and creates a gentle, nourishing soap.

YIELD: 2,000 to 2,286 grams of diluted liquid soap

START TO FINISH TIME: 2 to 3 hours to create soap paste, 24 hours to dilute

LYE DISCOUNT: 3%

SAFETY FIRST: Remember to wear goggles and gloves. Mix the lye solution in a well-ventilated area with access to a sink for flushing with water. Keep your work space free from distractions, small children, and pets.

EQUIPMENT

* Digital scale
* Microwave-safe batch container
* Slow cooker
* Silicone spatulas
* Lye solution container
* Dry lye container
* Stick blender

INGREDIENTS

Base Oils (600 grams)

* 240 grams (40%) olive oil
* 180 grams (30%) 76-degree coconut oil
* 180 grams (30%) high oleic sunflower oil

Lye Solution

* 405 grams distilled water
* 135 grams potassium hydroxide

Water for Dilution

* 857 to 1,143 grams distilled water

Step 1: Weigh the olive, coconut, and sunflower oils into the microwave-safe container.

Step 2: Heat the oils in the microwave until melted.

Step 3: Pour the oil mixture into your slow cooker, carefully scraping the bowl with a silicone spatula. Set your slow cooker to medium heat.

Step 4: Prepare your lye solution by weighing the water into your lye solution container.

Step 5: Weigh the potassium hydroxide into your dry lye container.

Step 6: Following safety precautions, pour the potassium hydroxide into the water while stirring. Turn your head and lean away from the lye solution. Stir until all the granules have dissolved.

Step 7: As soon as your lye solution has started to clear up, pour it into your melted oils and use a stick blender to mix until you reach a taffy-like trace, up to 20 minutes.

Step 8: Let your soap cook on medium heat until it tests neutral.

Step 9: Once your paste is done, you can dilute it using the 857 to 1,143 grams of water (see directions, page 187).

Step 10: Once diluted, you can choose a blend from Favorite Essential Oil Blends for Liquid Soap (page 191) to scent your soap.

Tip: *Be sure to use high oleic sunflower oil when making any kind of soap. It has a longer shelf life than regular sunflower oil, which can go rancid quickly.*

Jojoba Oil Liquid Soap Base

VEGAN

Jojoba oil is a liquid wax. It mirrors the sebum in our own skin and creates a barrier, trapping in moisture—this is a very good thing!

YIELD: 1,981 to 2,264 grams of diluted liquid soap

START TO FINISH TIME: 2 to 3 hours to create soap paste, 24 hours to dilute

LYE DISCOUNT: 3%

SAFETY FIRST: Remember to wear goggles and gloves. Mix the lye solution in a well-ventilated area with access to a sink for flushing with water. Keep your work space free from distractions, small children, and pets.

EQUIPMENT

* Digital scale
* Microwave-safe batch container
* Slow cooker
* Silicone spatulas
* Lye solution container
* Dry lye container
* Stick blender

INGREDIENTS

Base Oils (600 grams)

* 210 grams (35%) 76-degree coconut oil
* 240 grams (40%) olive oil
* 120 grams (20%) castor oil
* 30 grams (5%) jojoba oil

Lye Solution

* 399 grams distilled water
* 133 grams potassium hydroxide

Water for Dilution

* 849 to 1,132 grams distilled water

Step 1: Weigh the coconut, olive, castor, and jojoba oils into the microwave-safe container.

Step 2: Heat the oils in the microwave until melted.

Step 3: Pour the oil mixture into your slow cooker, carefully scraping the bowl with a silicone spatula. Set your slow cooker to medium heat.

Step 4: Prepare your lye solution by weighing the water into your lye solution container.

Step 5: Weigh the potassium hydroxide into your dry lye container.

Step 6: Following safety precautions, pour the potassium hydroxide into the water while stirring. Turn your head and lean away from the lye solution. Stir until all the granules have dissolved.

Step 7: As soon as your lye solution has started to clear up, pour it into your melted oils and use a stick blender to mix until you reach a taffy-like trace, up to 20 minutes.

Step 8: Let your soap cook on medium heat until it tests neutral.

Step 9: Once your paste is done, you can dilute it using the 849 to 1,132 grams of water (see directions, page 187).

Step 10: Once diluted, you can choose a blend from Favorite Essential Oil Blends for Liquid Soap (page 191) to scent your soap.

Tip: *Jojoba oil does contain unsaponifiables, which can cloud liquid soap, so I like to use it at 5 percent or less.*

Avocado Oil Liquid Soap Base

VEGAN

Avocado oil is high in vitamin E and other helpful vitamins for your skin. It is used especially for sensitive and older skin.

~~~~~~

YIELD: 2,016 to 2,304 grams of diluted liquid soap

START TO FINISH TIME: 2 to 3 hours to create soap paste, 24 hours to dilute

LYE DISCOUNT: 3%

SAFETY FIRST: Remember to wear goggles and gloves. Mix the lye solution in a well-ventilated area with access to a sink for flushing with water. Keep your work space free from distractions, small children, and pets.

~~~~~~

EQUIPMENT

* Digital scale
* Microwave-safe batch container
* Slow cooker
* Silicone spatulas
* Lye solution container
* Dry lye container
* Stick blender

INGREDIENTS

Base Oils (600 grams)

* 240 grams (40%) 76-degree coconut oil
* 150 grams (25%) olive oil
* 150 grams (25%) avocado oil
* 60 grams (10%) castor oil

Lye Solution

* 414 grams distilled water
* 138 grams potassium hydroxide

Water for Dilution

* 864 to 1,152 grams distilled water

Step 1: Weigh the coconut, olive, avocado, and castor oils into the microwave-safe container.

Step 2: Heat the oils in the microwave until melted.

Step 3: Pour the oil mixture into your slow cooker, carefully scraping the bowl with a silicone spatula. Set your slow cooker to medium heat.

Step 4: Prepare your lye solution by weighing the water into your lye solution container.

Step 5: Weigh the potassium hydroxide into your dry lye container.

Step 6: Following safety precautions, pour the potassium hydroxide into the water while stirring. Turn your head and lean away from the lye solution. Stir until all the granules have dissolved.

Step 7: As soon as your lye solution has started to clear up, pour the lye solution into your melted oils and use a stick blender to mix until you reach a taffy-like trace, up to 20 minutes.

Step 8: Let your soap cook on medium heat until it tests neutral.

Step 9: Once your paste is done you can dilute it using the 864 to 1,152 grams of water (see directions, page 187).

Step 10: Once diluted, you can choose a blend from the Favorite Essential Oil Blends for Liquid Soap (page 191) to scent your soap.

Rose Geranium Soap, page 228

Loofah Spa Soap, page 222

Java-Mint Scrub Soap, page 219

Lavender-Orange
Soap, page 224

Calendula & Grapefruit
Embed Soap, page 226

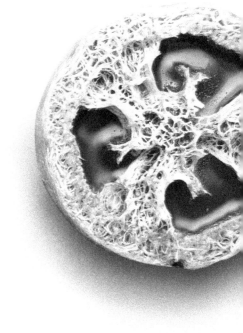

06

Melt-and-Pour Soapmaking

Melt-and-pour soapmaking is great fun and allows for endless creativity. It's a good way to try out soapmaking without handling lye. Lye was used to create the melt-and-pour soap base, but you won't have to work with it directly. You'll melt the base down to add scent, color, and additives, and then pour it into a mold to harden. Melt-and-pour is a particularly wonderful craft to do with kids.

Recipes

* Java-Mint Scrub Soap 219

* Loofah Spa Soap 222

* Lavender-Orange Soap 224

* Calendula & Grapefruit
  Embed Soap 226

* Rose Geranium Soap 228

* Seaweed & Lemon Soap 230

Melt-and-Pour Soapmaking Step-by-Step

Before you get started, let's go over the materials you'll need and techniques you'll use to make melt-and-pour soap.

Choose a Soap Base

Selecting a melt-and-pour base is a matter of preference. Soap bases range from simple white and clear bases to more exotic bases such as aloe, shea butter, goat milk, hemp, honey, olive, and more. I look for a soap base that is as natural as can be, made with organic ingredients. You can also find palm-free bases, although they are a bit more expensive.

Soap bases typically come in either clear or white. The white bases are whitened using titanium dioxide, which natural soapmakers typically avoid. As an alternative, I recommend buying a more natural clear base and whitening it with zinc oxide.

It's easy to estimate how much soap base you'll need to fill a mold. Fill the mold with water, place an empty container on a scale, hit the tare button to zero the scale, and then pour the water into the container to weigh. You'll need an equivalent amount of soap base to fill the mold.

Melt Your Soap Base

Melt-and-pour soap base can be melted using a few different methods:

Microwave: One of the easiest ways to melt soap is in the microwave. Cut your soap base into chunks, and place it into a heatproof container, such as a large glass measuring bowl. Cover with plastic wrap to prevent evaporation, and heat in 30-second bursts, stirring in between to ensure an even melt.

Double boiler: Using a double boiler to melt your soap base ensures that the soap doesn't burn. Use a lid or cover your top container with plastic wrap to prevent evaporation.

Slow cooker: If you plan on creating several melt-and-pour projects at once, you can melt a large amount of melt-and-pour in a slow cooker and leave it on warm or low to keep it fluid. Cover to prevent evaporation.

DISPERSE YOUR COLORANTS

If you add powdered herbs and spices directly to your melted soap base, they might clump and fail to mix in easily. Instead, disperse these colorants in isopropyl alcohol and mix in a small cup or shot glass. Mix again right before adding to your soap to make sure all your colorant is well mixed and not stuck to the bottom of your container.

SPRAY SOAP WITH ALCOHOL

Spraying your soap with alcohol after pouring into a mold helps pop any bubbles. Spraying between layers helps them adhere to one another and not come apart in the shower.

I recommend 99 percent isopropyl alcohol for spraying your soap or dispersing colorants. This high-proof alcohol leaves behind less water after evaporating. If you can't find this type of alcohol, using 91 percent or 70 percent is fine.

Make Your Soap

Let's make some melt-and-pour soap!

〜〜〜〜〜〜〜〜〜〜〜〜〜〜〜〜〜〜〜〜〜〜

SAFETY FIRST: Remember that melt-and-pour is hot once melted. Take care when heating and pouring your soap, especially if children are helping.

〜〜〜〜〜〜〜〜〜〜〜〜〜〜〜〜〜〜〜〜〜〜

Prep ahead: If you are pre-dispersing your colorants or additives in alcohol, get them measured and ready to go using the instructions on page 207. Weigh the essential oils for your batch into a glass container and set aside.

Step 1: Cut the soap base into even 1-inch cubes. This allows the soap to melt more evenly and quickly.

Step 2: Using a scale, weigh the desired amount of soap into a heat-proof container.

Step 3: Melt your melt-and-pour soap base.

Step 4: Add scent, color, and additives. Stir well.

Step 5: Pour the soap into your mold.

Step 6: Immediately spray the soap with alcohol to pop any bubbles on the surface. Your soap will start to harden and a thick skin will form.

Step 7: Let the soap harden and cool. This will take anywhere from minutes to hours, depending on the mold(s). Soaps in small individual cavities will cool in minutes, compared with a large loaf-style mold, which might take hours.

Step 2

Step 3

Step 4

Step 5

Step 6

Step 9

Step 8: Clean up: Rinse containers and utensils with hot water.

Step 9: Unmold the soap. If using loaf molds, you can cut the soap as soon as you unmold it. Slice the soap into bars.

Step 10: Immediately wrap the bars in plastic wrap or shrink wrap film to protect against sweating. Melt-and-pour soap is ready to use right away, with no curing necessary.

Melt-and-Pour Pro Tips

- Temperature matters when it comes to crafting with melt-and-pour soap. High temperatures can cause brittleness and dehydration. A good range is between 120°F and 130°F. Typically, you don't want to heat it above 140°F, but double-check the temperatures from the manufacturer of your soap base. I recommend using an infrared thermometer to easily check temperatures; stir the soap first since the thermometer takes the surface temperature.

- You can add superfat oils or butters to melt-and-pour, though most bases come already superfatted. Add ½ teaspoon per 450 grams of melt-and-pour base. Superfatting can diminish lather, so less is more.

- If your melt-and-pour starts solidifying before you get it poured, pop it back into the microwave and heat in 10-second bursts.

- If your additives or colorants are sinking to the bottom of your melt-and-pour, let your soap thicken before you pour it into the mold. Wait until the last possible second to pour. There are also suspension bases you can use that more easily suspend things like seeds, herb powders, pumice, etc.

- You can purchase a cold-process–like, low-sweat melt-and-pour base. This allows you to add melt-and-pour embeds (see Embedding Melt-and-Pour, page 216) to cold-process soap or to create melt-and-pour bars that won't sweat as much as regular bases.

- Melt only as much soap as you need. Remelting soap can cause dehydration, resulting in brittle or off-colored soap.

- Store any unused soap base in airtight containers.

- If your melt-and-pour soap bars have fingerprints from handling, spray them with alcohol to remove the prints.

Melt-and-Pour Troubleshooting

Issue: Layers come apart when cutting.

CAUSE/WAYS TO PREVENT: Spray a generous amount of 99 percent isopropyl alcohol on the first layer before pouring the second. This ensures they will stick together.

FIX: You can use the soap as is or melt and re-create your soap.

Issue: Layers or embeds melt.

CAUSE/WAYS TO PREVENT: Pour the soap at cooler temperatures. The melting occurs because your soap is too hot.

FIX: N/A

Issue: Bubbles on surface of soap.

CAUSE/WAYS TO PREVENT: Spray the top of your soap with 99 percent isopropyl alcohol to pop the bubbles immediately after you pour.

FIX: You can remelt, but this isn't usually a major issue.

Issue: Soap is sweating. The high glycerin content in melt-and-pour soap is a humectant and attracts moisture. This can show up as water droplets or a crystal-like covering.

CAUSE/WAYS TO PREVENT: Wrap your soap tightly in plastic wrap or shrink wrap. You can also use a low-sweat melt-and-pour base if you live in a humid climate.

FIX: You can try spraying with 99 percent isopropyl alcohol and then drying in front of a fan. Quickly wrap soap to prevent further sweating.

Issue: Soap boils when heated.

CAUSE/WAYS TO PREVENT: Melt-and-pour should never be boiled. You've overheated it. Use an infrared thermometer to check temperature, and melt in 30-second bursts if you're using the microwave.

FIX: Your melt-and-pour soap might end up gloppy and unpourable. This is an aesthetic issue.

Issue: Burnt soap. Off-smelling and/or yellow tinted.	**CAUSE/WAYS TO PREVENT:** Heat gently and check temperature as stated previously. **FIX:** You can use this soap; it just might have a faint burnt smell.
Issue: Botanicals on or in soap have turned brown.	**CAUSE/WAYS TO PREVENT:** Most herbs turn brown or black in soap. Try calendula, which might stay yellow. **FIX:** N/A
Issue: Soap turns tan or brown.	**CAUSE/WAYS TO PREVENT:** Your fragrance oil might contain vanilla. Check with your supplier for vanilla content. **FIX:** N/A
Issue: Clumps of color in soap.	**CAUSE/WAYS TO PREVENT:** Dissolve or disperse powder colorants in alcohol or liquid glycerin before adding to soap base. **FIX:** Remelt and stir the color in more.
Issue: Pockmarks on detailed bar of soap.	**CAUSE/WAYS TO PREVENT:** Spray the detailed soap mold with 99 percent isopropyl alcohol before pouring in the soap. This helps the soap spread and get into every little nook and cranny. **FIX:** Remelt and try again.
Issue: Soap is stuck in mold.	**CAUSE/WAYS TO PREVENT:** This just happens at times. You probably didn't do anything wrong. Humidity can cause soap to stick in the mold. **FIX:** Freeze your soap, and see if that shrinks it enough to remove from mold.
Issue: Soap is oozing essential oil.	**CAUSE/WAYS TO PREVENT:** The scent has not been thoroughly blended. **FIX:** Try remelting and mix more, or you can use the soap as is.

Layering Melt-and-Pour

Because melt-and-pour cools quickly, it's easy to create crisp, clean layers. You can create a soap design using as many layers as you're brave enough to try, from two colors to 20!

Prep ahead: Prepare your colorants if you plan to disperse them in alcohol, and weigh your essential oils.

Step 1: Cut your soap base into even 1-inch cubes. You will need a heat-proof container for each color you are using.

Step 2: Use a scale to weigh the desired amount of soap into each heat-proof container. Use equal amounts for even layers, or divide unevenly for thinner or thicker layers.

Step 3: Melt the soap base for the first layer.

Step 4: Add scent and color. If you are creating two equal layers, add about half of the total amount to each layer. If you are creating four layers, add 25 percent to each layer.

Step 2

Step 3

Step 4

→

Step 5

Step 7

Step 7, continued

Step 7, continued

Step 5: Pour the soap into the mold and immediately spray the surface with 99 percent isopropyl alcohol to pop any bubbles.

Step 6: Allow the first layer to harden enough to support the next layer. To test if the first layer is hard enough, tilt the mold a bit to see if the soap moves underneath the skin that has formed. If you have a ripple, let it harden a bit longer. You can also blow on the skin that has formed and see if it ripples or stays solid.

Step 7, continued   Step 9

Step 7: Once the first layer has hardened, repeat steps 3 to 6 for each additional layer. Right before you pour a layer, generously spray the set layer with 99 percent isopropyl alcohol. This will help the next layer adhere and prevent your soap from breaking apart during use. Keep the temperature for each additional layer closer to 120°F (see Melt-and-Pour Pro Tips, page 210) so it doesn't melt the layer you're pouring onto.

Step 8: Spray the surface of the final layer with alcohol to pop any bubbles.

Step 9: Let the soap harden. Unmold and cut the soap, immediately wrapping in plastic to protect against sweating.

Embedding Melt-and-Pour

Embedding soap is when you place pre-hardened pieces of melt-and-pour soap into a new batch of melt-and-pour soap. The embed soaps can be shapes cut out using a cookie cutter, pieces grated to look like confetti, curls made using a vegetable peeler, or cut-up chunks. This technique allows you to make unique and funky soap designs. Suppliers also sell long tube embed molds in different shapes such as hearts, moons, and flowers. This tutorial uses premade melt-and-pour soaps cut into simple square chunks as embeds.

Prep ahead: Prepare your colorants if you plan to disperse them in alcohol, and weigh your essential oils. Next, prepare the melt-and-pour embeds. I like to take two existing bars of melt-and-pour soap and cut them into ¼- to ½-inch chunks. Set aside. These will remain whole; do not melt.

Step 1: Cut soap base into even 1-inch cubes.

Step 2: Use a scale to weigh the desired amount of soap into a heat-proof container.

Step 3: Melt the soap base.

Step 4: Add the scent and color.

Step 5: Pour enough soap into the mold to create about a ¼-inch layer and immediately spray the surface with 99 percent isopropyl alcohol to pop bubbles. By pouring a bit of

Prep ahead

Step 2

Step 3

Step 4

Step 5

Step 7

Step 7, continued

soap into the mold and allowing it to harden, you are creating a platform for your embeds to rest on. Otherwise, they will sink to the bottom.

Step 6: Allow the first layer to harden enough to support the next layer. To test if the first layer is hard enough, tilt the mold a bit to see if the soap moves underneath the skin that has

formed. If you have a ripple, let it harden a bit longer. You can also blow on the skin that has formed and see if it ripples or if it stays solid.

Step 7: Spray the set layer and the embeds generously with alcohol. This will ensure that the layers stick and that the embeds don't fall out of the soap during use.

→

Step 8

Step 9

Step 10

Step 8: Pour the rest of the melted base into the mold, covering the embeds. Make sure the temperature is close to 120°F so the embeds don't melt.

Step 9: After pouring, spray the surface with alcohol to pop any bubbles.

Step 10: Let the soap harden. Unmold and cut the soap, immediately wrapping with plastic to protect against sweating.

Java-Mint Scrub Soap

VEGAN · EXFOLIATING · MINTY · CITRUS

Who doesn't love coffee? If you do, this scrubby soap is perfect to keep beside your kitchen sink for when your hands need an extra good cleaning.

~~~~~~

YIELD: 550 grams | 4 bars (138 grams each)

START TO FINISH TIME: 1 hour to create soap, 2 to 4 hours to unmold and cut

SCENT: Peppermint and orange

SAFETY FIRST: Remember that melt-and-pour is hot once melted. Take care when heating and pouring your soap, especially if children are helping.

~~~~~~

EQUIPMENT

* Digital scale
* Glass container
* Small plastic or glass cup
* Infrared thermometer
* 2 (16-ounce) heatproof glass measuring cups
* Silicone spatulas
* Measuring spoons
* 4-inch silicone loaf mold
* Fine-mist spray bottle with 99 percent isopropyl alcohol
* Plastic wrap

INGREDIENTS

Scent

* 3 grams peppermint essential oil
* 8 grams orange folded essential oil

Melt-and-Pour Soap Base

* 550 grams clear melt-and-pour soap base, divided

Colorants/Additives

* ½ teaspoon zinc oxide powder
* ¼ teaspoon 99 percent isopropyl alcohol
* 1 teaspoon finely ground coffee

→

Prep ahead: Weigh the essential oils into a glass container; blend together. In the small cup, mix the zinc oxide and alcohol.

Step 1: Cut the soap base into even 1-inch cubes.

Step 2: Use a scale to weigh 450 grams into one heatproof container and 100 grams into the other.

Step 3: Melt the 450 grams of soap for the first layer. The first layer will be the coffee scrub layer.

Step 4: Add about 8 grams of the essential oil blend and the coffee. Stir well to disperse the coffee. Allow the soap to cool until it starts to thicken up to help suspend the coffee.

Step 5: Pour the soap into the mold and immediately spray with alcohol to pop any bubbles.

Step 6: Let this first layer harden enough to support the next layer.

Step 7: Melt the 100 grams of soap.

Step 8: Add the zinc oxide mixture and the rest of the essential oils to the melted soap and mix well.

Step 9: Generously spray the set coffee scrub layer with rubbing alcohol.

Step 10: Check the temperature of the white soap base and make sure that it is 125°F or below.

Step 11: Pour the white layer over the coffee scrub layer. Spray the surface with alcohol to pop any bubbles.

Step 12: Let the soap harden. Unmold and cut the soap, immediately wrapping it in plastic to protect against sweating.

Tip: *Remember to spray each layer with alcohol before pouring the next layer or your layers will break apart.*

Loofah Spa Soap

VEGAN · BODY · EXFOLIATING · CITRUS

This fun soap uses a dried loofah embed. I used to think that loofah came from the sea, but I was wrong. Loofah grows in the garden and resembles a large cucumber. After harvest, they are left to dry and then used as scrubbing sponges—very exfoliating!

YIELD: 450 grams | 5 bars (90 grams each)

START TO FINISH TIME: 1 hour to create soap, 2 to 4 hours to unmold and cut

SCENT: Lemon and patchouli

SAFETY FIRST: Remember that melt-and-pour is hot once melted. Take care when heating and pouring your soap, especially if children are helping.

EQUIPMENT

* Digital scale
* Glass container
* Small plastic or glass cup
* Infrared thermometer
* Heatproof glass measuring cup
* Silicone spatulas
* Measuring spoons
* Round silicone mold (with at least 5 cavities)
* Fine-mist spray bottle with 99 percent isopropyl alcohol
* Plastic wrap

INGREDIENTS

Scent

* 4 grams lemon essential oil
* 2 grams patchouli essential oil
* 2 grams litsea essential oil
* 1 gram ylang-ylang essential oil

Melt-and-Pour Soap Base

* 450 grams clear melt-and-pour soap base

Colorants/Additives

* ⅛ teaspoon pre-reduced indigo crystals
* ½ teaspoon 99 percent isopropyl alcohol
* 5 (⅞-inch) slices loofah (2¼- to 2½-inch in diameter)

Prep ahead: Weigh the lemon, patchouli, litsea, and ylang-ylang essential oils into a glass container; blend together. Set aside. In the small cup, prepare your colorant by combining the indigo crystals and alcohol. Soak your whole or sliced loofah in water (see tip).

Step 1: Cut the soap base into even 1-inch cubes.

Step 2: Use a scale to weigh the soap base into a heatproof container.

Step 3: Melt the soap base.

Step 4: While the soap base is melting, wring out each loofah slice and place it into a mold cavity.

Step 5: Once the soap is melted, add the scent and color. Start by adding 4 to 6 drops of the prepared indigo solution to your soap and mix. Add more if you want a deeper blue—a little goes a long way.

Step 6: Spray each loofah in the mold with alcohol.

Step 7: Pour soap into each cavity; immediately spray the surface with alcohol to pop any bubbles.

Step 8: Let the soap harden. Unmold the soap, immediately wrapping it in plastic to protect against sweating.

Tip: *You can purchase sliced or whole loofah. If you purchase a whole loofah, use a serrated knife to slice it after soaking.*

Lavender-Orange Soap

VEGAN · BODY · FLORAL · CITRUS

This geometric design is easy to accomplish, using simple layering techniques in a tilted mold. The lavender and orange essential oil combo is refreshing and balancing. This is one of my favorite melt-and-pour soaps to make for friends and family. Once you get the basic concept down, you can use more colors and create a really stunning design.

YIELD: 550 grams | 4 bars (138 grams each)

START TO FINISH TIME: 1 hour to create soap, 2 to 4 hours to unmold and cut

SCENT: Lavender and orange

SAFETY FIRST: Remember that melt-and-pour is hot once melted. Take care when heating and pouring your soap, especially if children are helping.

EQUIPMENT

* Digital scale
* Glass container
* 2 small plastic or glass cups
* Infrared thermometer
* 2 heatproof glass measuring cups
* Silicone spatulas
* Measuring spoons
* 4-inch silicone loaf mold
* Fine-mist spray bottle with 99 percent isopropyl alcohol
* Plastic wrap

INGREDIENTS

Scent

* 6 grams orange folded essential oil
* 5 grams lavender essential oil

Melt-and-Pour Soap Base

* 550 grams clear melt-and-pour soap base, divided

Colorants/Additives

* ⅛ teaspoon alkanet powder
* ¼ teaspoon zinc oxide powder, divided
* 1 teaspoon 99 percent isopropyl alcohol, divided
* ⅛ teaspoon turmeric powder

Prep ahead: Weigh the essential oils into a glass container; blend together. Set aside. Prepare your colorants. In one small cup, mix the alkanet powder with ¼ teaspoon of zinc oxide and ½ teaspoon of alcohol. In the other small cup, mix the turmeric powder with the remaining ¼ teaspoon of zinc oxide and ½ teaspoon of alcohol. Set aside.

Step 1: Cut the soap base into even 1-inch cubes.

Step 2: Use a scale to weigh 275 grams of soap base into each glass measuring cup.

Step 3: Melt the soap base in the first measuring cup.

Step 4: Add 5 grams of the essential oil blend and the prepared alkanet and zinc oxide colorant.

Step 5: Tilt your mold about 30 degrees by placing a spoon underneath one of the long sides of the mold.

Step 6: Pour half of the alkanet-colored soap into the mold, and immediately spray with alcohol to pop any bubbles.

Step 7: Let the first layer harden completely. Once hard, tilt the mold in the opposite direction by moving the spoon under the opposite long side, then prepare the next layer.

Step 8: Melt the other soap base.

Step 9: Add the remaining 6 grams of the essential oil blend and the prepared turmeric and zinc oxide colorant.

Step 10: Spray the already-set alkanet layer with alcohol.

Step 11: Pour half of the turmeric-colored soap into the mold, and immediately spray with alcohol to pop bubbles.

Step 12: Let this second layer harden completely.

Step 13: Once hard, tilt the mold in the opposite direction again and prepare the third layer.

Step 14: Remelt the leftover alkanet soap.

Step 15: Spray the already-set turmeric layer with alcohol.

Step 16: Pour the rest of the alkanet soap into the mold.

Step 17: Once the alkanet layer has hardened, spray with alcohol and pour the last turmeric layer. The mold should be flat on your surface and not tilted for this last layer.

Step 18: Let the soap harden. Unmold and cut the soap, immediately wrapping it in plastic to protect against sweating.

Calendula & Grapefruit Embed Soap

VEGAN · BODY · EXFOLIATING · CITRUS

Using embeds in soap is great fun, because you never know exactly what you'll get until you cut. This bright and vibrant soap uses little square embeds to create a joyful, artistic design. The calendula gives the soap an interesting texture and lightly exfoliates.

YIELD: 550 grams | 4 bars (138 grams each)

START TO FINISH TIME: 1 hour to create soap, 2 to 4 hours to unmold and cut

SCENT: Grapefruit, orange, and lemongrass

SAFETY FIRST: Remember that melt-and-pour is hot once melted. Take care when heating and pouring your soap, especially if children are helping.

EQUIPMENT

* Digital scale
* Glass container
* 2 small plastic or glass cups
* Infrared thermometer
* 3 heatproof glass measuring cups
* Silicone spatulas
* Measuring spoons
* 4-inch silicone loaf mold
* Square silicone mold (with at least 4 cavities)
* Fine-mist spray bottle with 99 percent isopropyl alcohol
* Plastic wrap

INGREDIENTS

Scent

* 6 grams grapefruit essential oil
* 3 grams orange essential oil
* 2 grams lemongrass essential oil

Melt-and-Pour Soap Base (550 grams)

* 550 grams clear melt-and-pour soap base, divided

Colorants/Additives

* ⅛ teaspoon madder root powder
* 1 teaspoon 99 percent isopropyl alcohol, divided
* ⅛ teaspoon turmeric powder
* 1 tablespoon dried calendula petals

Prep ahead: Weigh the essential oils into a glass container; blend together. Set aside. Prepare your colorants. In the first small cup, mix the madder root powder with ½ teaspoon of the alcohol. In the second cup, mix the turmeric with the remaining ½ teaspoon of alcohol. Set aside.

Step 1: Cut the soap base into even 1-inch cubes.

Step 2: Use a scale to weigh 75 grams of soap into each of two heatproof measuring cups.

Step 3: Melt the soap base in the first measuring cup.

Step 4: Once the soap is melted, add 2 grams of essential oil blend. Add ¼ teaspoon of prepared madder root solution to your soap and mix well. Add more for a deeper color.

Step 5: Pour the soap into two of the square cavities of your mold. Immediately spray with alcohol to pop any bubbles.

Step 6: Repeat steps 3 to 5 with the other 75 grams of soap base, but use the turmeric solution to color it. You should now have 4 square bars of soap: 2 yellow and 2 red/orange.

Step 7: Allow these soaps to completely harden. Once hard, unmold and chop into ¼- to ½-inch cubes to use as embeds. The sizes and shapes of the embeds are completely up to you.

Step 8: Place the remaining 400 grams of soap base into the third heatproof measuring cup and melt.

Step 9: Once the soap is melted, add the remaining essential oil blend. Add the calendula petals and mix well.

Step 10: Place the loaf mold onto a scale, hit tare, and weigh 30 grams of soap base into the mold. Spray with alcohol, and let this layer harden. This layer will allow the embeds to suspend in the middle of the soap bars instead of sinking to the bottom.

Step 11: Spray the hardened layer of soap with alcohol. Spray the embeds with alcohol, and place them on top of the hardened layer of soap.

Step 12: Remelt the rest of the soap base.

Step 13: Once melted, pour the rest of the soap base over the embeds. Make sure the temperature is under 125°F or the embeds might melt. Spray with alcohol to pop bubbles.

Step 14: Let the soap harden. Unmold and cut the soap, immediately wrapping them in plastic to protect against sweating.

Rose Geranium Soap

VEGAN · BODY · FLORAL

Rose soap is a classic. This beautiful soap is colored a delicate pink using rose clay. Lavender and geranium essential oils create a pleasant and bright floral scent.

YIELD: 550 grams | 4 bars (138 grams each)

START TO FINISH TIME: 1 hour to create soap, 2 to 4 hours to unmold and cut

SCENT: Lavender and geranium

SAFETY FIRST: Remember that melt-and-pour is hot once melted. Take care when heating and pouring your soap, especially if children are helping.

EQUIPMENT

* Digital scale
* Glass container
* Small plastic or glass cup
* Infrared thermometer
* 2 heatproof glass measuring cups
* Silicone spatulas
* Measuring spoons
* 4-inch silicone loaf mold
* Fine-mist spray bottle with 99 percent isopropyl alcohol
* Plastic wrap

INGREDIENTS

Scent

* 6 grams lavender essential oil
* 5 grams geranium essential oil

Melt-and-Pour Soap Base

* 550 grams clear melt-and-pour soap base, divided

Colorants/Additives

* ⅛ teaspoon rose clay powder
* ½ teaspoon 99 percent isopropyl alcohol
* 1 tablespoon dried rose petals

Prep ahead: Weigh the lavender and geranium essential oils into a glass container; blend together. Set aside. In the small cup, prepare your colorant by mixing the rose clay and alcohol.

Step 1: Cut the soap base into even 1-inch cubes.

Step 2: Use a scale to weigh 400 grams of soap base into one glass measuring cup and 150 grams into the other.

Step 3: Melt the 400 grams of soap base.

Step 4: Add 7 grams of the essential oil blend and all the prepared rose clay color to the soap and mix.

Step 5: Pour the soap into the mold and immediately spray it with alcohol to pop any bubbles.

Step 6: Let this first layer harden enough to support the next layer (for more details, see step 6 on page 214).

Step 7: Melt the 150 grams of soap base.

Step 8: Add the rest of the essential oils and the dried rose petals and mix well. Keep a pinch of the petals to sprinkle on top.

Step 9: Spray the already-set rose clay layer with alcohol.

Step 10: Pour the soap on top of the rose clay layer and immediately spray with alcohol. Quickly sprinkle the leftover rose petals on top.

Step 11: Let the soap harden. Unmold and cut the soap, immediately wrapping in plastic to protect against sweating.

Seaweed & Lemon Soap

VEGAN · BODY · HERBAL · CITRUS

Kelp powder gives soap a wonderful natural green color. It does have a slight smell, but it's masked by the bright essential oil blend we use. Your friends and family are sure to love this ocean-inspired soap.

~~~~~~

YIELD: 550 grams | 4 bars (138 grams each)

START TO FINISH TIME: 1 hour to create soap, 2 to 4 hours to unmold and cut

SCENT: Lemon, litsea, and rosemary

SAFETY FIRST: Remember that melt-and-pour is hot once melted. Take care when heating and pouring your soap, especially if children are helping.

~~~~~~

EQUIPMENT

* Digital scale
* Glass container
* Small plastic or glass cup
* Infrared thermometer
* 2 heatproof glass measuring cups
* Silicone spatulas
* Measuring spoons
* 4-inch silicone loaf mold
* Fine-mist spray bottle with 99 percent isopropyl alcohol
* Plastic wrap

INGREDIENTS

Scent

* 5 grams lemon essential oil
* 4 grams litsea essential oil
* 1 gram rosemary essential oil

Melt-and-Pour Soap Base

* 550 grams clear melt-and-pour soap base, divided

Colorants/Additives

* ⅛ teaspoon seaweed (kelp) powder
* ½ teaspoon 99 percent isopropyl alcohol

Prep ahead: Weigh the lemon, litsea, and rosemary essential oils into a glass container; blend together. Set aside. In the small cup, prepare your colorant by combining the kelp powder and alcohol.

Step 1: Cut the soap base into even 1-inch cubes.

Step 2: Use a scale to weigh 400 grams of soap base into one glass measuring cup, and 150 grams into the other.

Step 3: Melt the 400 grams of soap base.

Step 4: Add 7 grams of the essential oil blend and all of the prepared seaweed color and mix.

Step 5: Pour the soap into the mold and immediately spray it with alcohol to pop any bubbles.

Step 6: Let this first layer harden enough to support the next layer (for more details, see step 6 on page 214).

Step 7: Melt the 150 grams of soap base.

Step 8: Add the rest of the essential oils and mix well.

Step 9: Spray the already-set seaweed layer with alcohol.

Step 10: Pour the melted soap on top of the seaweed layer and immediately spray with alcohol.

Step 11: Let the soap harden. Unmold and cut the soap, immediately wrapping in plastic to protect against sweating.

Charcoal & Anise Soap, page 245

Oatmeal, Honey & Turmeric Soap, page 248

O7

Hand-Milling Soap

Hand-milling is when you take an existing cold-process or hot-process soap, shred it, melt it, add scent, color, and additives, and then spoon it into molds. The resulting soap has a rustic appearance, but that's part of its handmade charm.

Recipes

* Charcoal & Anise Soap 245

* Oatmeal, Honey & Turmeric Soap 248

* Cornmeal Kitchen Soap 250

* Almond & Oats Soap 252

Hand-Milling Step-by-Step

Hand-milling is a useful process for soapmakers to master for several reasons. First, it's a great way to re-batch (make again) cold-process or hot-process soap that didn't come out quite as expected. I'm a believer that most batches of cold-process and hot-process soap that go wrong can be saved by re-batching. Don't be afraid to experiment. Here are some circumstances in which you might use the hand-milling process to fix a soap:

* You forgot to add an oil to your batch. Fix: Add the forgotten oil to the shreds during the cook. Mix well.

* You forgot to add scent. Fix: Add scent after the shreds have cooked.

* Your design didn't come out as planned. Fix: Re-batch to create a new design.

* Your soap separated in the mold. Fix: Chop or break into chunks, dump it into a slow cooker, and cook.

Some soapmakers actually prefer to purchase loaves of unscented and uncolored cold-process soap to hand-mill. As with melt-and-pour, if you purchase a premade base, you don't have to work with lye. Others like to make batches of unscented and uncolored cold-process soap just to hand-mill. Since the lye in hand-milled soap is already gone, the hand-milling process is easier on essential oils and more sensitive additives.

Next, you'll find some essential tips and a step-by-step process to walk you through the art of hand-milling.

Choose a Base to Hand-Mill

You can create your own soap base to hand-mill by selecting a recipe from this book and making it with just the base oils, lye, and water, leaving out the scent, color, or additives, which will be added later. As soon as the soap is saponified, usually after 24 to 48 hours, you can shred it to hand-mill. You can also use old soap, but since water evaporates out of soap over time, you'll need to add more water. Adding water helps it cook down to a consistency that can be stirred and spooned into a mold.

Add Water to Your Base

Water makes a big difference. If you add too much, your soap might shrink or warp as it evaporates during the cure. Not adding enough will cause your soap to be dry and thick, and it might look clumpy and *really* rustic.

I recommend adding 1 to 3 tablespoons of water per 450 grams of soap shreds. Use less if the soap is fresh and hasn't lost water to evaporation; use more if you're working with soap that has been curing for two or more weeks.

Melt Your Soap Base

Hand-milled soap can be melted using the same techniques as melt-and-pour (page 207). You can use a microwave, double boiler, or slow cooker. You can also put your shredded soap in a covered stainless-steel pot and cook it in the oven on the lowest setting, usually around 170°F.

Consistency Is Key

It can be tricky to know exactly when your hand-milled soap is done. Your shreds will start off opaque and eventually turn translucent as they cook. As you stir, the soap will melt together into a thick consistency, like mashed potatoes.

You can keep your soap thick and lumpy, or add more water and heat to make it more fluid. Just keep in mind that it will take longer for fluid soap to cure, as the water needs to evaporate.

You might have bits of unmelted soap in the finished product. I usually do, and I embrace the mottled look.

Disperse Your Colorants

If you add powdered herbs and spices directly to melted hand-milled soap base, they might clump and not mix in easily. Disperse your colorant in twice the amount of alcohol and mix it in a small cup or shot glass. Mix again right before you add it to your soap to make sure all your colorant is added, and not stuck to the bottom of the container.

Make Your Soap

Let's make some hand-milled soap!

SAFETY FIRST: Remember that hand-milled soap is hot once heated. Take care when heating and pouring your soap, especially if children are helping.

Prep ahead: If you are premixing your colorants or additives in 99 percent isopropyl alcohol, get them measured and ready to go. Measure the colorant or powder additive into a small cup. Add the alcohol, mix well, and set aside. Weigh the essential oils for your batch into a glass container, blend together, and set aside.

Step 1: Shred your soap. You can use a cheese grater, food processor, or my favorite tool, an electric grater. Be sure to weigh the shreds so you know how much scent, color, and additives to use.

Step 2: Wet the shreds. I recommend adding 1 to 3 tablespoons of water per 450 grams of soap shreds. Use less if the soap is fresh and hasn't lost water to evaporation. Use more if you're working with soap that has been curing for 2 or more weeks.

Step 3: Heat the shreds until they resemble translucent, lumpy mashed potatoes. Depending on the age of your soap base and how much water you use, you might have a thicker or thinner consistency from batch to batch. Stir periodically as it cooks.

Step 1

Step 2

Step 3

→

Step 3, continued

Step 5

Step 5, continued

Step 6

Step 8

Step 4: Remove the soap from the heat. Work quickly through the following steps, as the soap will harden as it cools.

Step 5: Add the prepared scent, color, and additives if you are using any. Mix gently.

Step 6: Once you have all the ingredients incorporated, spoon the soap into the mold.

Step 7: Clean up: Rinse containers and utensils with hot water.

Step 8: Once the soap is hardened, you can unmold it. If you are using individual cavity molds, your soap will harden in under an hour. Loaves or larger molds might take several hours to harden completely. If you used a loaf mold, you can cut your soap as soon as you unmold it.

Step 9: Let the soap cure for a minimum of 2 weeks. During the cure, your soap will become milder and water will evaporate, leaving you with a harder, longer-lasting bar of soap.

Hand-Milling Pro Tips

- To help your soap shreds melt easier, you can let them sit and dry a day or two and then process using a food processor. The smaller the pieces of soap, the smoother the melt.

- Do not stir your cooking soap vigorously. Fold it over and move your spoon around gently, or else you'll create foam or air bubbles.

- Experiment with adding different water amounts to your shredded base. Remember, more water equals a smoother and more fluid soap, but it can be sticky and soft upon unmolding. Less water equals a lumpier or more rustic soap that's easier to unmold and cut.

- If you don't have soap molds, you can use plastic yogurt containers, silicone ice cube trays, or small boxes lined with freezer paper.

- Instead of using water, you can add milk for a creamier lather in your finished soap!

Hand-Milling Troubleshooting

Issue: Botanicals on or in soap have turned brown.

CAUSE/WAYS TO PREVENT: Most herbs turn brown or black in soap. Calendula is one botanical that might stay yellow.

FIX: N/A

Issue: Soap turns tan or brown.

CAUSE/WAYS TO PREVENT: Your fragrance oil might contain vanilla.

FIX: N/A

Issue: Clumps of color in soap.

CAUSE/WAYS TO PREVENT: Dissolve or disperse powder colorants in alcohol or liquid glycerin before adding to soap base.

FIX: Re-shred, heat, and stir the color in more, or just use as is.

Issue: Soap is stuck in the mold.

CAUSE/WAYS TO PREVENT: You might have added too much water, which has made the soap too sticky. Try adding less next time.

FIX: Freeze the soap and see if it shrinks enough to remove from the mold.

Issue: Soap has warped or shrunk during the cure.

CAUSE/WAYS TO PREVENT: You might have added too much water. Add less next time.

FIX: N/A

Issue: Soap is oozing essential oil.

CAUSE/WAYS TO PREVENT: The scent has not been thoroughly blended.

FIX: Re-shred, heat, and stir the scent in more, or just use as is.

Hand-Milling Decorative Techniques

Swirling Hand-Milled Soap

It's simple to make swirled hand-milled soap by using a "spoon plop" technique. You won't get the fine, wispy swirls that you get by swirling cold-process soap, but you'll get some interesting patterns! Use a loaf mold for this design technique.

Step 1: Heat the soap using one of the techniques on page 207.

Step 2: Once the soap is fluid, divide it into two or more containers.

Step 3: Add color and scent to each container and mix.

Step 4: The soap won't be pourable, but you can spoon it out. Alternate spoonfuls of each colored soap into your mold. Work quickly so the soap doesn't dry in between spoonfuls. You can swirl after you plop into the mold, but it isn't necessary.

Step 1

Step 2

Step 3

→

Step 4

Step 4, continued

Step 4, continued

Step 5

Step 5: Once the soap has hardened in the mold, remove it and cut it into bars.

Step 6: Cure for a minimum of 2 weeks to allow water to evaporate.

Layering Hand-Milled Soap

Layering hand-milled soap is a great way to create an artistic bar. Choose contrasting colors so each layer stands out.

Step 1: Heat the soap using one of the techniques on page 207.

Step 2: Once the soap is fluid, divide it into two or more containers.

Step 3: Add color and scent to each container and mix.

Step 4: Spoon one color into your mold. Bang your mold onto a hard surface to flatten the layer. Spray it generously with alcohol. This helps keep the top wet so the next layer adheres.

Step 5: Immediately spoon the next color on top of the first layer. Again, bang your mold onto a hard surface to flatten. Repeat this step if you're doing more than two layers.

Step 6: Once the soap has hardened in the mold, remove it and cut it into bars.

Step 7: Cure for a minimum of 2 weeks.

Step 4

Step 5

Step 6

Decorating Hand-Milled Soap with Dried Flowers

One quick and easy way to decorate hand-milled soap is to press dried flowers into it when it's freshly molded. The only thing is you must work quickly!

Step 1: Follow the hand-milling process up to the point where you spoon your soap into a mold.

Step 2: As soon as you spoon the soap into your mold, press flowers into the soap. Rosebuds work well, as they have a small stem that can be pressed into the soap to help anchor the buds.

You can use dried flowers of any type or size; however, make sure they have a bit of a stem to push into the soap.

Step 3: Once the soap has hardened in the mold, remove it and cut it into bars if you used a loaf mold.

Step 4: Cure for a minimum of 2 weeks.

Step 2

Step 3

Hand-Milling Recipes
Charcoal & Anise Soap

VEGAN · FACE · ACNE-FIGHTING · FLORAL · MINTY

This soap is stark black and smells like licorice. Charcoal draws impurities, oils, and toxins out of the skin and has been used to clear up acne for decades. (Do not premix charcoal powder, as it repels water.) When using this soap, allow it to sit on your skin like a mask for about a minute before you rinse it off. This gives it time to work its magic.

YIELD: 450 grams | 4 bars (113 grams each)

START TO FINISH TIME: 1 hour to create soap, 2 to 4 hours to unmold, 2 weeks to cure

SCENT: Anise, peppermint, and lavender

SAFETY FIRST: Remember that hand-milled soap is hot once melted. Take care when heating and pouring your soap, especially if children are helping.

EQUIPMENT

* Digital scale
* Glass container
* 1 (16-ounce) heatproof glass measuring cup
* Silicone spatulas
* Measuring spoons
* Oval silicone mold (with at least 4 cavities)

INGREDIENTS

Scent
* 4 grams lavender essential oil
* 4 grams anise essential oil
* 2 grams peppermint essential oil

Hand-Milled Soap Base
* 450 grams unscented and uncolored soap shreds

Colorants/Additives
* ½ tablespoon charcoal powder
* 1 tablespoon dried rose petals

Prep ahead: Weigh the lavender, anise, and peppermint essential oils for your batch; blend together. Set aside.

Step 1: Wet the shreds.

Step 2: Heat the shreds until they resemble translucent, lumpy mashed potatoes.

Step 3: Remove the soap from the heat. Work quickly through the following steps, as the soap will harden as it cools.

Step 4: Add the prepared essential oil blend and charcoal to the cooked soap and mix well.

Step 5: Divide the rose petals among each mold cavity.

Step 6: Quickly spoon your soap into each mold cavity, covering the rose petals. Use a spatula to smooth it down.

Step 7: Once the soap has hardened, you can unmold it.

Step 8: Cure for a minimum of 2 weeks.

Oatmeal, Honey & Turmeric Soap

BODY · SKIN-SOOTHING · MINTY · CITRUS · WOODSY

Oatmeal is soothing to the skin, and honey and turmeric have been used as healing tonics for ages. Your family will love this nourishing soap. Turmeric is one of my favorite natural colorants and produces a bright yellow-orange bar of soap.

~~~~~~

YIELD: 450 grams | 4 bars (113 grams each)

START TO FINISH TIME: 1 hour to create soap, 2 to 4 hours to unmold, 2 weeks to cure

SCENT: Peppermint, cedarwood, spruce, and orange

SAFETY FIRST: Remember that hand-milled soap is hot once melted. Take care when heating and pouring your soap, especially if children are helping.

~~~~~~

EQUIPMENT

* Digital scale
* Glass container
* 1 (16-ounce) heatproof glass measuring cup
* Silicone spatulas
* Measuring spoons
* Oval silicone mold (with at least 4 cavities)

INGREDIENTS

Scent

* 4 grams orange essential oil
* 2 grams cedarwood essential oil
* 2 grams peppermint essential oil
* 2 grams spruce essential oil

Hand-Milled Soap Base

* 450 grams unscented and uncolored soap shreds

Colorants/Additives

* 1 teaspoon turmeric powder
* 1 teaspoon 99 percent isopropyl alcohol
* 1 teaspoon ground oats
* 1 teaspoon honey

Prep ahead: Weigh the orange, cedarwood, peppermint, and spruce essential oils; blend together. Set aside. In the small cup, prepare your colorant by mixing the turmeric powder with the alcohol.

Step 1: Wet the shreds.

Step 2: Heat the shreds until they resemble translucent, lumpy mashed potatoes.

Step 3: Remove the soap from the heat. Work quickly through the following steps, as the soap will harden as it cools.

Step 4: Add the prepared essential oil blend, ground oats, honey, and turmeric blend and mix well.

Step 5: Quickly spoon your soap into each mold cavity. Use a spatula to smooth it down.

Step 6: Once the soap has hardened, you can unmold it.

Step 7: Cure for a minimum of 2 weeks.

Tip: *Whole oats are scratchy in soap. I recommend grinding them down to a powder.*

Cornmeal Kitchen Soap

VEGAN · EXFOLIATING · HERBAL

This scrubby soap uses cornmeal as an exfoliant. The essential oil blend is bright and a bit medicinal smelling because of the tea tree oil. Keep this soap by the kitchen sink to scrub your hands after cooking or a day in the garden.

~~~~~~

YIELD: 450 grams | 4 bars (113 grams each)

START TO FINISH TIME: 1 hour to create soap, 2 to 4 hours to unmold, 2 weeks to cure

SCENT: Litsea, tea tree, and ginger

SAFETY FIRST: Remember that hand-milled soap is hot once melted. Take care when heating and pouring your soap, especially if children are helping.

~~~~~~

EQUIPMENT

* Digital scale
* Glass container
* 1 (16-ounce) heatproof glass measuring cup
* Silicone spatulas
* Measuring spoons
* Oval silicone mold (with at least 4 cavities)

INGREDIENTS

Scent

* 4 grams litsea essential oil
* 4 grams tea tree essential oil
* 2 grams ginger essential oil

Hand-Milled Soap Base

* 450 grams unscented and uncolored soap shreds

Colorants/Additives

* 1 teaspoon pink clay powder
* 1 teaspoon 99 percent isopropyl alcohol
* 1 teaspoon cornmeal

Prep ahead: Weigh the litsea, tea tree, and ginger essential oils for your batch; blend together. Set aside. In the small cup, combine the pink clay and alcohol. Set aside.

Step 1: Wet the shreds.

Step 2: Heat the shreds until they resemble translucent, lumpy mashed potatoes.

Step 3: Remove the soap from the heat. Work quickly through the following steps, as the soap will harden as it cools.

Step 4: Add the prepared essential oil blend, cornmeal, and rose clay mixture and mix well.

Step 5: Quickly spoon your soap into each mold cavity. Use a spatula to smooth it down.

Step 6: Once the soap has hardened, you can unmold it.

Step 7: Cure for a minimum of 2 weeks.

Tip: *I like to grind my cornmeal using a coffee grinder to create a powder that's less scratchy than whole cornmeal.*

Almond & Oats Soap

VEGAN · BODY · SKIN–SOOTHING · CITRUS

Bitter almond is one of my favorite essential oils. It is super potent, and a little goes a long way. I especially love it in holiday blends to add a certain bakery note. Use a food processor to finely grind your oats if you don't want an exfoliating soap. Leave them whole or slightly ground for a scratchy soap.

~~~~~~

YIELD: 450 grams | 4 bars (113 grams each)

START TO FINISH TIME: 1 hour to create soap, 2 to 4 hours to unmold, 2 weeks to cure

SCENT: Almond and orange

SAFETY FIRST: Remember that hand-milled soap is hot once melted. Take care when heating and pouring your soap, especially if children are helping.

~~~~~~

EQUIPMENT

* Digital scale
* Glass container
* 1 (16-ounce) heatproof glass measuring cup
* Silicone spatulas
* Measuring spoons
* Oval silicone mold (with at least 4 cavities)

INGREDIENTS

Scent

* 7 grams orange essential oil
* 3 grams bitter almond essential oil (50/50 blend; see tip)

Hand-Milled Soap Base

* 450 grams unscented and uncolored soap shreds

Colorants/Additives

* 1 tablespoon ground oats

Prep ahead: Weigh the orange and bitter almond essential oils for your batch; blend together. Set aside.

Step 1: Wet the shreds.

Step 2: Heat the shreds until they resemble translucent, lumpy mashed potatoes.

Step 3: Remove the soap from the heat. Work quickly through the following steps, as the soap will harden as it cools.

Step 4: Add the prepared essential oil blend and oats and mix well.

Step 5: Quickly spoon your soap into each mold cavity. Use a spatula to smooth it down.

Step 6: Once the soap has hardened, you can unmold it.

Step 7: Cure for a minimum of 2 weeks.

Tip: *Bitter almond essential oil cannot be sold pure; it comes blended (50/50) with almond carrier oil. It contains prussic acid, which is regulated by the DEA, so it must be diluted.*

08

Finishing Touches

I'm hoping that you caught the soapmaking bug, and are now interested in taking your talents and creativity to new heights. This chapter will explore some of the places you can go from here, including how to create your own recipe, and even how to package, label, and sell your own signature soaps!

Creating Your Own Cold-Process Soap Recipe

Soon after you make your first few successful batches, you're going to want to make, or formulate, your own soap recipe. Here's why:

Formulating your own soap recipes is good if you plan to go into business. You don't want someone else's recipe to be the basis for your business. Create your own.

Occasionally, a customer will ask for a custom soap. By learning how to formulate, you can easily create soaps for different skin types and purposes.

When you have a better grasp on formulation, you can more easily modify a recipe to your liking.

This section will lay out steps you can follow to formulate a new soap recipe. Before you begin doing so, be sure to review the carrier oils on pages 14 to 16.

Step 1: Decide on the purpose of your soap.

Will it be extra moisturizing, scrubby, vegan, or extra cleansing? What will be the end user's experience with the soap?

Step 2: Choose your base oils.

Most soapmakers start with specific percentages of oils and then add specialty oils and butters.

The "trifecta" is the most popular oil blend for those who want to make soap using palm oil, lard, or tallow. These three oils have similar properties and can be used interchangeably to give a soap hardness, body, and stable lather. The trifecta blend uses equal parts olive oil, coconut oil, and palm, lard, or tallow. The starting formula would look like this:

34% olive oil, 33% coconut oil, and 33% palm, lard, or tallow

If you want to use a specialty oil or butter, substitute other liquid oils for some of the olive oil and cosmetic butters for some of the palm, lard, or tallow. For example, instead of using 34% olive oil, you could use 28% olive oil and 6% argan oil. Instead of using 33% lard, use 25% lard and 8% shea butter.

If you want to create a palm-free and vegan soap, you'll need to get a little more creative. Both rice bran oil and avocado oil are high in palmitic acid. They don't create as hard a soap as palm oil, but combined with a butter, such as shea or cocoa, they make good substitutes.

Here is my favorite basic palm-free and vegan starting formula:

34% olive oil, 33% coconut oil, 15% cocoa butter, 9% avocado oil, and 9% rice bran oil

Step 3: Determine how much soap you want to make.

Most recipes in this book use 900 grams of oil (about 2 pounds). They fit into a 10-inch silicone loaf mold. When creating your own recipe, you'll need to determine how much soap your mold will hold. Most mold suppliers will tell you how much soap or what size of base oil recipe will fit in their mold. If you need to determine the amount yourself, there is a formula to help you out (see How Much Soap Will Your Mold Hold?, page 258).

Once you determine your total oil quantities, multiply the total oil amount by each individual oil percentage in your formula to determine the amount of each oil needed.

A common 10-inch silicone loaf mold will require a 900-gram oil recipe. Multiply each oil percentage by 900 to determine the amount of each oil. For example, using the palm-free formula:

* 900 x .34 = 306 grams olive oil
* 900 x .33 = 297 grams coconut oil
* 900 x .15 = 135 grams cocoa butter
* 900 x .09 = 81 grams avocado oil
* 900 x .09 = 81 grams rice bran oil

You now have your base recipe.

Step 4: Determine your superfat/lye discount.

Using a superfat or lye discount ensures that your soap will have unsaponified oil. This free-floating oil gives the soap emollient and moisturizing properties.

I recommend staying in the range of 5 to 8 percent. Superfatting lower than 5 percent can cause the finished soap to be harsh or drying. Superfatting higher than 8 percent can cause the soap to be soft, with too little lather. Keep in mind, the higher the percentage of unsaponified oils, the greater the risk of the soap becoming rancid.

Step 5: Run the base oils and superfat percentage through a lye calculator.

Now that you know what oils and the percentage of superfat you want to use, plug the numbers into a lye calculator to tell you how much lye you'll need. You can calculate your lye amount by hand, but using an online lye calculator is easier and leaves less room for error (see Lye & Essential Oil Calculators, page 271).

How Much Soap Will Your Mold Hold?

The following formulas will help you determine the total oil weight of your batch. Please note that this excludes water and lye, so it is just an estimate. If you use a water discount or if you want high peaks on your soap, you might need to add a few more ounces of oil to fill your mold.

It is important to note that all calculations here use inches and ounces. You can convert the ounces of oils to grams after you've used the formula, if you wish.

For a square or rectangular mold (loaf or slab), use the formula: (length) x (width) x (height) x 0.4

* Example: Loaf mold measures 10 inches x 3.625 inches x 2.25 inches

* Calculation: 10 x 3.625 x 2.25 x 0.4 = 32.625

* This mold would hold about 32.625 ounces of oils. You can round up or down.

For a round mold (such as a PVC or mail tube), use the formula: 3.14 x (radius) x (radius) x (height) x 0.4

* Radius equals half of the width. For a 3-inch-wide PVC pipe, the radius is 1.5 inches.

* Example: PVC pipe measures 9 inches tall and 3 inches wide (diameter).

* Calculation: 3.14 x 1.5 x 1.5 x 9 x 0.4 = 25.434

* This mold would hold about 25.434 ounces of oils. You can round up or down.

Step 6: Determine your water amount.

I use a 1:2 ratio of lye to water. More water will create a soap that is slow moving to trace, but will take longer to unmold and cut and might be sticky. Generally, discounting the water will create a soap that is faster to trace and quicker to unmold and cut. Don't be afraid to experiment with different water amounts to find out what works best with your recipe.

You can plug water percentages or ratios into a lye calculator, but this can be confusing. I use a lye calculator to determine the lye amount needed based on my superfat percentage, and then multiply the lye amount by two to obtain my water amount.

Step 7: Determine your scent, color, and/or additives.

Read through the earlier sections of the book to understand how much scent, color, and additives you can add to a soap. Learn about essential oil rates on page 2, natural colorants on page 8, and additives on page 18.

Step 8: Make your soap. Cure. Evaluate.

After a 4- to 6-week cure, evaluate your soap to see if you like it. Give it a try. What do you like about it? What don't you like about it? Ask for feedback from friends or family.

Step 9: Modify your recipe, if needed.

Here are some ideas for modifying a soap recipe to address common problems.

Your soap is too soft. You want a harder bar.

Raise the percentage of oils high in palmitic acid and stearic acid, such as palm oil, lard, tallow, shea butter, cocoa butter, mango butter, etc.

Your soap is too drying.

Raise the percentage of oils high in oleic acid, such as olive oil and other liquid oils (excluding castor).

Please note that if you raise the percentage of oils high in oleic acid, the soap will be less hard.

You can also try using a higher superfat percentage. If you used 5 percent, try 8 percent.

Your soap doesn't have much lather.

Raise the percentage of oils high in lauric acid, such as coconut oil.

Add 5 percent castor oil to the formula. Castor oil helps soap to lather by creating more solubility.

When formulating recipes, you don't always have to start from scratch. Sometimes formulating is more about modifying a recipe to make it your own. The preceding tips can help you modify a recipe.

SAFETY TIP: Any time you modify the oils in a recipe, run the new recipe through a lye calculator to obtain the required amount of lye. Each oil has its own saponification value.

Packaging Soap

Packaging puts the finishing touches on your handmade soap—it's now a beautiful gift or marketable luxury item. Different types of soap require different types of packaging. This section will help get you started.

PACKAGING COLD-PROCESS, HOT-PROCESS, AND HAND-MILLED SOAPS

These three types of soaps are all packaged in the same manner. The best packaging allows the soap to breathe; you don't want packaging that traps in moisture and doesn't allow the water to continue to evaporate out of the bar. Here are some ideas:

Cigar-style band labels: You can find templates online or even design your own. These labels wrap around the soap and leave much of it exposed. You can find printable labels at www.DIYSoapLabels.com.

Cardboard soap boxes: You can find many soap boxes online that fit bars cut from common soap molds. You can find solid boxes or more decorative boxes with cutouts.

Bags with woven material: Common materials include muslin, jute, and organza. These bags will allow the soap to breathe, and they come in a variety of colors and sizes.

Breathable shrink wrap: You can find shrink wrap made for these types of soaps that allow them to breathe.

Avoid the following packaging materials for cold-process, hot-process, and hand-milled soaps:

* Plastic wrap
* Non-breathable shrink wrap
* Plastic boxes
* Plastic bags

PACKAGING MELT-AND-POUR SOAPS

Because of the natural glycerin in melt-and-pour soap, it can easily become wet with glycerin dew if left out in the air. So, unlike the other soap styles, melt-and-pour soap should be packaged in airtight packaging, such as the following:

* Plastic wrap
* Non-breathable shrink wrap
* Plastic boxes
* Plastic bags

PACKAGING LIQUID SOAP

Liquid soap can be packaged in a variety of containers. Plastic or glass bottles are available in many shapes and sizes. Find pump tops that fit, and you're ready to go.

Labeling Soap

If you want to sell your soap, you'll need to label it. These labeling guidelines are for soapmakers in the United States. If you're in another country, you'll need to research your local regulations.

If you are selling soap and making no claims other than that it cleans, your soap will fall under Consumer Product Safety Commission (CPSC) labeling guidelines.

If you are selling soap and making cosmetic claims, such as that it is moisturizing, cleansing, beautifying, conditioning, or exfoliating, your soap is now a cosmetic and falls under the labeling laws of the Food and Drug Administration (FDA).

Here is what you'll need to include on your label:

* For soap without cosmetic claims: Identity of the product (in this case, soap), net weight, and name and address of the manufacturer. (No ingredients need to be listed, although you can certainly choose to add ingredients to your label.)

* For soap with cosmetic claims: Identity of the product (in this case, soap), net weight, name and address of the manufacturer, and ingredients declaration. An ingredients declaration is a listing of ingredients used to create a product, listed in descending order (from largest amount used to smallest amount used).

For more information on labeling soap, visit www.MarieGale.com.

Selling Soaps

It is common for bars of soap to take over your home as you experiment with different ingredients and recipes. Friends, family, and coworkers might start encouraging you to pursue a new business venture. You might have the idea that you'd like to sell your soap to at least cover the cost of making it.

Many soapmakers naturally evolve from hobbyists to businesspeople. Selling soap can be a great way to bring in a bit of extra income or completely replace your full-time income. Creating a business, however, no matter what kind, takes time, planning, and hustle.

ARE YOU READY?

It takes time to understand the chemistry, learn from poorly made batches, and perfect your recipes and process. There isn't a magic timeline or even a magic batch number that indicates your readiness to start selling your products.

Instead, you'll need to answer this one main question.

Do I know how my soap will cure and perform at one month, two months, or even six months?

This is important, because when people buy soap, they might not use it right away. You need to be sure that your formula is shelf-stable and that the scent and color will hold up without fading. A customer will be upset if they get your soap home and a few weeks later they can no longer smell the wonderful fragrance.

You might be ready after six months of intense research, product-making, and trial and error. Or it might take you closer to a year, or even longer. This experience is important to make sure you're not selling lye-heavy or unstable soap.

SETTING UP YOUR BUSINESS

Once you decide you're ready, the following process will help you set up your business. These steps are for those in the US. If you are outside of the US, you'll need to research the requirements for your country.

Step 1: Choose a business name. You'll want a name that reflects your brand and speaks to your potential customers. Make sure the website URL and social media pages are available. Perform an Internet, social media, and United States Patent and Trademark Office trademark database search to make sure no one else is using the name to conduct business.

Step 2: Create a business by deciding on a business structure, registering with your state, obtaining any needed licenses, and acquiring an EIN (Employer Identification Number) from the IRS. Every state has a small business administration website that lays out the steps to follow. Perform an Internet search for "*[your state] small business administration*" and you'll find what you need.

Step 3: Get insurance! If you're operating as a business and selling soap, you need insurance to protect yourself in today's litigious society. At minimum, you need general liability and product liability insurance. Most craft fairs and farmers' markets require general liability in case someone is injured at your booth. Product liability covers you in case someone is injured by your product or your product damages someone's property. The Handcrafted Soap and Cosmetics Guild, Handmade Insurance, and Indie Business Network all offer insurance for soapmakers.

Step 4: Open a bank account. You'll need to keep your business income and spending separate from your personal accounts. Once you obtain an EIN, you'll be able to open a business checking account.

Step 5: Decide how you'll accept payments. Both Square and PayPal are popular payment processors. They come with card readers so that you can swipe credit and debit cards at shows and markets. You can also hook them up to your e-commerce website, should you decide to create one.

Step 6: Decide on accounting software. You'll need to track money coming into your business and money going out so that you can correctly file your taxes. I recommend QuickBooks or Fresh-Books. It's also an excellent idea to consult with a professional accountant to make sure you are setting everything up correctly. You'll also need help planning for tax season.

Step 7: Collect and pay local sales tax. As a business, it is your duty to charge sales tax to your customers and then pay it to the state. Be sure you know your local rates and how to pay.

PRICING YOUR SOAP

Pricing your soap takes careful thought and planning. The biggest mistake that new businesses make is to underprice their products. It's important to determine what it costs to make soap, down to the penny.

I recommend two software programs that can help figure out the cost of your soap: SoapMaker and Craftybase.

Aside from the cost of the raw materials that go into each bar, you'll also need to determine the other costs of doing business and figure them into your product pricing. They can include:

* Rent
* Maintenance
* Utility bills
* Business loan payback
* Bank fees
* Membership dues
* State/government fees

* Dues and subscriptions
* Office supplies
* Printing
* Postage/parcel delivery
* Advertising and promotion
* Merchant account fees

On many resources, you'll see a formula for selling that states something like *cost x 2 = wholesale* and *wholesale x 2 = retail*.

This might work for some businesses, but if your brand is top-notch and you're trying to sell your soap in a high-end market, you might be selling yourself short. Take into consideration your brand when it comes to pricing. You might price your soap as high as $12 per bar, depending on your target market.

WHERE TO SELL YOUR SOAP

There are a few different sales avenues to consider. You can choose one or try them all.

Shows: There are countless farmers' markets, craft fairs, and maker fairs that allow soapmakers to sign up as vendors. You'll need to plan a design for your booth. I recommend looking at Pinterest for booth-setup inspiration. Be sure to have various heights of displays on your table and clear signage.

Online: You can create an e-commerce website to sell your soap. I recommend Shopify or WordPress with WooCommerce installed. You want your website to sit on your domain. There are also marketplace websites that host many different makers, such as Etsy. Etsy is a good place to test the waters, but it can be oversaturated with soap. If you choose to go with Etsy, I still recommend setting up your own website on your business URL in case you want to move there later or even sell on both.

Wholesale: You can create a wholesale program to sell directly to local stores and boutiques. You'll need to come up with wholesale pricing, a product catalog, and terms and conditions. I recommend choosing your top four to six soaps to offer wholesale. This will allow you to try it out. When it comes to wholesale, managing a program with fewer products is easier than offering every single soap you make.

Selling soap can be challenging and fun. I hope these tips help you in starting your business journey. Making soap is easy; turning it into a business will require self-education on general business topics, selling, marketing, and even basic accounting. But don't be afraid to learn new things—you've learned so much already, and with that, I welcome you to the soapmaking community!

Measurement Conversions

Volume Equivalents (Liquid)

US STANDARD (OUNCES)	US STANDARD (APPROXIMATE)	METRIC
2 tablespoons	1 fl. oz.	30 mL
¼ cup	2 fl. oz.	60 mL
½ cup	4 fl. oz.	120 mL
1 cup	8 fl. oz.	240 mL
1½ cups	12 fl. oz	355 mL
2 cups or 1 pint	16 fl. oz.	475 mL
4 cups or 1 quart	32 fl. oz.	1 L
1 gallon	128 fl. oz.	4 L

Oven Temperatures

FAHRENHEIT (F)	CELSIUS (C) (APPROXIMATE)
250°F	120°C
300°F	150°C
325°F	165°C
350°F	180°C
375°F	190°C
400°F	200°C
425°F	220°C
450°F	230°C

Volume Equivalents (Dry)

US STANDARD	METRIC (APPROXIMATE)
⅛ teaspoon	0.5 mL
¼ teaspoon	1 mL
½ teaspoon	2 mL
¾ teaspoon	4 mL
1 teaspoon	5 mL
1 tablespoon	15 mL
¼ cup	59 mL
⅓ cup	79 mL
½ cup	118 mL
⅔ cup	156 mL
¾ cup	177 mL
1 cup	235 mL
2 cups or 1 pint	475 mL
3 cups	700 mL
4 cups or 1 quart	1 L

Weight Equivalents

US STANDARD	METRIC (APPROXIMATE)
½ ounce	15 g
1 ounce	30 g
2 ounces	60 g
4 ounces	115 g
8 ounces	225 g
12 ounces	340 g
16 ounces or 1 pound	455 g

Glossary

Acid: A substance with a pH less than 7. In soapmaking, base oils are acidic.

Base: Also called an alkali; a substance with a pH greater than 7. In soapmaking, sodium hydroxide and potassium hydroxide are bases.

Cure: The drying period of the soapmaking process.

Dreaded orange spots (DOS): Little bright orange dots that show up when there is rancid oil in your bars of soap.

Emulsion: The point at which your oil and lye solution is mixed and should not separate.

Fatty acids: The building blocks of soapmaking base oils. They include lauric, myristic, stearic, palmitic, oleic, ricinoleic, linoleic, and linolenic acids.

Gel phase: The heating phase of saponification. Soap will start to turn translucent as it heats up and saponifies.

Lye calculator: An online tool used to determine how much lye is needed to turn a specific amount of soapmaking oils into soap.

Lye discount: Similar to superfat; this is when you use less lye than you need to fully saponify the oils in a recipe. This leaves behind unsaponified oils and butters, giving the soap emollient properties.

Saponification: The chemical reaction that occurs during the soapmaking process where sodium hydroxide or potassium hydroxide turns fatty acids into soap.

Superfat: Excess base oils in a recipe that are not saponified by lye.

Trace: When soap has emulsified and is thick enough to leave a mark on the surface when you drizzle raw soap from a spatula or stick blender while mixing.

Zap test: Also called "tongue test"; when you touch a soap to your tongue to test for active lye. If your soap is neutral, you won't feel anything. If your soap has active lye, it will sting a bit, sort of like touching your tongue to a battery. Some soapmakers wet their finger, rub it on the soap, and then touch their finger to their tongue to test for active lye.

Resources

SOAPMAKING SUPPLIERS (US)
Bramble Berry – www.brambleberry.com
Bulk Apothecary – www.bulkapothecary.com
Ciberia Soap Supply – www.cibariasoapsupply.com
Costco (local store) – for pure olive oil
Essential Depot – www.essentialdepot.com
Glory Bee – www.glorybee.com
Jedwards – www.bulknaturaloils.com
Mad Micas – www.madmicas.com
Majestic Mountain Sage – www.thesage.com
Mountain Rose Herbs – www.mountainroseherbs.com
Muddy Soap Co – www.muddysoapco.com
Nurture Soap Supply – www.nurturesoap.com
Rustic Escentuals – www.rusticescentuals.com
San Francisco Herb Co. – www.sfherb.com
Soaper's Choice – www.soaperschoice.com
Soaper's Supplies – www.soaperssupplies.com
The Lye Guy – www.thelyeguy.com
Wholesale Supplies Plus – www.wholesalesuppliesplus.com

SOAPMAKING SUPPLIERS (AUSTRALIA/NEW ZEALAND)
Auroma – www.auroma.com.au
Aussie Soap Supplies – www.aussiesoapsupplies.com.au
Australian Wholesale Oils – www.awo.com.au
Escentials of Australia – www.escentialsofaustralia.com
Heirloom Body Care – www.heirloombodycare.com.au
Herb Wholesalers – www.herbwholesalers.com
New Directions Australia – www.newdirections.com.au
Southern Skies Soap Supplies – www.southernskiessoapsupplies.com.au

SOAPMAKING SUPPLIERS (CANADA)
Candora Soap Supplies – www.candorasoap.ca
Creations from Eden – www.creationsfromeden.com

Voyageur Soap & Candle – www.voyageursoapandcandle.com
Windy Point Soap Making Supplies – www.windypointsoap.com

SOAPMAKING SUPPLIERS (UK)
Fresholi – www.fresholi.co.uk
Gracefruit – www.gracefruit.com
New Directions UK – www.newdirectionsuk.com
The Soapmakers Store – www.soapmakers-store.com
The Soap Kitchen – www.thesoapkitchen.co.uk
Soap Supplier – https://soapsupplier.co.uk
Summer Naturals – www.summernaturals.co.uk

RECOMMENDED MELT-AND-POUR BRANDS
Bulk Apothecary – www.bulkapothecary.com
SFIC - www.sficcorp.com
Stephenson - www.stephensonpersonalcare.com

ESSENTIAL OIL SUPPLIERS
Many of the soapmaking suppliers offer essential oils as well, but I've found better pricing and quality essential oils from these suppliers:
Lebermuth – www.lebermuth.com
Liberty Natural Products – www.libertynatural.com
New Directions Aromatics – www.newdirectionsaromatics.com
Rainbow Meadow* – www.rainbowmeadow.com
   *Great source for bitter almond essential oil, which can be hard to find.

SOAP CUTTERS
Bud's Woodshop – www.etsy.com/shop/budhaffner
For Crafts Sake — www.forcraftssake.com
Soap Equipment – www.soapequipment.com

LYE & ESSENTIAL OIL CALCULATORS
Essential Oil Calc – www.eocalc.com
Majestic Mountain Sage – www.thesage.com
SoapCalc – www.soapcalc.com
Soapee – www.soapee.com

SOAPMAKING LABELS
DIY Soap Labels – www.diysoaplabels.com

SOAPMAKING BLOGS
Lovin' Soap – www.lovinsoap.com
The Nerdy Farm Wife – www.thenerdyfarmwife.com
Soap Queen – www.soapqueen.com

SOAPMAKING FATTY ACID PROFILES AND SAP VALUES
www.lovinsoap.com/oils-chart
www.soaperschoice.com (view product list)

SOAPMAKING E-CLASSES AND ONLINE COURSES
www.lovinsoap.com

MORE BOOKS BY AMANDA GAIL AARON (AMAZON.COM)
Goat Milk Soapmaking
Making Salt Bars
How to Teach Your Craft
Men's Grooming Recipe Book

SOAPMAKING BUSINESS BOOKS (AMAZON.COM)
When you're ready to move from hobby to business, I recommend these books by Benjamin Aaron:
Creating a Soap and Skincare Brand
How to Wholesale Your Handcrafted Soap
Pricing Handmade Soap for Profit

ESSENTIAL OIL EDUCATION AND SAFETY
Essential Oil Safety by Robert Tisserand and Rodney Young
The Unspoken Truth About Essential Oils by Stacey Haluka and Kayla Fioravanti
Aromamedical – www.aromamedical.org
Atlantic Institute – www.atlanticinstitute.com/blog
Robert Tisserand – www.roberttisserand.com

SOAPMAKING INSURANCE

Handcrafted Soap & Cosmetic Guild – www.soapguild.org
HandMade Artisan Insurance – www.handmadeinsurance.com
Indie Business Network – www.indiebusinessnetwork.com
RLI – www.rlicorp.com

Recipe Label Index

A

Acne-fighting
Charcoal & Anise Soap, 245–246
Charcoal Soap, 72–73
Kombucha Soap, 106–108
100% Coconut Oil Soap—20% Superfat, 66–67

B

Body
Almond Orange Soap, 82–83
Apple Cider Vinegar Soap, 100–101
Basic Beginner Soap—Lard or Tallow, 56–57
Basic Beginner Soap—Vegan, 58–59
Basil, Lavender & Mint Soap, 121–122
Bastile Soap with Coconut Oil, 62–63
Bastile Soap with Shea Butter, 64–65
Bay Rum Soap, 84–85
Carrot & Honey Soap, 128–129
Calendula & Grapefruit Embed Soap, 226–227
Castile Soap, 60–61
Chamomile Tea Soap, 86–87
Charcoal Soap, 72–73
Citrus Zest Kitchen Soap, 148–149
Clay & Agave Swirled Soap, 174–175
Cocoa & Honey Soap, 90–91
Coconut Milk & Cedarwood Soap, 88–89
Coffee Scrub Soap, 98–99
Cucumber Scrub Soap, 169–171
Cypress, Lavender & Sage Soap, 102–103

Dandelion, Nettle & Aloe Soap, 92–93
Egg & Turmeric Soap, 109–111
Garden Herb Soap, 118–120
Herb & Hemp Soap, 162–163
Honey & Clove Soap, 158–159
Juniper's Soap, 80–81
Kombucha Soap, 106–108
Lavender & Geranium Soap, 96–97
Lavender Mint Soap, 76–77
Lavender-Orange Soap, 224–225
Lavender Soap, 178–179
Lemon & Poppy Seed Soap, 166–168
Lemon Turmeric Soap, 104–105
Loofah Spa Soap, 222–223
Mocha Mint Soap, 176–177
Neem Soap, 78–79
Nourishing Oatmeal & Honey Soap, 150–151
Oatmeal, Honey & Tumeric Soap, 248–249
Oatmeal Soap, 70–71
Ocean Breeze Soap, 130–131
100% Coconut Oil Soap—20% Superfat, 66–67
Orange Spice Soap, 152–153
Patchouli Orange Soap, 124–125
Peppermint Lime Soap, 154–155
Plantain-Infused Lavender Soap, 126–127
Pumpkin Purée Soap, 164–165
Red Wine Soap, 156–157
Rose Clay Soap, 74–75
Rose Geranium Soap, 228–229

Body *(continued)*
   Sea Clay & Avocado Soap, 115–117
   Sea Clay & Eucalyptus Soap, 94–95
   Seaweed & Lemon Soap, 230–231
   Seaweed & Pumice Soap, 160–161
   Shea Butter & Geranium Soap, 172–173
   Tomato & Herb Soap, 112–114

C

Citrus
   Almond & Oats Soap, 252–253
   Almond Orange Soap, 82–83
   Apple Cider Vinegar Soap, 100–101
   Bay Rum Soap, 84–85
   Calendula & Grapefruit Embed Soap,
      226–227
   Carrot & Honey Soap, 128–129
   Chamomile Tea Soap, 86–87
   Citrus Zest Kitchen Soap, 148–149
   Cocoa & Honey Soap, 90–91
   Coconut Milk & Cedarwood Soap, 88–89
   Coffee Scrub Soap, 98–99
   Dandelion, Nettle & Aloe Soap, 92–93
   Egg & Turmeric Soap, 109–111
   Honey & Clove Soap, 158–159
   Java-Mint Scrub Soap, 219–220
   Kombucha Soap, 106–108
   Lavender-Orange Soap, 224–225
   Lemon & Poppy Seed Soap, 166–168
   Lemon Turmeric Soap, 104–105
   Loofah Spa Soap, 222–223
   Neem Soap, 78–79
   Nourishing Oatmeal & Honey Soap,
      150–151

Oatmeal, Honey & Turmeric Soap,
   248–249
Orange Spice Soap, 152–153
Patchouli Orange Soap, 124–125
Pumpkin Purée Soap, 164–165
Rose Clay Soap, 74–75
Seaweed & Lemon Soap, 230–231
Seaweed & Pumice Soap, 160–161
Tomato & Herb Soap, 112–114

E

Exfoliating
   Calendula & Grapefruit Embed Soap,
      226–227
   Citrus Zest Kitchen Soap, 148–149
   Coffee Scrub Soap, 98–99
   Cornmeal Kitchen Soap, 250–251
   Cucumber Scrub Soap, 169–171
   Garden Herb Soap, 118–120
   Herb & Hemp Soap, 162–163
   Java-Mint Scrub Soap, 219–220
   Lavender Mint Soap, 76–77
   Lemon & Poppy Seed Soap, 166–168
   Loofah Spa Soap, 222–223
   Mocha Mint Soap, 176–177
   Sea Clay & Eucalyptus Soap, 94–95
   Seaweed & Pumice Soap, 160–161

F

Face
   Apple Cider Vinegar Soap, 100–101
   Bastile Soap with Coconut Oil, 62–63
   Bastile Soap with Shea Butter, 64–65
   Carrot & Honey Soap, 128–129
   Castile Soap, 60–61

Chamomile Tea Soap, 86–87

Charcoal & Anise Soap, 245–246

Charcoal Soap, 72–73

Clay & Agave Swirled Soap, 174–175

Coconut Milk & Cedarwood Soap, 88–89

Cucumber Scrub Soap, 169–171

Cypress, Lavender & Sage Soap, 102–103

Dandelion, Nettle & Aloe Soap, 92–93

Egg & Turmeric Soap, 109–111

Kombucha Soap, 106–108

Lavender & Geranium Soap, 96–97

Lavender Soap, 178–179

Lemon Turmeric Soap, 104–105

Neem Soap, 78–79

Oatmeal Soap, 70–71

Peppermint Lime Soap, 154–155

Plantain-Infused Lavender Soap, 126–127

Rose Clay Soap, 74–75

Sea Clay & Avocado Soap, 115–117

Sea Clay & Eucalyptus Soap, 94–95

Shea Butter & Geranium Soap, 172–173

Floral

Apple Cider Vinegar Soap, 100–101

Chamomile Tea Soap, 86–87

Charcoal & Anise Soap, 245–246

Clay & Agave Swirled Soap, 174–175

Cocoa & Honey Soap, 90–91

Cucumber Scrub Soap, 169–171

Cypress, Lavender & Sage Soap, 102–103

Garden Herb Soap, 118–120

Herb & Hemp Soap, 162–163

Honey & Clove Soap, 158–159

Juniper's Soap, 80–81

Kombucha Soap, 106–108

Lavender & Geranium Soap, 96–97

Lavender Mint Soap, 76–77

Lavender-Orange Soap, 224–225

Lavender Soap, 178–179

Neem Soap, 78–79

Oatmeal Soap, 70–71

Patchouli Orange Soap, 124–125

Plantain-Infused Lavender Soap, 126–127

Red Wine Soap, 156–157

Rose Clay Soap, 74–75

Rose Geranium Soap, 228–229

Sea Clay & Avocado Soap, 115–117

Shea Butter & Geranium Soap, 172–173

G

Gentle

Almond Orange Soap, 82–83

Bastile Soap with Coconut Oil, 62–63

Bastile Soap with Shea Butter, 64–65

Carrot & Honey Soap, 128–129

Castile Soap, 60–61

Cypress, Lavender & Sage Soap, 102–103

Herb & Hemp Soap, 162–163

Kombucha Soap, 106–108

Lavender & Geranium Soap, 96–97

Lavender Soap, 178–179

Neem Soap, 78–79

Nourishing Oatmeal & Honey Soap,
150–151

Oatmeal Soap, 70–71

Peppermint Lime Soap, 154–155

Plantain-Infused Lavender Soap, 126–127

Red Wine Soap, 156–157

Shea Butter & Geranium Soap, 172–173

Tomato & Herb Soap, 112–114

H

Herbal
  Basil, Lavender & Mint Soap, 121–122
  Charcoal Soap, 72–73
  Clay & Agave Swirled Soap, 174–175
  Coffee Scrub Soap, 98–99
  Cornmeal Kitchen Soap, 250–251
  Dandelion, Nettle & Aloe Soap, 92–93
  Egg & Turmeric Soap, 109–111
  Garden Herb Soap, 118–120
  Herb & Hemp Soap, 162–163
  Kombucha Soap, 106–108
  Red Wine Soap, 156–157
  Sea Clay & Eucalyptus Soap, 94–95
  Seaweed & Lemon Soap, 230–231
  Tomato & Herb Soap, 112–114
High-cleansing
  100% Coconut Oil Soap—Laundry Soap,
    68–69
Household
  100% Coconut Oil Soap—Laundry Soap,
    68–69

M

Minty
  Basil, Lavender & Mint Soap, 121–122
  Carrot & Honey Soap, 128–129
  Charcoal & Anise Soap, 245–246
  Charcoal Soap, 72–73
  Cocoa & Honey Soap, 90–91
  Coffee Scrub Soap, 98–99
  Cucumber Scrub Soap, 169–171
  Garden Herb Soap, 118–120
  Java-Mint Scrub Soap, 219–220
  Lavender Mint Soap, 76–77

Mocha Mint Soap, 176–177
Oatmeal, Honey & Turmeric Soap,
  248–249
Ocean Breeze Soap, 130–131
Peppermint Lime Soap, 154–155
Pumpkin Purée Soap, 164–165
Sea Clay & Avocado Soap, 115–117
Sea Clay & Eucalyptus Soap, 94–95
Seaweed & Pumice Soap, 160–161

S

Skin-soothing
  Almond & Oats Soap, 252–253
  Oatmeal, Honey & Turmeric Soap,
    248–249
Spicy
  Bay Rum Soap, 84–85
  Cucumber Scrub Soap, 169–171
  Honey & Clove Soap, 158–159
  Nourishing Oatmeal & Honey Soap,
    150–151
  Orange Spice Soap, 152–153
  Pumpkin Purée Soap, 164–165

V

Vegan
  Almond & Oats Soap, 252–253
  Almond Orange Soap, 82–83
  Apple Cider Vinegar Soap, 100–101
  Avocado Oil Liquid Soap Base, 202–203
  Basic Beginner Soap—Vegan, 58–59
  Basil, Lavender & Mint Soap, 121–122
  Bastile Soap with Coconut Oil, 62–63
  Bastile Soap with Shea Butter, 64–65
  Bay Rum Soap, 84–85

Calendula & Grapefruit Embed Soap, 226–227

Castile Soap, 60–61

Chamomile Tea Soap, 86–87

Charcoal & Anise Soap, 245–246

Charcoal Soap, 72–73

Citrus Zest Kitchen Soap, 148–149

Clay & Agave Swirled Soap, 174–175

Coconut Milk & Cedarwood Soap, 88–89

Coconut Oil Cleaning Liquid Soap Base, 196–197

Coffee Scrub Soap, 98–99

Cornmeal Kitchen Soap, 250–251

Cucumber Scrub Soap, 169–171

Cypress, Lavender & Sage Soap, 102–103

Dandelion, Nettle & Aloe Soap, 92–93

Garden Herb Soap, 118–120

Herb & Hemp Soap, 162–163

Java-Mint Scrub Soap, 219–220

Jojoba Oil Liquid Soap Base, 200–201

Juniper's Soap, 80–81

Kombucha Soap, 106–108

Lavender & Geranium Soap, 96–97

Lavender Mint Soap, 76–77

Lavender-Orange Soap, 224–225

Lavender Soap, 178–179

Lemon & Poppy Seed Soap, 166–168

Lemon Turmeric Soap, 104–105

Loofah Spa Soap, 222–223

Mocha Mint Soap, 176–177

Neem Soap, 78–79

Oatmeal Soap, 70–71

Ocean Breeze Soap, 130–131

Olive Oil Liquid Soap Base, 193–194

100% Coconut Oil Soap—20% Superfat, 66–67

Orange Spice Soap, 152–153

Patchouli Orange Soap, 124–125

Peppermint Lime Soap, 154–155

Plantain-Infused Lavender Soap, 126–127

Pumpkin Purée Soap, 164–165

Red Wine Soap, 156–157

Rose Clay Soap, 74–75

Rose Geranium Soap, 228–229

Sea Clay & Avocado Soap, 115–117

Sea Clay & Eucalyptus Soap, 94–95

Seaweed & Lemon Soap, 230–231

Seaweed & Pumice Soap, 160–161

Shea Butter & Geranium Soap, 172–173

Sunflower Oil Liquid Soap Base, 198–199

Tomato & Herb Soap, 112–114

W

Woodsy

Coconut Milk & Cedarwood Soap, 88–89

Coffee Scrub Soap, 98–99

Cypress, Lavender & Sage Soap, 102–103

Oatmeal, Honey & Turmeric Soap, s248–249

Index

A

Additives, 3, 18–20

Alcohol, 207

Almond & Oats Soap, 252–253

Almond Orange Soap, 82–83

Aloe vera liquid, 93

Apple Cider Vinegar Soap, 100–101

Ash, 43

Avocado Oil Liquid Soap Base, 202–203

B

Basic Beginner Soap—Lard or Tallow, 56–57

Basic Beginner Soap—Vegan, 58–59

Basil, Lavender & Mint Soap, 121–122

Bastile Soap with Coconut Oil, 62–63

Bastile Soap with Shea Butter, 64–65

Bay Rum Soap, 84–85

Businesses, starting, 262–265

Butters, 16

C

Calendula & Grapefruit Embed Soap, 226–227

Carrier oils, 14–17

Carrot & Honey Soap, 128–129

Castile Soap, 60–61

Castor oil, 16

Chamomile Tea Soap, 86–87

Charcoal, cosmetic, 18

Charcoal & Anise Soap, 245–246

Charcoal Soap, 72–73

Citrus Zest Kitchen Soap, 148–149

Clay, 18

Clay & Agave Swirled Soap, 174–175

Cocoa & Honey Soap, 90–91

Coconut Milk & Cedarwood Soap, 88–89

Coconut oil, 14

Coconut Oil Cleaning Liquid Soap Base, 196–197

Coffee, 19

Coffee Scrub Soap, 98–99

Cold-process soaps

  about, 4, 25

  coloring, 29

  creating new recipes, 256–260

  decorative techniques, 39–55

  essential oil blends, 22

  essential oil usage rate, 22

  gel phase, 35

  melting oils, 29

  modifying for hot-process, 136

  packaging, 260–261

  recipes, 56–131

  steps, 30–33

  tips, 36

  trace process, 34

  troubleshooting, 37–38

Colorants, 3, 11, 17–18

Consumer Product Safety Commission (CPSC), 262

Containers, 11, 13

Cornmeal Kitchen Soap, 250–251

Cucumber Scrub Soap, 169–171

Cutters, 10

Cypress, Lavender & Sage Soap, 102–103

D

Dandelion, Nettle & Aloe Soap, 92–93

Decorative techniques

    cold-process soaps, 39–55

    dried flowers, 244

    embedding, 216–218

    embossing and stamping, 39

    hand-milled soaps, 241– 244

    hot-process soaps, 142– 147

    layering, 52–55, 142–143, 213–215, 243

    melt-and-pour soaps, 213–218

    swirling, 40–51, 144–147, 241–242

E

Egg & Turmeric Soap, 109–111

Embedding, 216–218

Embossing, 39

Emollient oils, 2

Emulsification, 2, 34

Equipment, 10–12

Essential oils, 11, 20–23

    blends for cold-process soaps, 22

    blends for liquid soaps, 190–192

F

Fatty acids, 2

Flowers, dried, 20, 244

Food and Drug Administration (FDA), 262

G

Garden Herb Soap, 118–120

Gel phase, 35

Gloves, 12, 13, 23

Glycerin, 2

H

Hand-milled soaps

    about, 5, 7, 233–235

    adding water to the base, 235

    choosing a base, 235

    consistency in, 236

    decorative techniques, 241– 244

    dispersing colorants, 236

    essential oil usage rate, 22

    melting the base, 236

    packaging, 260–261

    recipes, 245–253

    steps, 237–239

    tips, 239

    troubleshooting, 240

Herb & Hemp Soap, 162–163

Herbs, 17–18, 20

High linoleic liquid oils, 16

High oleic liquid oils, 15

Honey & Clove Soap, 158–159

Hot-process soaps

    about, 4, 133

    coloring, 135

    cooking, 135

    decorative techniques, 142– 147

    essential oil usage rate, 22

    modifying cold-process recipes, 136

    packaging, 260–261

    recipes, 148–179

    steps, 137–140

    tips, 140

    troubleshooting, 141

I

Infusions, 17, 19

J

Java-Mint Scrub Soap, 219–220

Jojoba oil, 16

Jojoba Oil Liquid Soap Base, 200–201

Juniper's Soap, 80–81

K

Kombucha Soap, 106–108

L

Labeling soaps, 261–262

Lard, 15

Lavender & Geranium Soap, 96–97

Lavender Mint Soap, 76–77

Lavender-Orange Soap, 224–225

Lavender Soap, 178–179

Layering

    cold-process soaps, 52–55

    hand-milled soaps, 243

    hot-process soaps, 142–143

    melt-and-pour soaps, 213–215

Lemon & Poppy Seed Soap, 166–168

Lemon Turmeric Soap, 104–105

Linolenic liquid oils, 16

Liquid soaps

    about, 4–5, 181–183

    cooking, 183

    diluting, 187–188

    essential oil blends, 190–192

    essential oil usage rate, 22

    packaging, 261

    recipes, 193–203

    steps, 184–186

    tips, 188

    troubleshooting, 189

Loofah Spa Soap, 222–223

Lye

    about, 2, 13–14

    calculators, 14

    cleaning up, 12

    containers, 11

    safety, 5–7

M

Measuring spoons, 11

Melt-and-pour soaps

    about, 5, 7, 13, 205–206

    alcohol spraying, 207

    choosing a base, 206

    decorative techniques, 213–218

    dispersing colorants, 207

    essential oil usage rate, 22

    melting the base, 207

    packaging, 261

    recipes, 219–231

    steps, 208–209

    tips, 210

    troubleshooting, 211–212

Milk frothers, 10

Milk powders, 20

Mocha Mint Soap, 176–177

Molds, 10, 13

    calculating oil weights for, 258

N

Natural, use of term, 2–3

Neem Soap, 78–79

Nourishing Oatmeal & Honey Soap, 150–151

O

Oatmeal, 19

Oatmeal, Honey & Turmeric Soap, 248–249

Oatmeal Soap, 70–71

Ocean Breeze Soap, 130–131

Oils

calculating weights for molds, 258

carrier, 14–17

essential, 11, 20–23, 190–192

infusions, 17, 19

Olive oil, 15

Olive Oil Liquid Soap Base, 193–194

100% Coconut Oil Soap—20% Superfat, 66–67

100% Coconut Oil Soap—Laundry Soap, 68–69

Orange Spice Soap, 152–153

P

Packaging soaps, 260–261

Palmitic acid, 15

Palm oil, 3, 17

Patchouli Orange Soap, 124–125

Peppermint Lime Soap, 154–155

Plantain-Infused Lavender Soap, 126–127

Potassium hydroxide, 5–6, 12, 13

Pumpkin Purée Soap, 164–165

R

Red Wine Soap, 156–157

Rice bran oil, 15

Ricing, 38

Rose Clay Soap, 74–75

Rose Geranium Soap, 228–229

S

Safety

carrier oils, 14

essential oils, 23

gear, 12

lye, 5–7

Salt, 20

Saponification, 2, 14

Scales, digital, 10

Scents, 3

Sea Clay & Avocado Soap, 115–117

Sea Clay & Eucalyptus Soap, 94–95

Seaweed & Lemon Soap, 230–231

Seaweed & Pumice Soap, 160–161

Seeds, 18

Selling soaps, 262–265

Shea Butter & Geranium Soap, 172–173

Slow cookers, 11

Soapmaking. *See also specific techniques*
  cleaning up, 12–13
  equipment, 10–12
  safety, 5–7
  science of, 2
  techniques, 4–5
Sodium hydroxide, 5–6, 12, 13
Spices, 17–18
Stamps, 39
Stick blenders, 10, 13
Substitutions, 14
Sugars, 20
Sunflower Oil Liquid Soap Base, 198–199
Swirling
  hand-milled soaps, 241–242
  hot-process soaps, 144–145
  in-the-mold loaf, 49–51
  in-the-pot cold-process, 40–42
  in-the-pot hot-process, 146–147
  slab, 44–46
  tiger stripe, 47–48

T
Tallow, 15
Thermometers, 11
Tomato & Herb Soap, 112–114
Trace, 34
Troubleshooting
  cold-process soaps, 37–38
  hand-milled soaps, 240
  hot-process soaps, 141
  liquid soaps, 189
  melt-and-pour soaps, 211–212

U
Usage rates, 22–23
Utensils, 10

Z
Zinc oxide, 18

Acknowledgments

Thank you, Benjamin, for supporting me while I worked on this whirlwind project. Thanks to Brandy for finding me online and being the perfect matchmaker. And to all the team at Callisto for being so wonderful to work with.

About the Author

Amanda Gail Aaron has built her career around providing education in her craft, soapmaking. She has taught in classrooms all over the United States and presents annually at conferences and seminars put on by the handcrafted soap industry's top guilds and organizations. In 2008, after learning the craft of soapmaking, Amanda started an educational blog at LovinSoap.com, which features step-by-step, full-color photographic tutorials, articles, troubleshooting advice, and general information about soapmaking. She publishes books, e-books, and e-courses on the topic of soapmaking and has written for industry publications such as *Handmade Magazine*, *Saponifier*, and *Soap Collaborative*. In 2009, she started teaching classes in Dallas and Austin, providing hands-on workshops where students could totally immerse themselves in and confidently learn the craft of soapmaking. Students from all over the United States have attended her hands-on workshops, and a few students have even traveled to her classes from outside of the country.

In 2013, after a heart-moving trip to Haiti to teach a group of women who lived in a tent camp how to make soap, she decided that she would use her love of teaching to help as many women in the same situation as she could. Along with her partner, Benjamin Aaron, she created a nonprofit whose aim is to teach women in developing nations the craft and the business of soapmaking, tackling two of poverty's biggest issues—lack of access to hygiene and lack of economic opportunity for women. The Lovin' Soap Project is a registered 501(c)(3) currently working in Haiti, Uganda, China, India, Senegal, Kenya, and Fiji, and it will continue to expand to other areas where women need opportunity.

You can connect with Amanda online in her Facebook group, Saponification Nation, where more than 30,000 soapmakers talk soap, share photos, and get soapmaking help and advice.

CPSIA information can be obtained
at www.ICGtesting.com
Printed in the USA
BVHW062327010419
544270BV00001B/1/P